# the roller art book

## drawing & painting

**Sig Purwin**

**North Light Publishers**
**Fairfield, Connecticut**

Published by NORTH LIGHT, an imprint of
WRITER'S DIGEST BOOKS,
9933 Alliance Road, Cincinnati, Ohio 45242.



Manufactured in U.S.A.
First Printing 1983

**Library of Congress Cataloging in Publication Data**

Purwin, Sig.
The roller art book.

1. Roller painting. 2. Drawing — Technique.
I. Title.
ND1536.P87 1982 751.4'9 82-24641
ISBN 0-89134-056-4 (pbk.)

Edited by Carla Dennis
Designed by Sig Purwin
Composed in Helvetica by Stet-Shields, Inc.
Printed and bound by The Book Press, Inc.

# Contents


| | |
|---|---|
| introduction | 8 |
| materials | 9 |
| strokes and rolls | 14 |
| roller scraping | 22 |
| impressions | 30 |
| spatter and blotting | 42 |
| animals | 46 |
| human figure | 59 |
| caricaturing | 66 |
| motivity | 74 |
| indoor painting | 80 |
| outdoor painting | 93 |
| murals | 105 |
| demonstrations/workshops | 109 |
| dialogue | 119 |

Acknowledgements:

| | |
|---|---|
| Michael de Punte | Photography & Imagery consultant |
| Dr. James Oschman | Technical help and encouragement |
| Millie | My wife, for her continuous help — personal and creative |

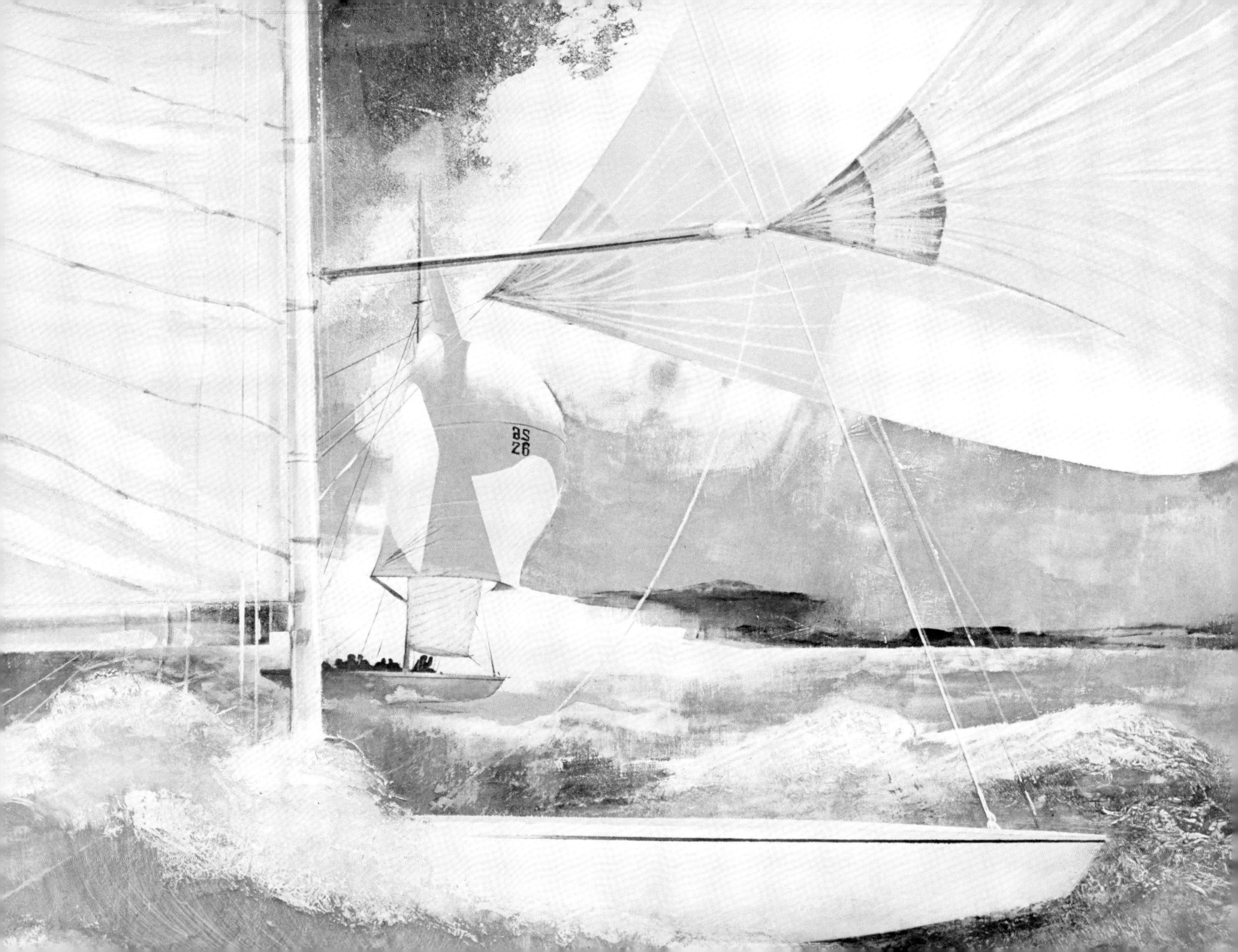
as
26

# introduction

The Roller Art book has three purposes:

A documentation of my experiences in brayer painting and drawing.

To use extensively visual and pictorial techniques as an alternative to the more usual how-to presentations.

To make brayer drawing and painting a readily understandable experience.

This book is intended as a reference guide for beginners as well as the more advanced artist. It can be studied and read from start to finish before you actually begin to work.

Or you can select specific chapters with diagrams and go from there.

# materials

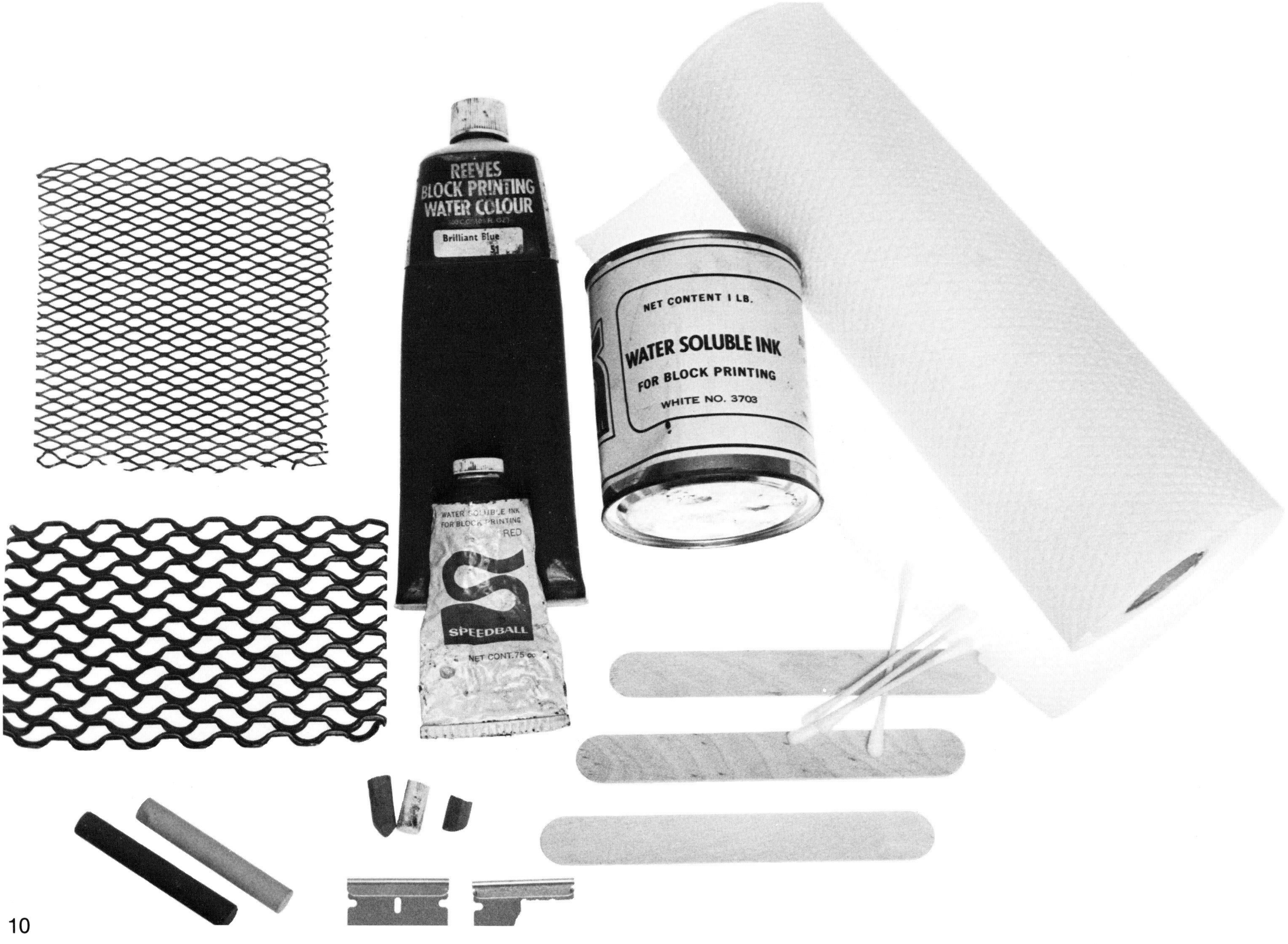
REEVES
BLOCK PRINTING
WATER COLOUR
Brilliant Blue
51
NET CONTENT I LB.
WATER SOLUBLE INK
FOR BLOCK PRINTING
WHITE NO. 3703
WATER SOLUBLE INK
FOR BLOCK PRINTING
RED
SPEEDBALL
NET CONT. 75 cc

**basic materials essential for roller art plus your choice of working surfaces***

1 expanded metal mesh (fine grade)
2 expanded metal mesh (course grade)
3 tube inks (water soluble or oil base)
4 one lb. can inks (water soluble or oil base)
5 paper towels
6 cotton swabs
7 tongue depressors
8 single-edge razor blades (shaped to fit)
9 oil crayons, chalks (various colors, sizes)

*From ordinary wrapping or newspaper to the more permanent art papers, hot or cold press, gesso-coated papers, panels of masonite or wood.

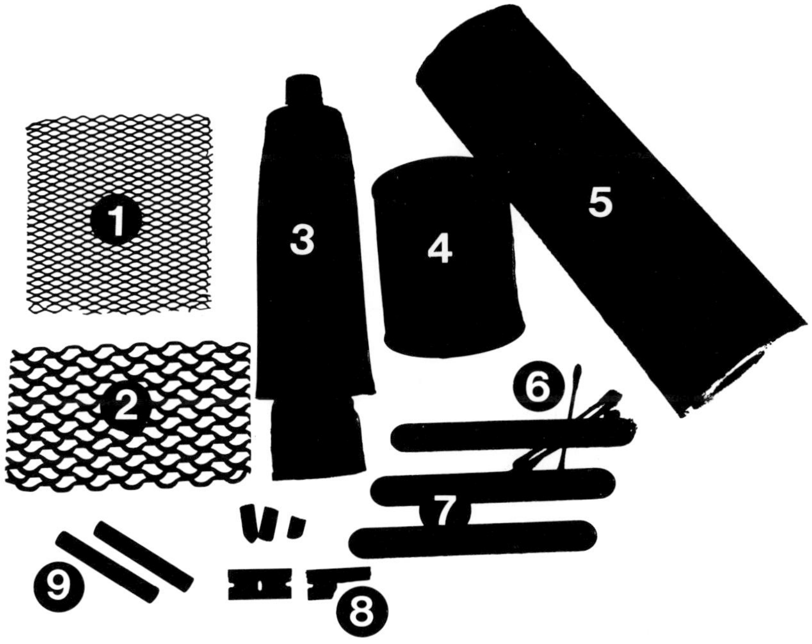

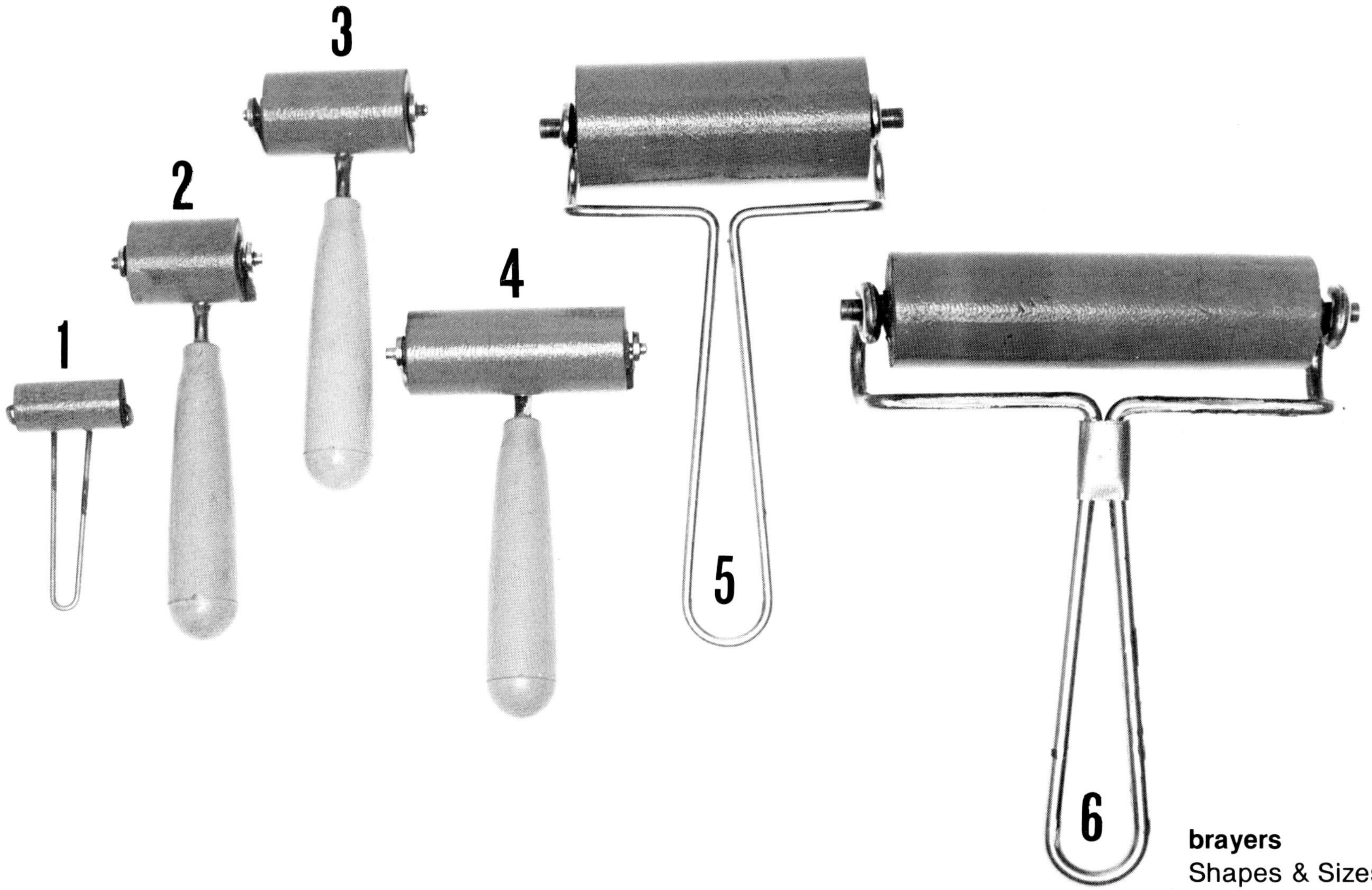


**brayers**
Shapes & Sizes:
1 1½ x ¾-inch diameter
2 1½ x 1¼-inch diameter
3 2 x 1¼-inch diameter
4 3 x 1¼-inch diameter
5 4 x 1¾-inch diameter
6 5½ x 1½-inch diameter

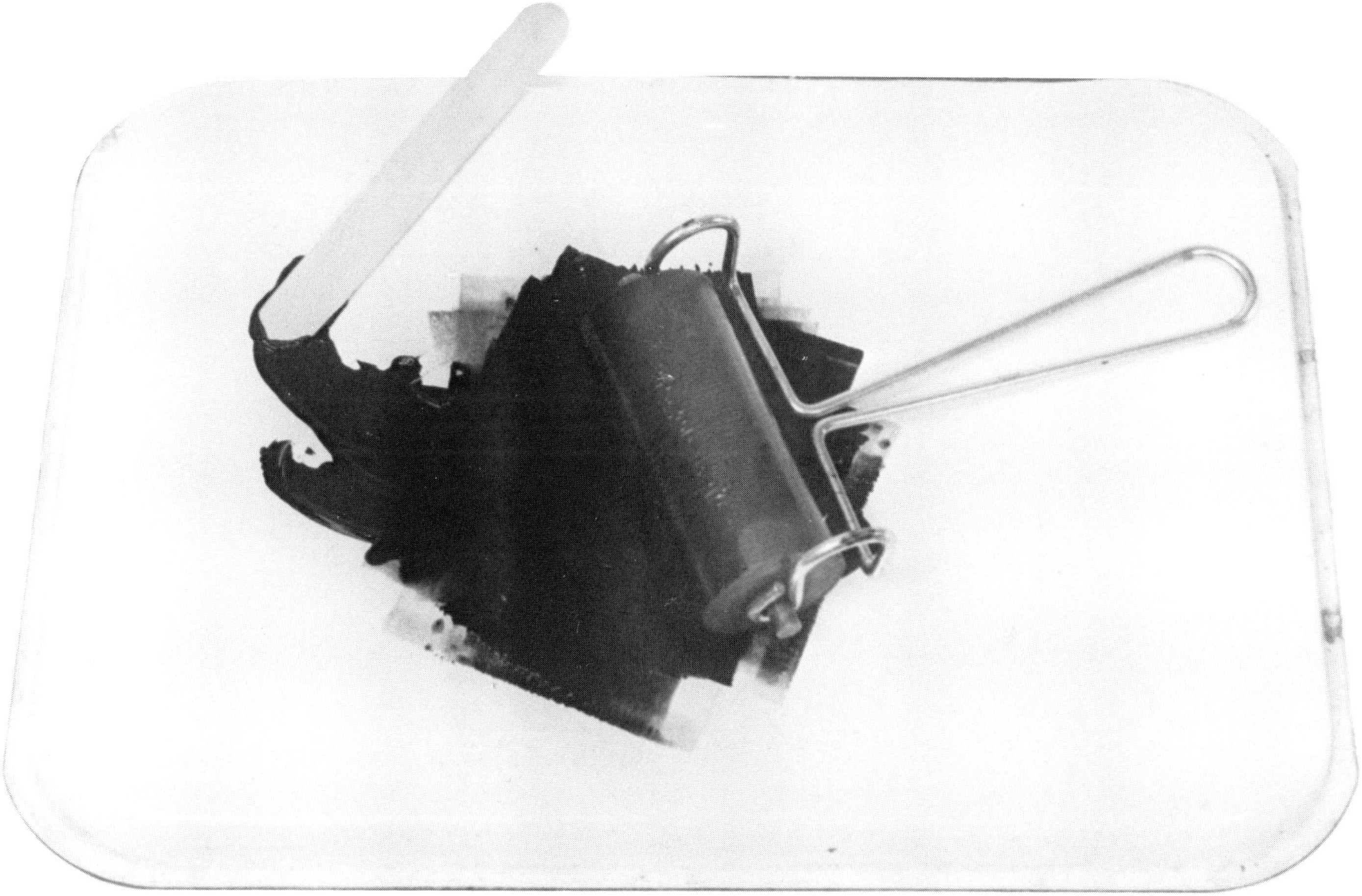

Dab the pigment (ink or paint) from the container onto the palette. Spread the pigment with a spreader prior to spreading further with the brayer. (Wood tongue depressors make excellent, expendable spreaders.)

# strokes and rolls

On the following pages there are photographs and diagrams illustrating the brayer in action. Get acquainted with the brayer by filling several sheets of paper with these exercises. Your strokes and rolls will vary and that is good. Start experimenting with your own configurations after you've become familiar with the brayer.

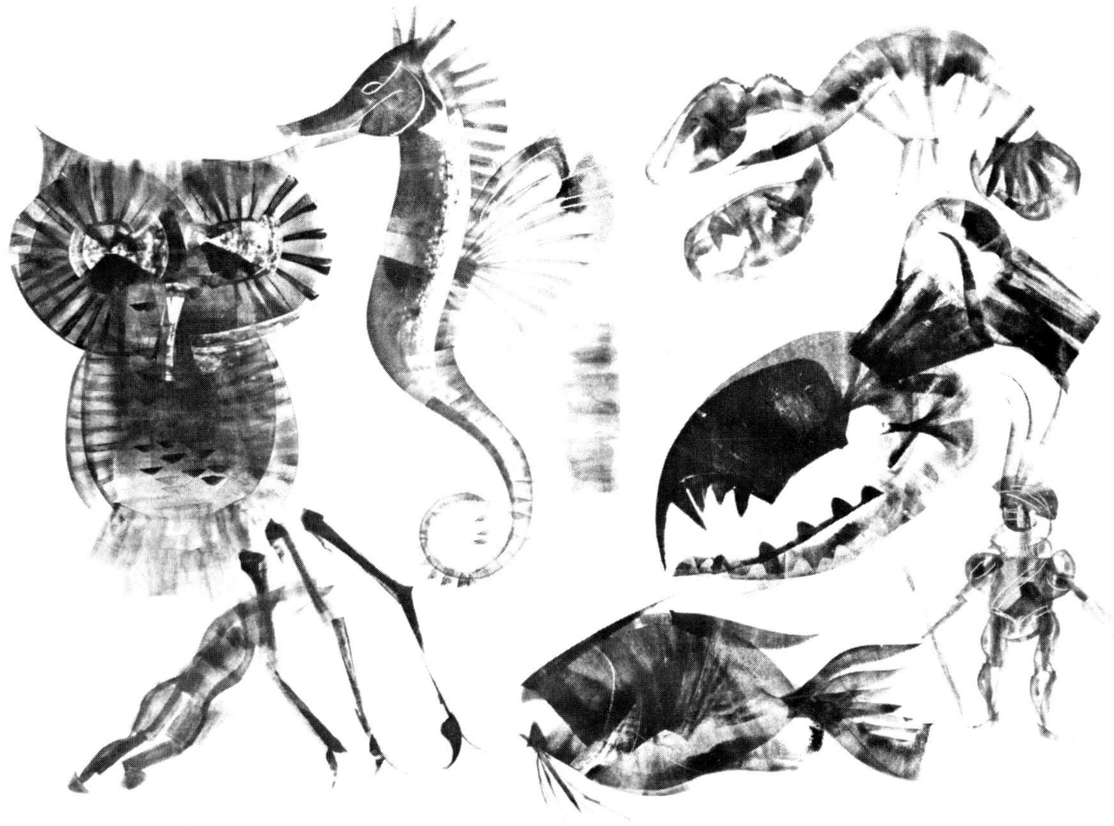

A

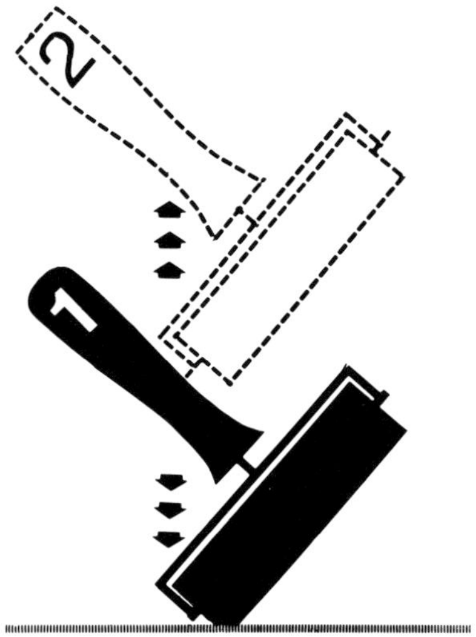


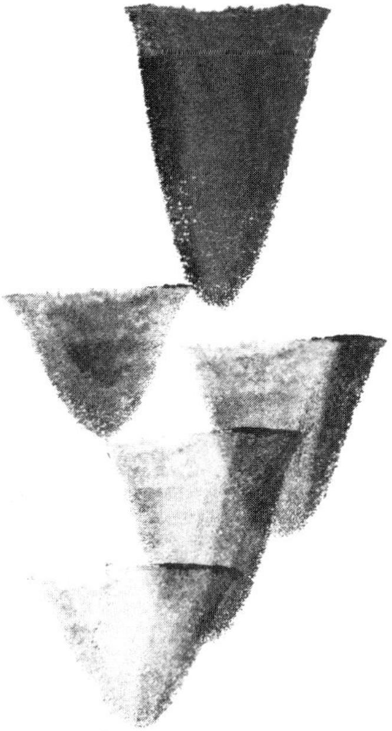

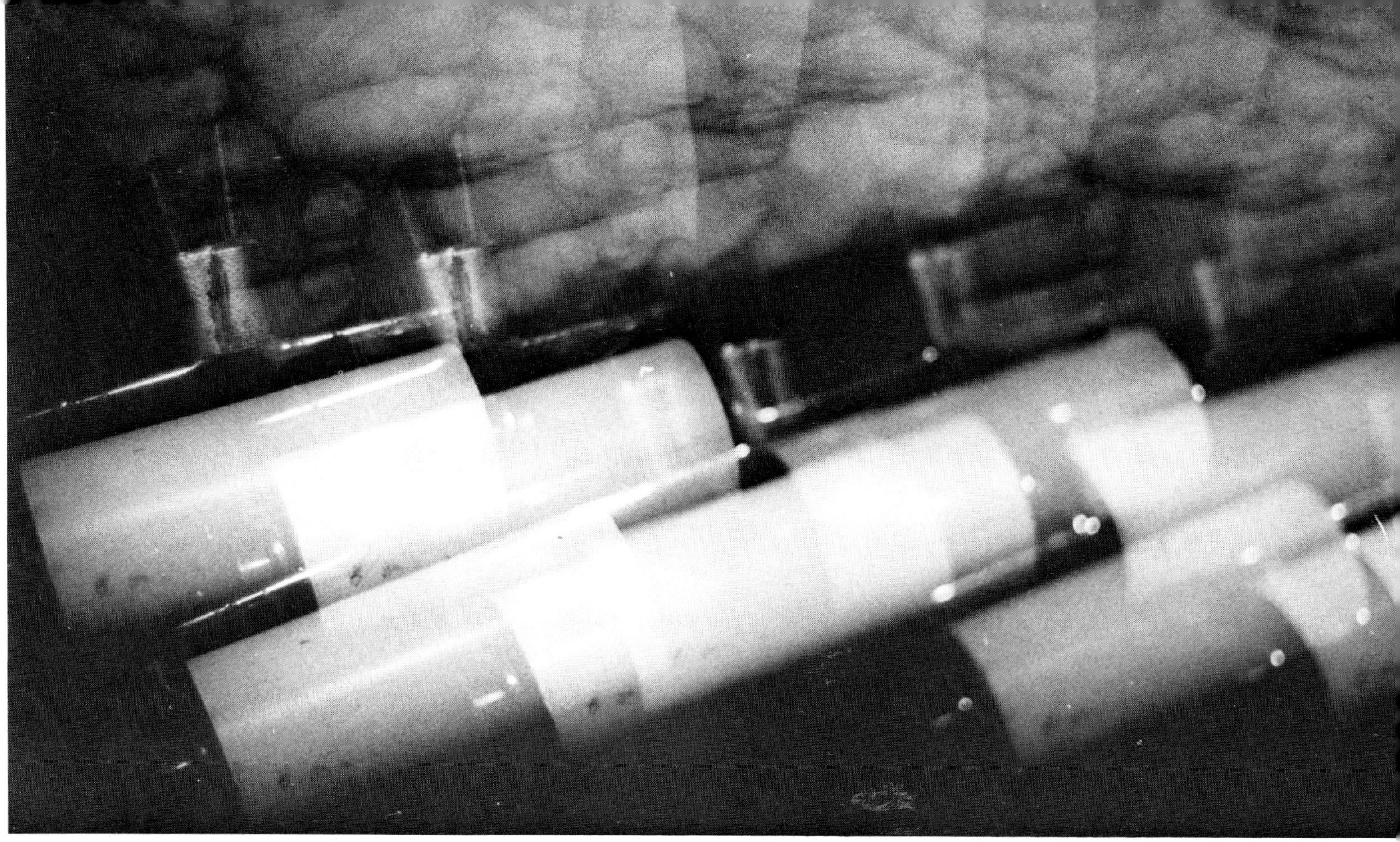

**the edge bounce stroke**

The photograph illustrates the vertical action of the brayer as it bounces across the surface of the paper.

Diagram A illustrates the correct position of the brayer for this stroke and the results.

B

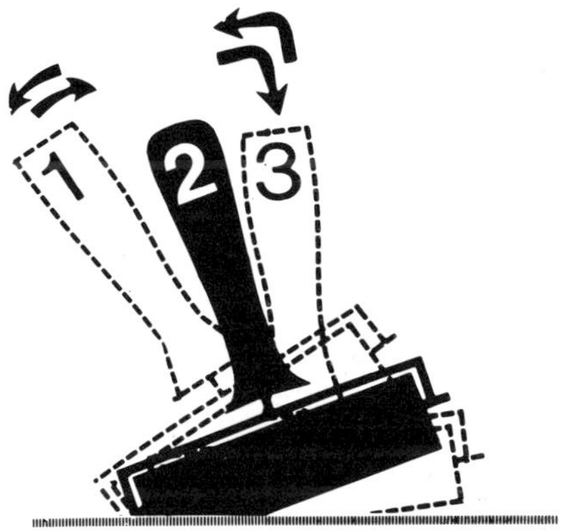


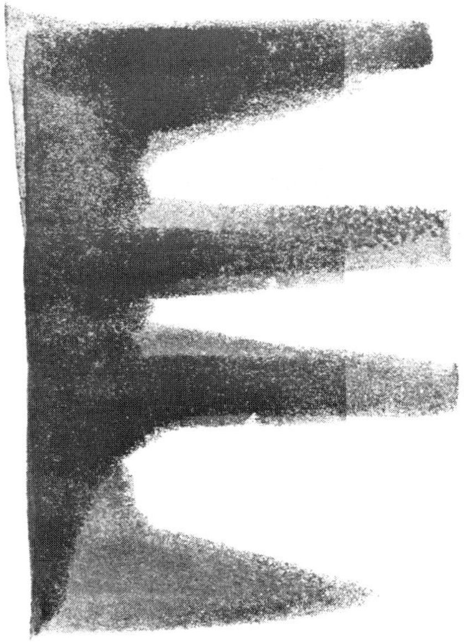

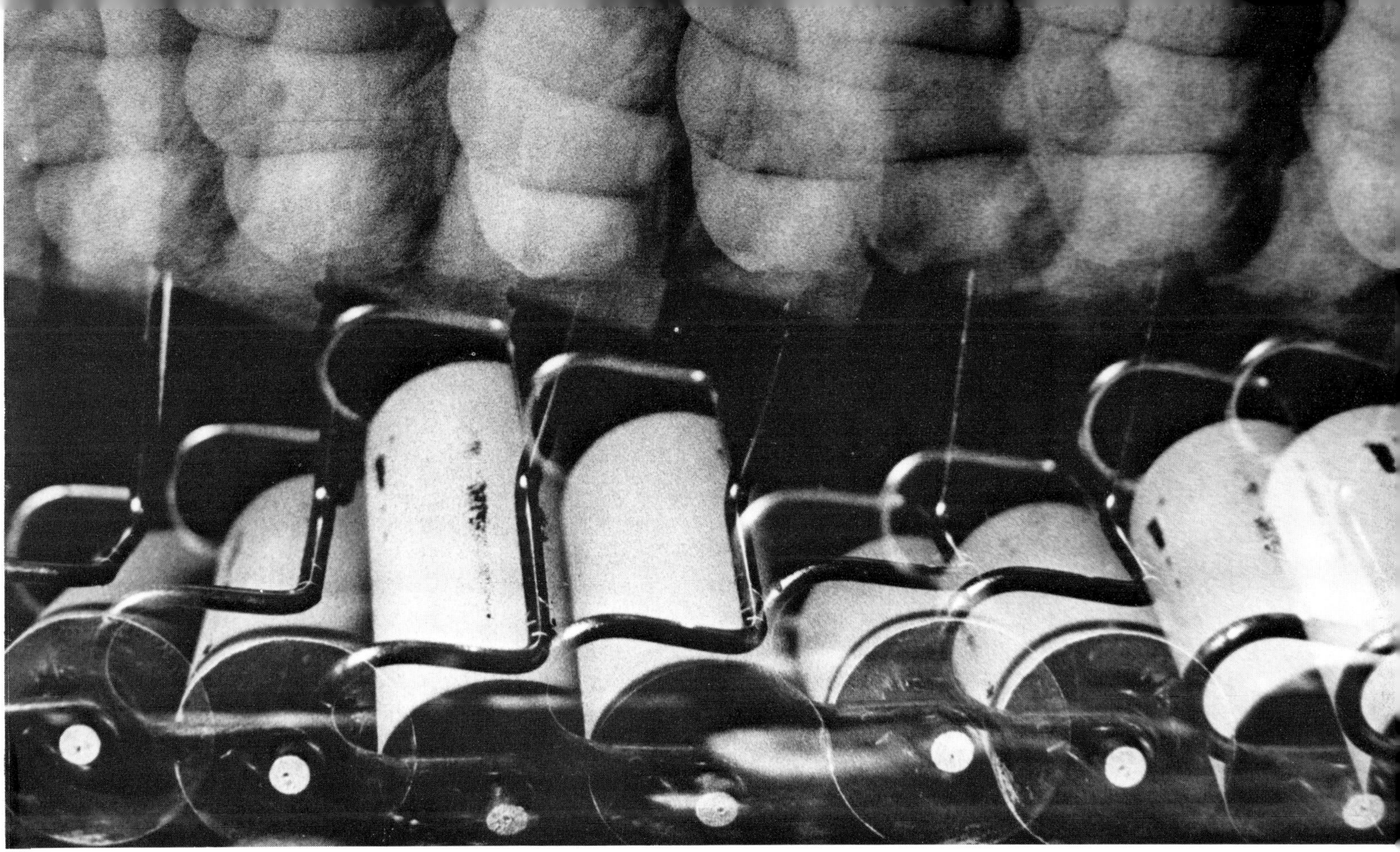

**the wiggle roll**

This illustrates the one side action of the up and down movement of the brayer as it rolls across the surface of the paper.

Diagram B shows the correct position of the brayer as it swings from side #1 to #3 with the results.

C

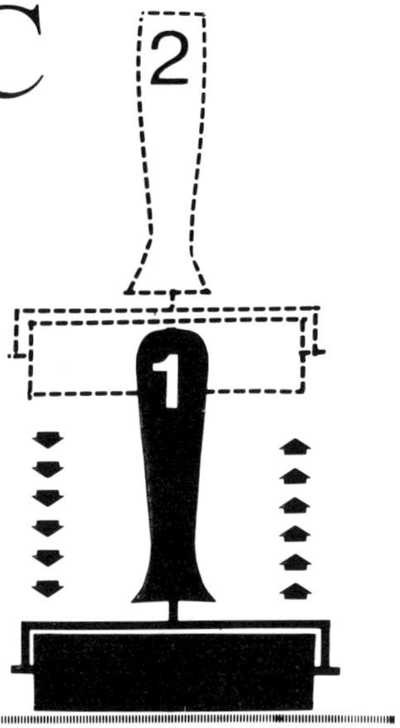

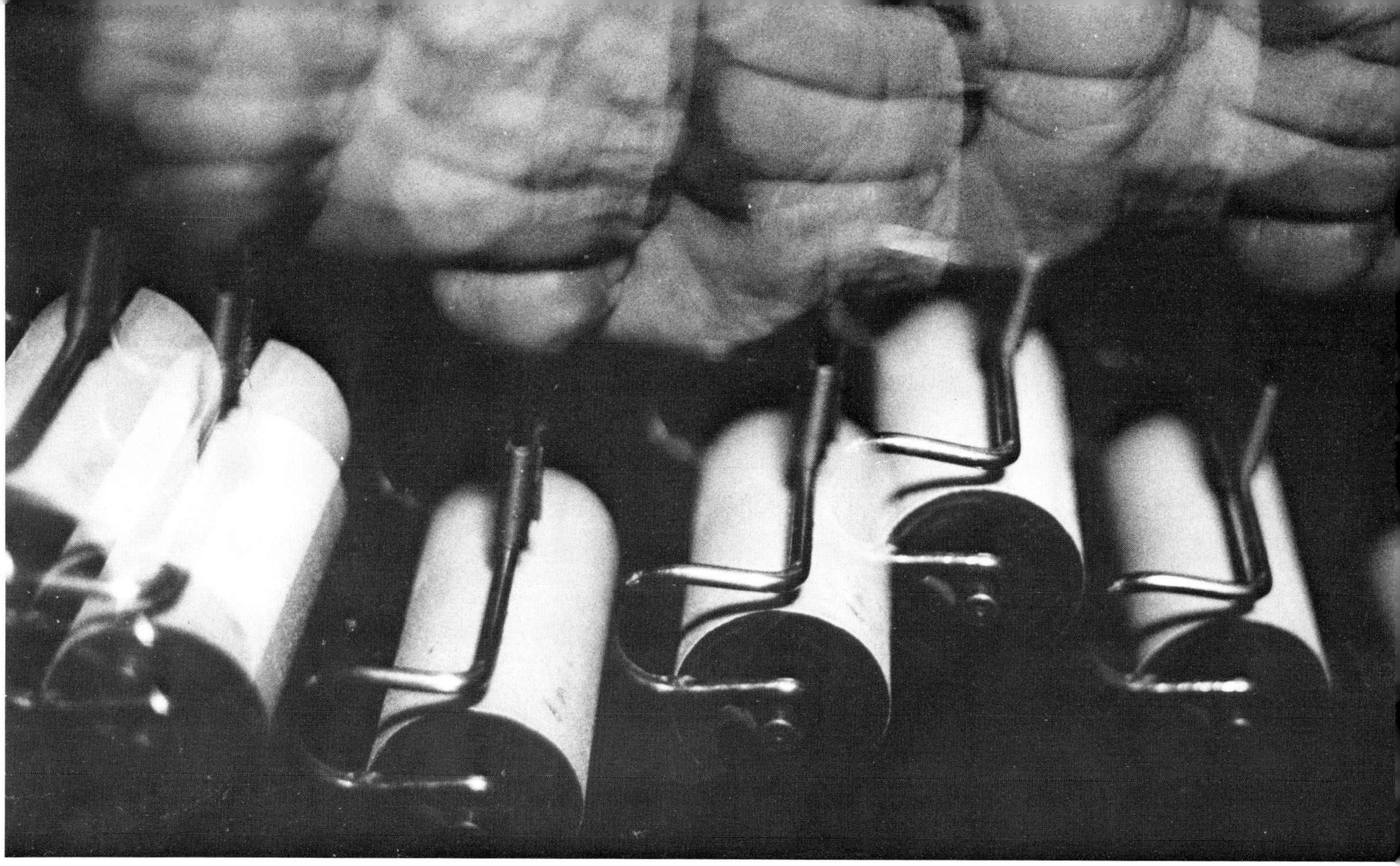

**the flat bounce**

The photograph illustrates the vertical bounce as well as the horizontal action across the surface of the paper.

Diagram C illustrates the correct position of the brayer as it contacts the paper in an up and down action with resulting images.

D

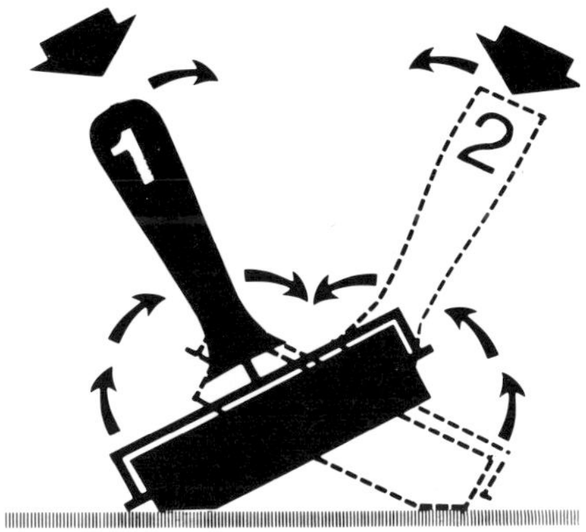


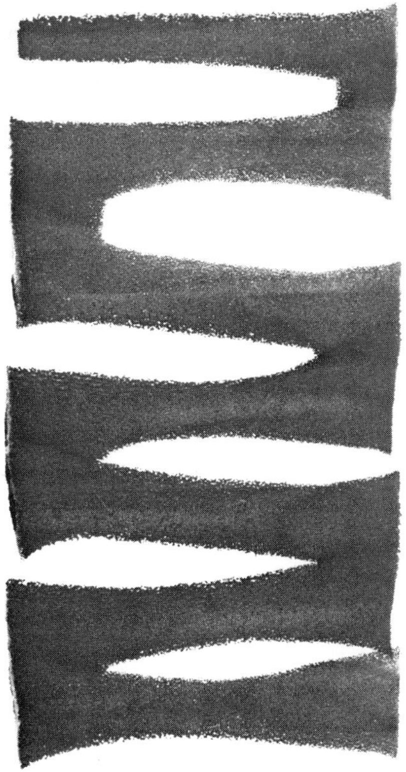

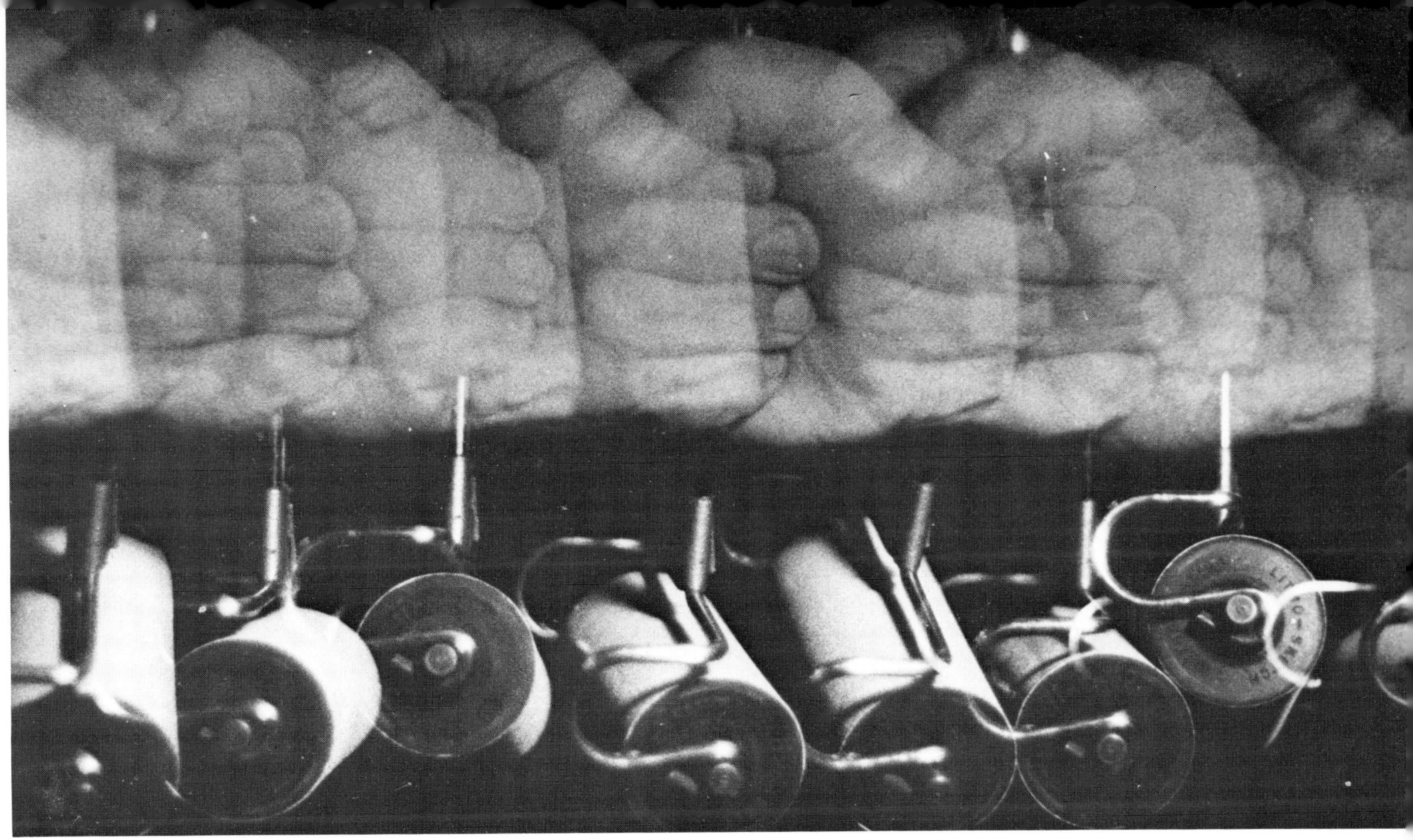

**the wiggle/waggle roll**

Here you see the side to side action as the brayer rolls across the paper surface.

Diagram D shows the correct position of the brayer as it swings from #1 to #2 with resulting images.

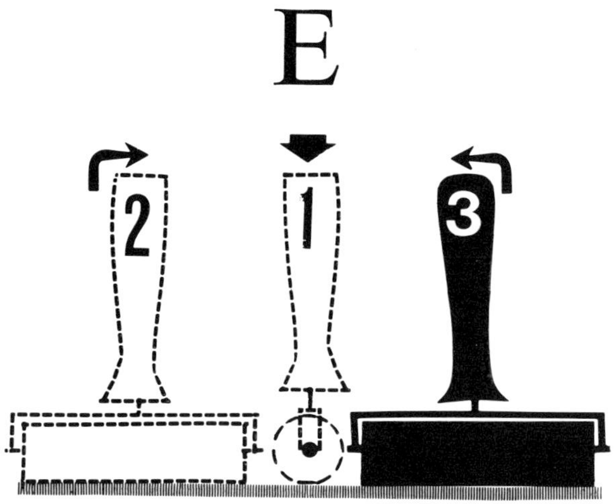


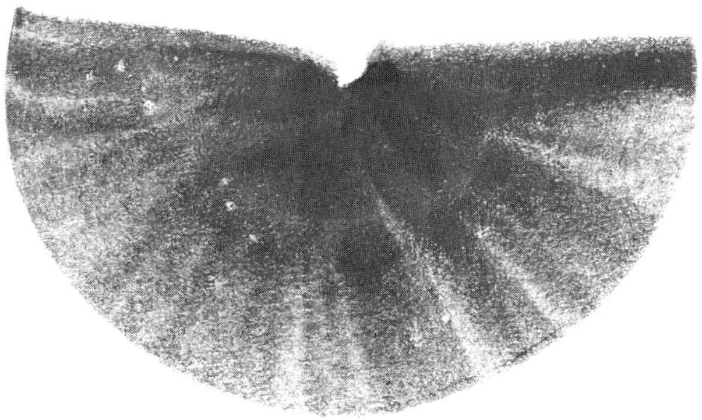

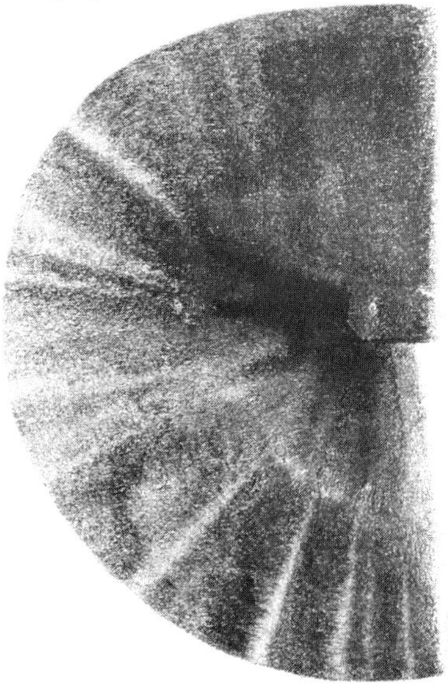

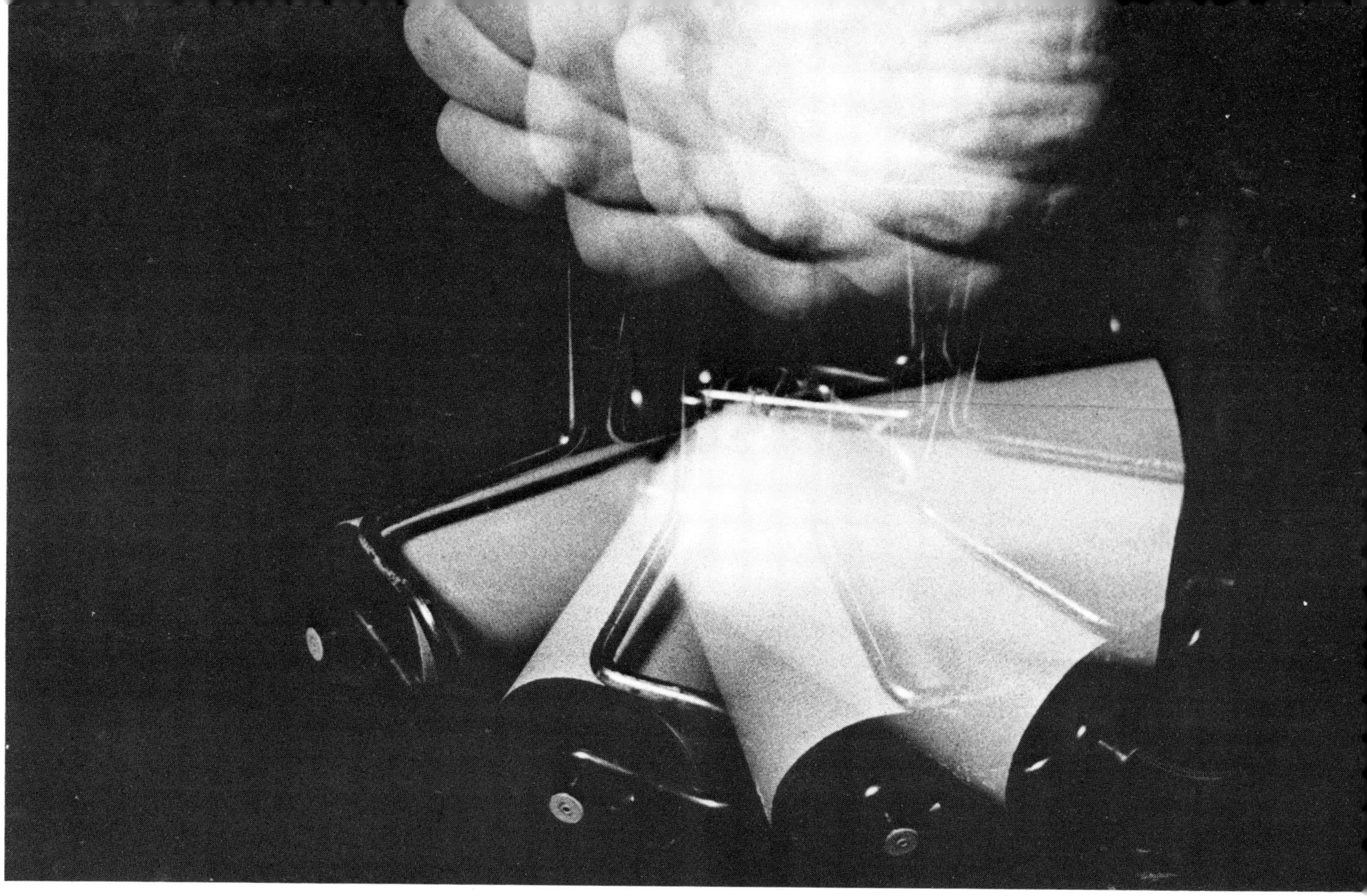

**the pivot/swivel roll**

This is the pivot action as the drag swivels the roller of the brayer.

Diagram E illustrates the placement of the brayer #1, then left or right to #2 or #3. The resulting images are indicated below.

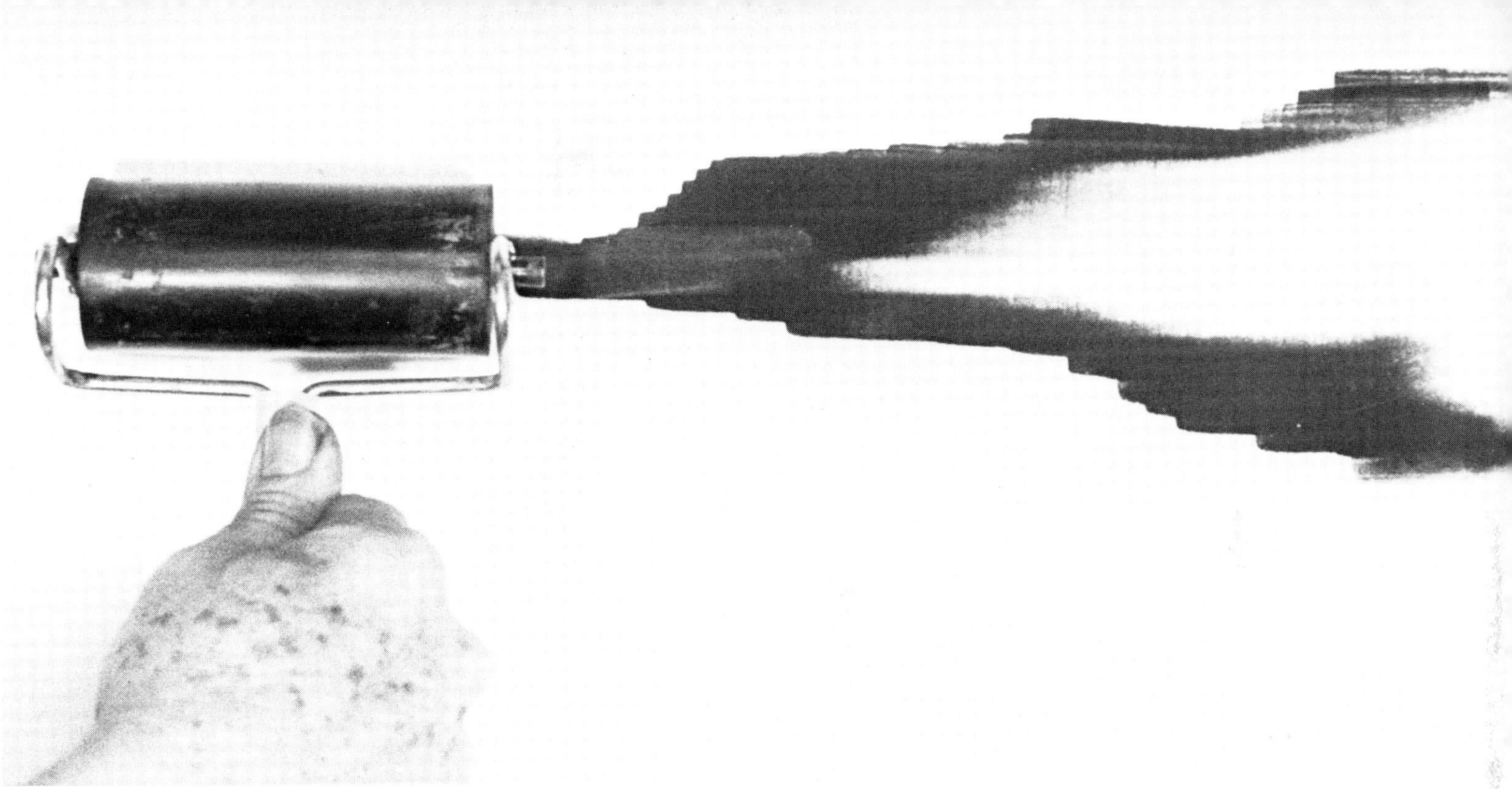

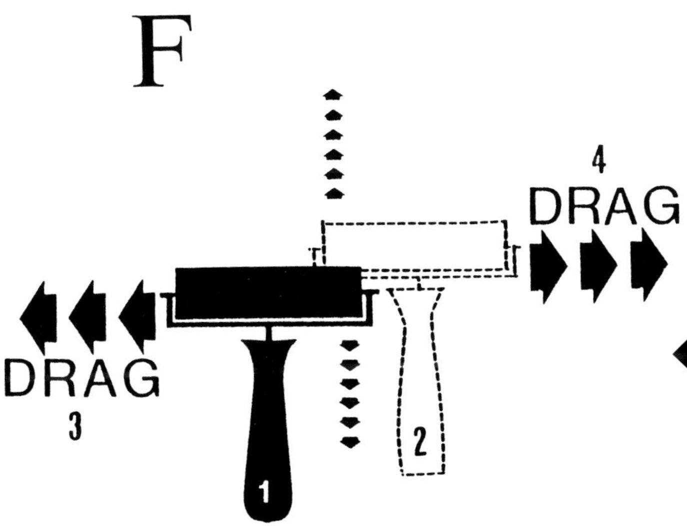


**the up/down and drag roll**

Here you see the short up/down stroke as you drag the brayer across the paper in a horizontal manner.

Diagram F shows the placement of the brayer #1, the drag across the paper #2, and simultaneously moving the tool as per #3 and #4.

## roller scraping

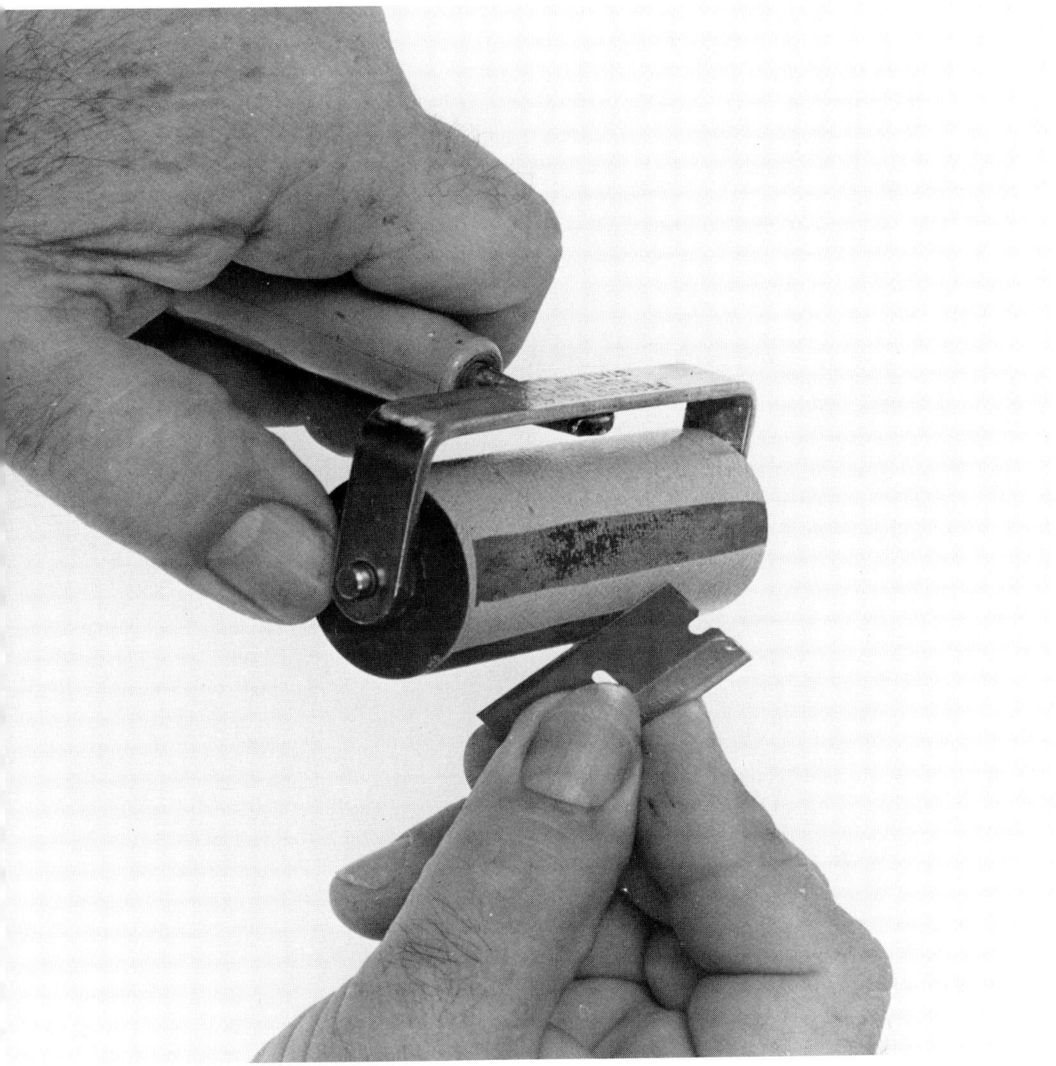

**the roller scraping technique**

Hold the ink coated roller of the brayer firmly with your thumb as shown, thus retaining the roller in position as illustrated in the photograph. Now, with the razor blade or some other metal scraper, carefully scrape away some of the ink from the roller's surface. With your left thumb, rotate or move the roller to the next area to be scraped. Repeat this scraping method and keep rotating until you complete the cycle.

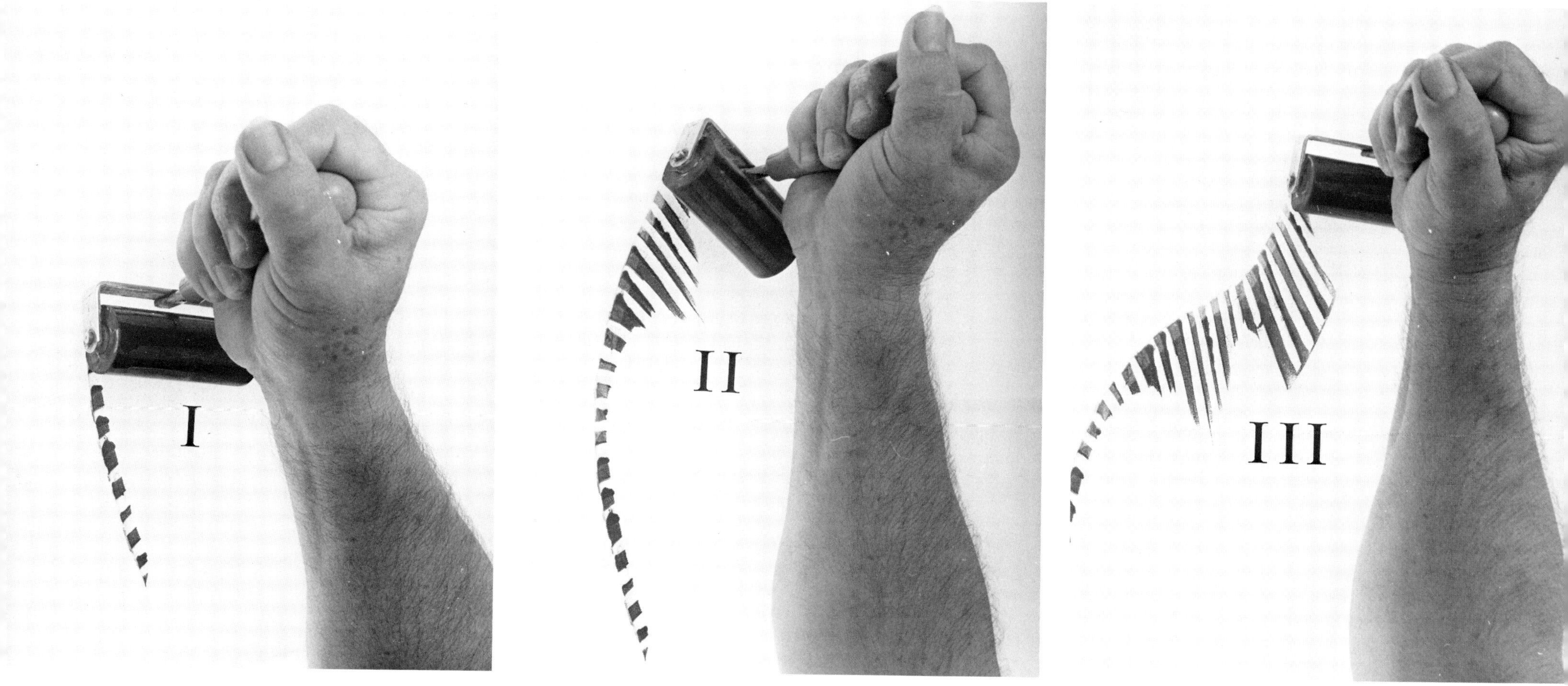


With the prepared roller ready, here, in three steps you see the brayer in action and the results.

**seated cat**
Diagram A
Prepare your roller as illustrated. These initial rolls set the character of the subject.

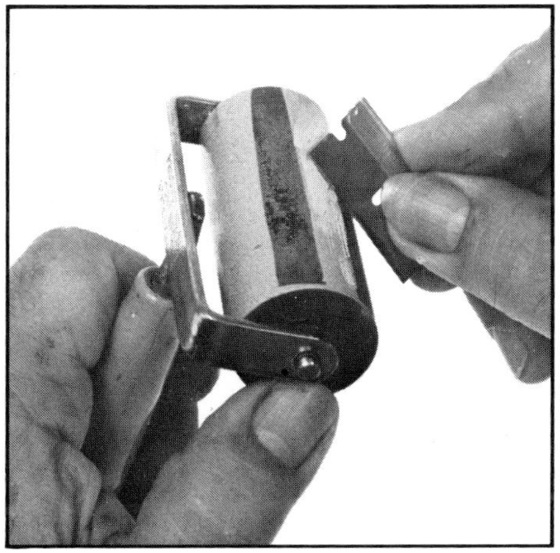

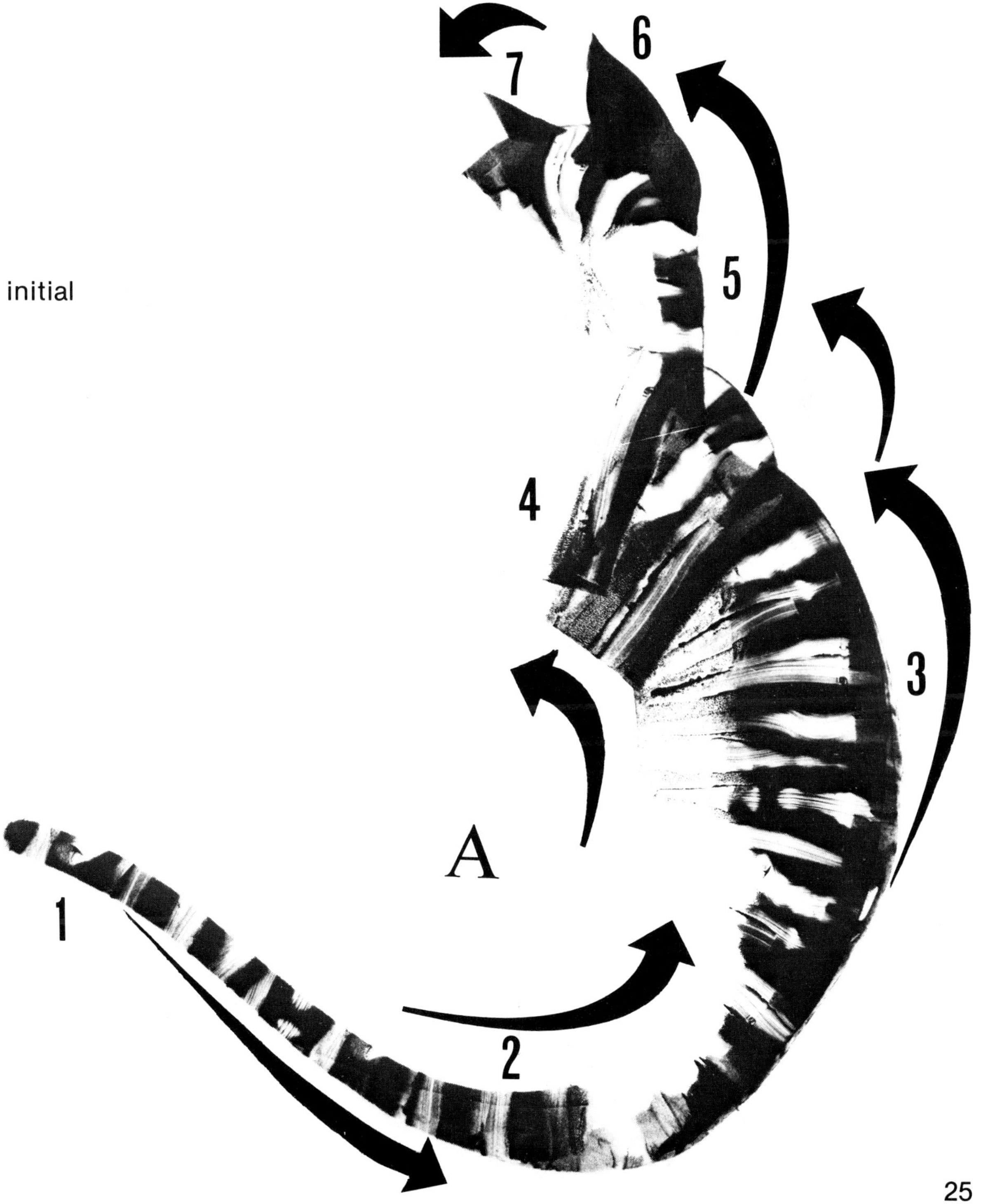

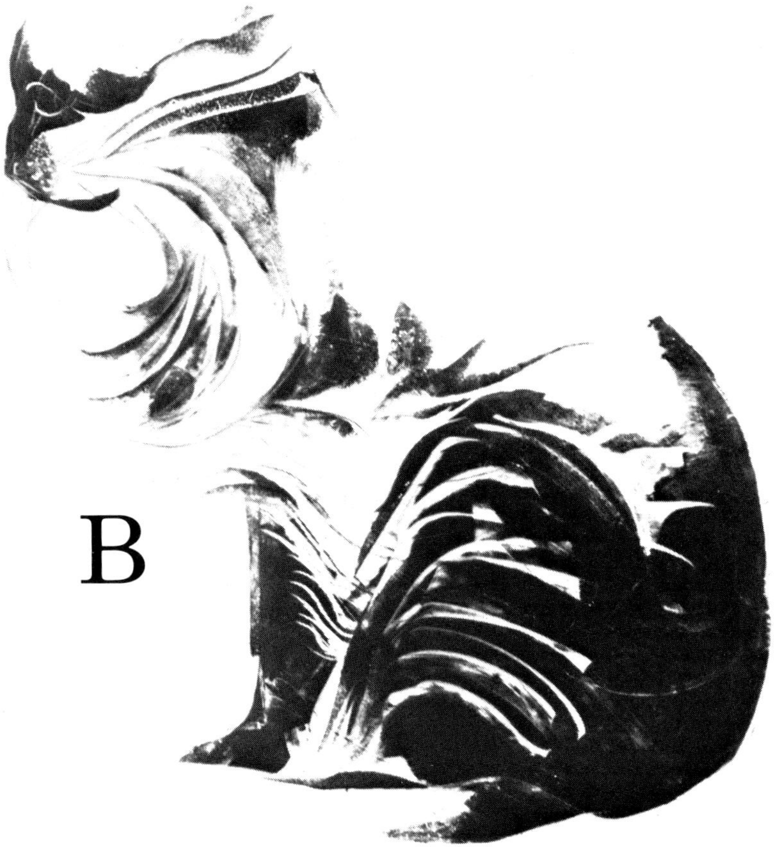

B

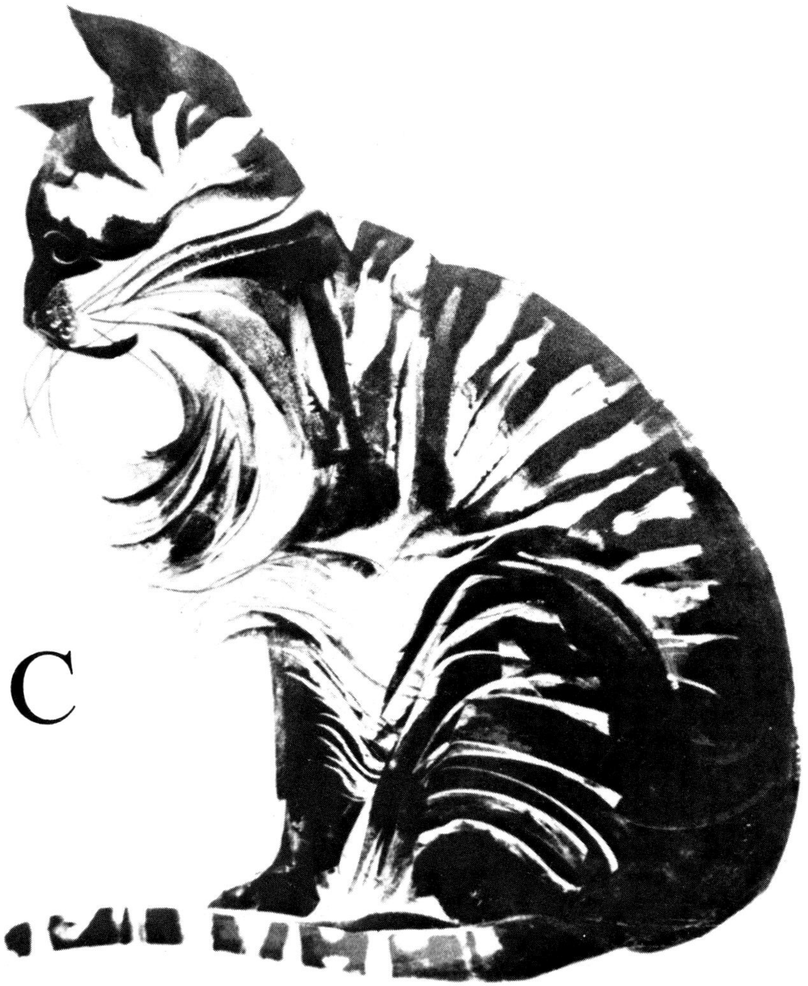

C

**seated cat**

You can practice your follow-up strokes separately and in greater confidence by working on a transparent overlay such as acetate, without risk of destroying or damaging the original image (A). When satisfied with your results, remove the acetate and proceed (B) with your roller strokes on image A.

Image C is the complete illustration of the seated cat. It's the result of a combination of A and B.

Size: actual art 18 inches high, black and white.

**wild goats**

Diagram A illustrates the initial preparation of roller.

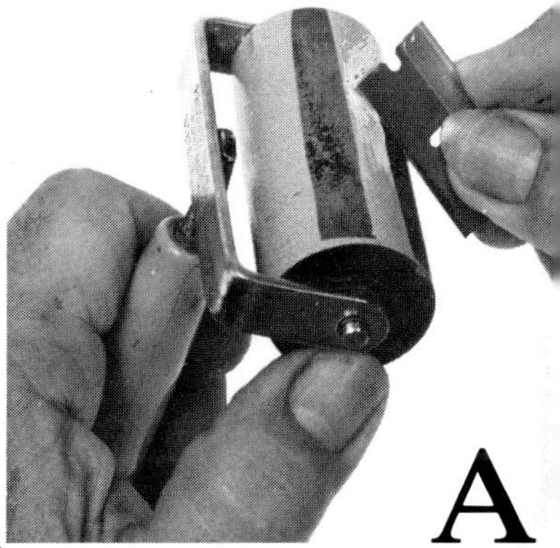

A

Below: three steps illustrating the roller action.

1

2

3

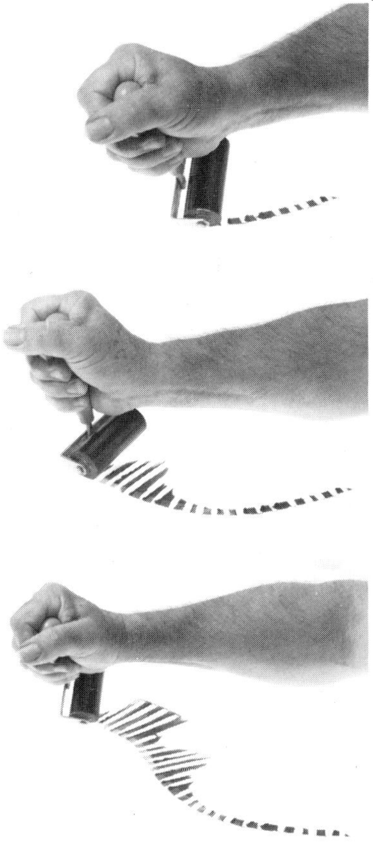

Results of the first important strokes.

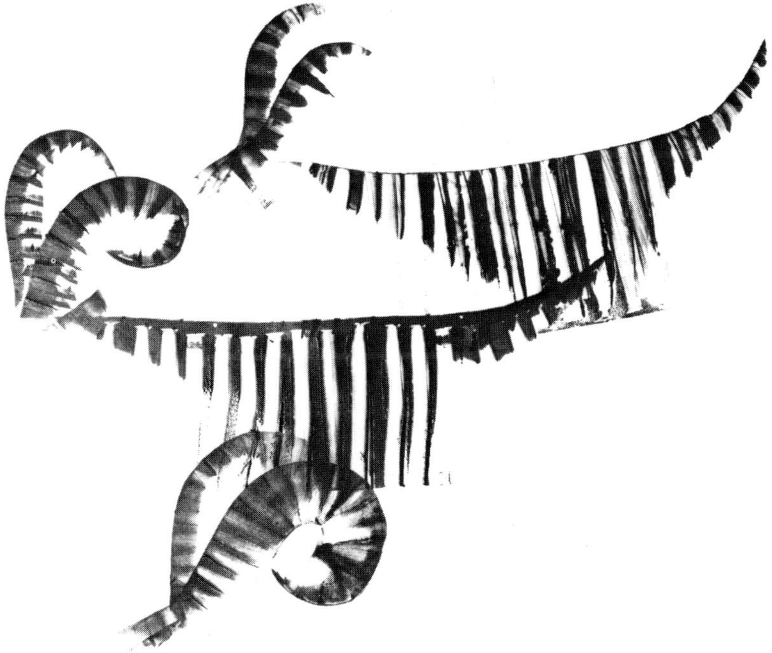

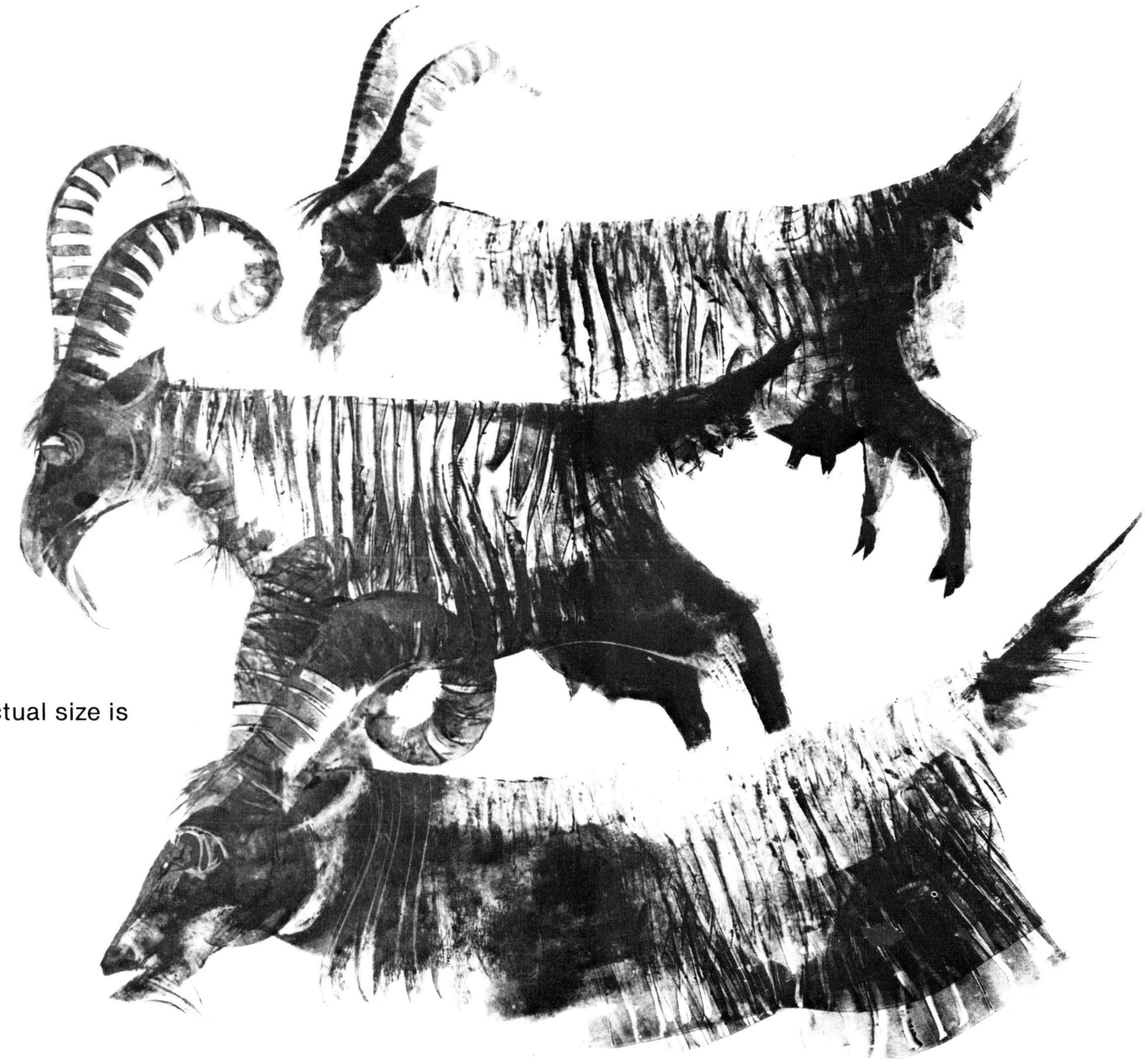

**wild goats**
Black and white, oil on paper. Actual size is three times larger than shown.

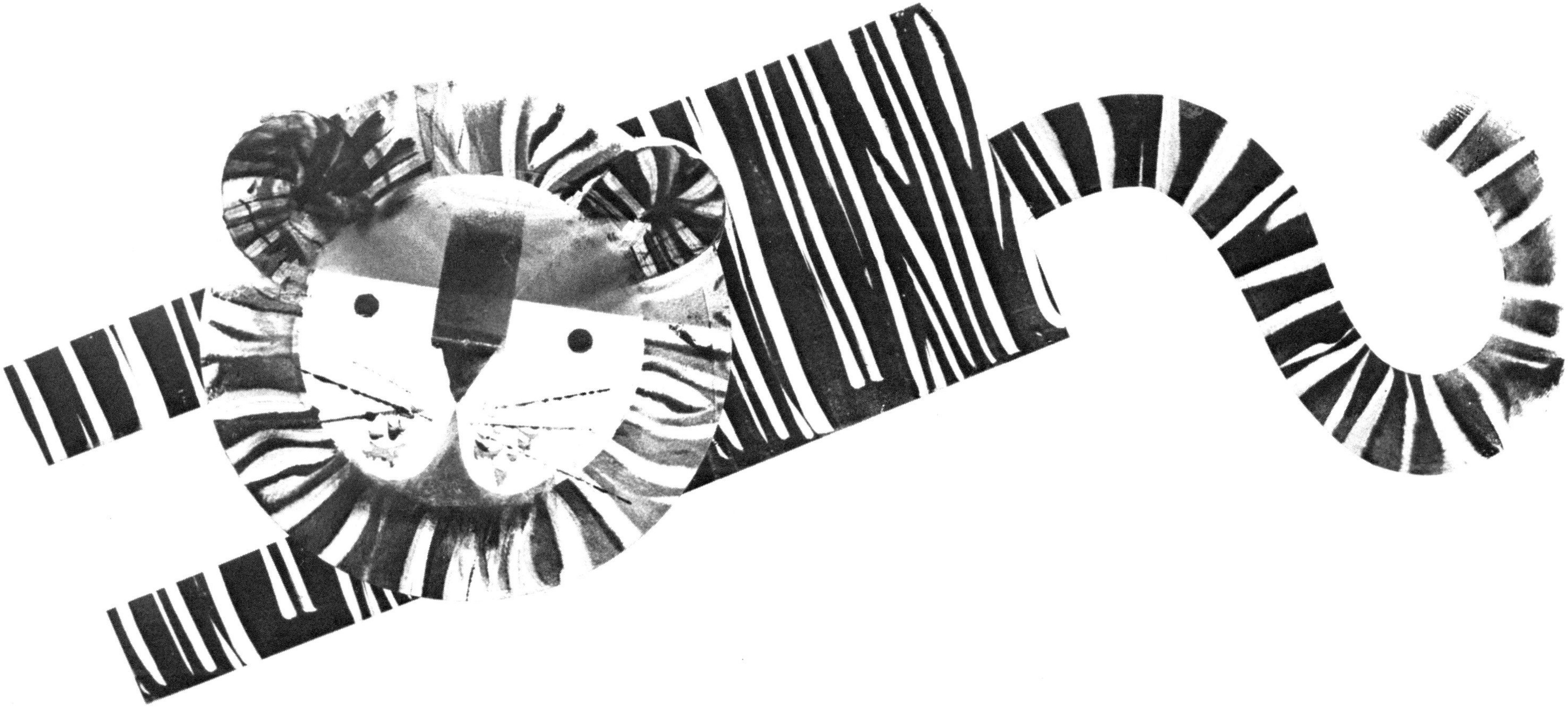

**scraping and scratching cat caricature**

20 inches long, one color.

## impressions

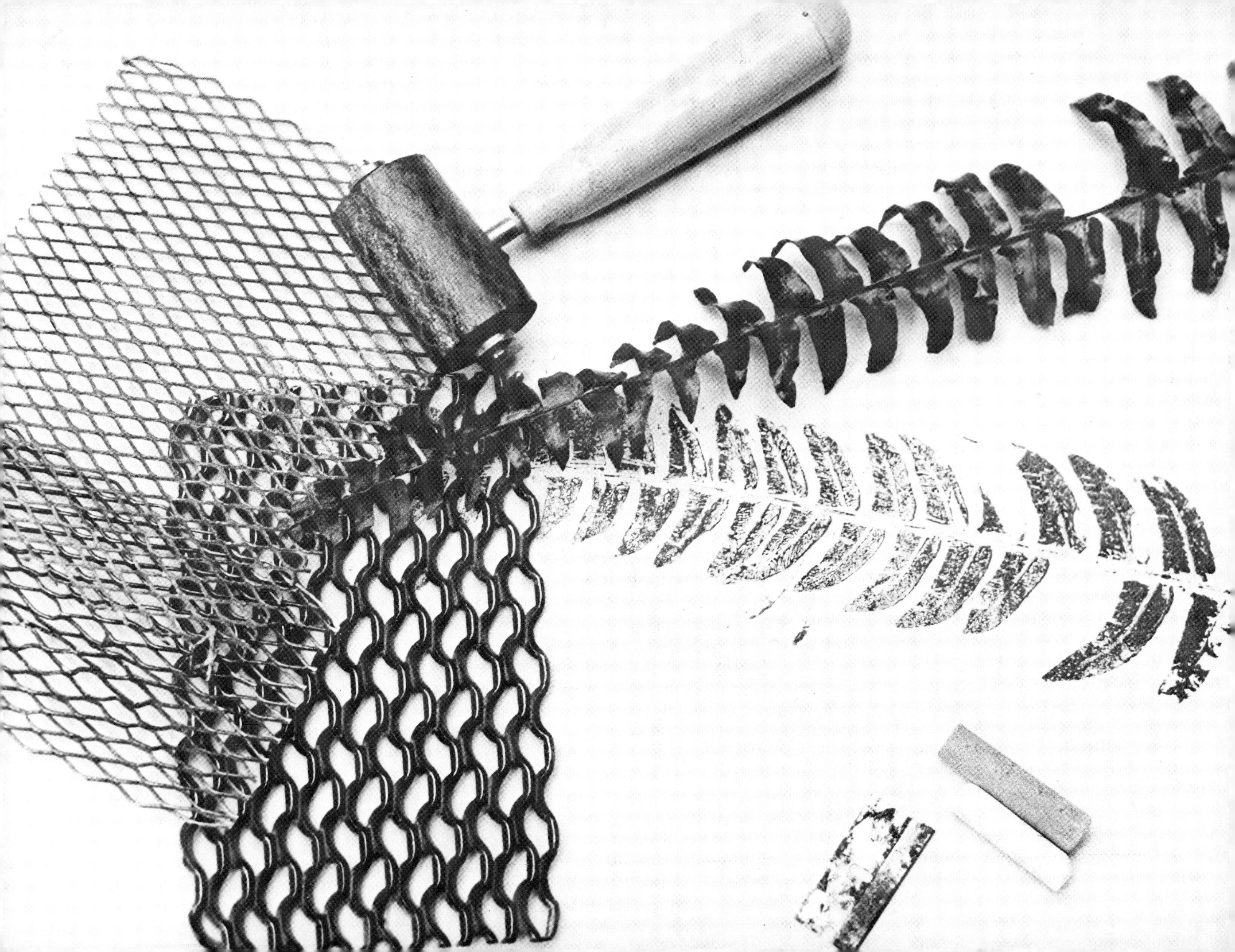

**the chalk resist technique**
With your white chalk write the word CHALK on a heavy piece of paper or illustration board. Prepare to roll with an inked brayer. ⟶

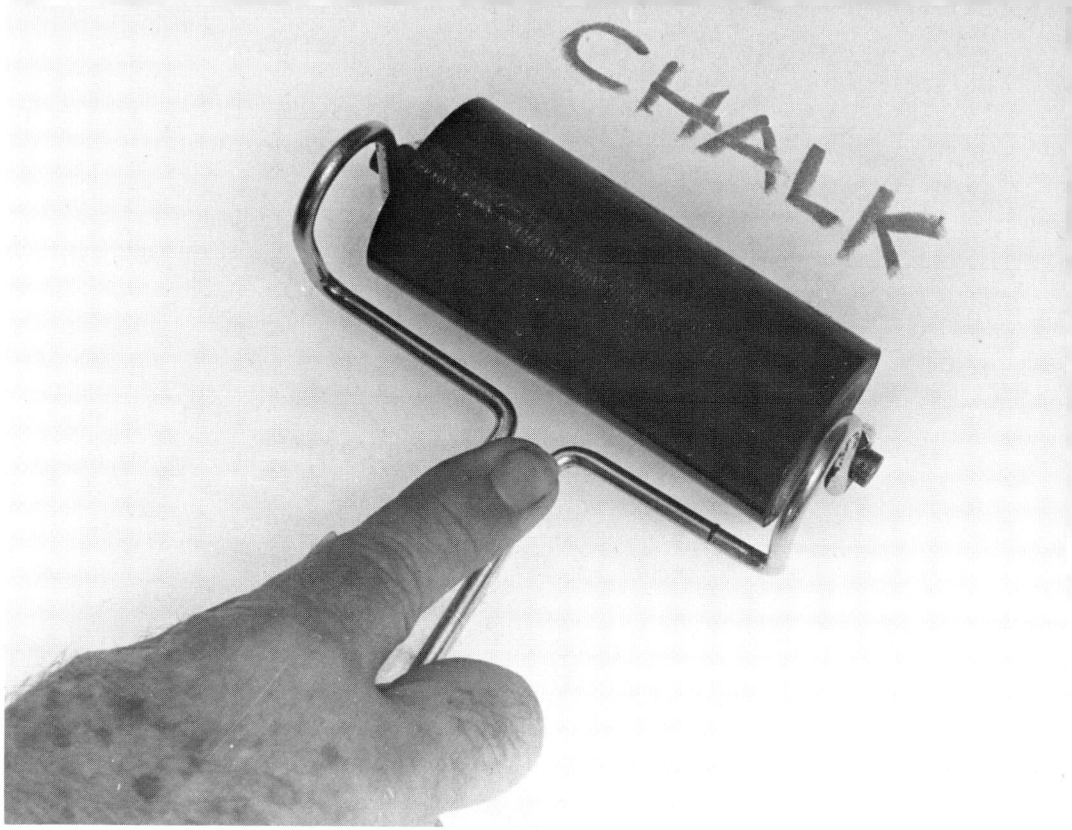


Make a single pass across the word CHALK. This shows the resist of the chalk to the ink, leaving a reverse chalk image on the roller itself.

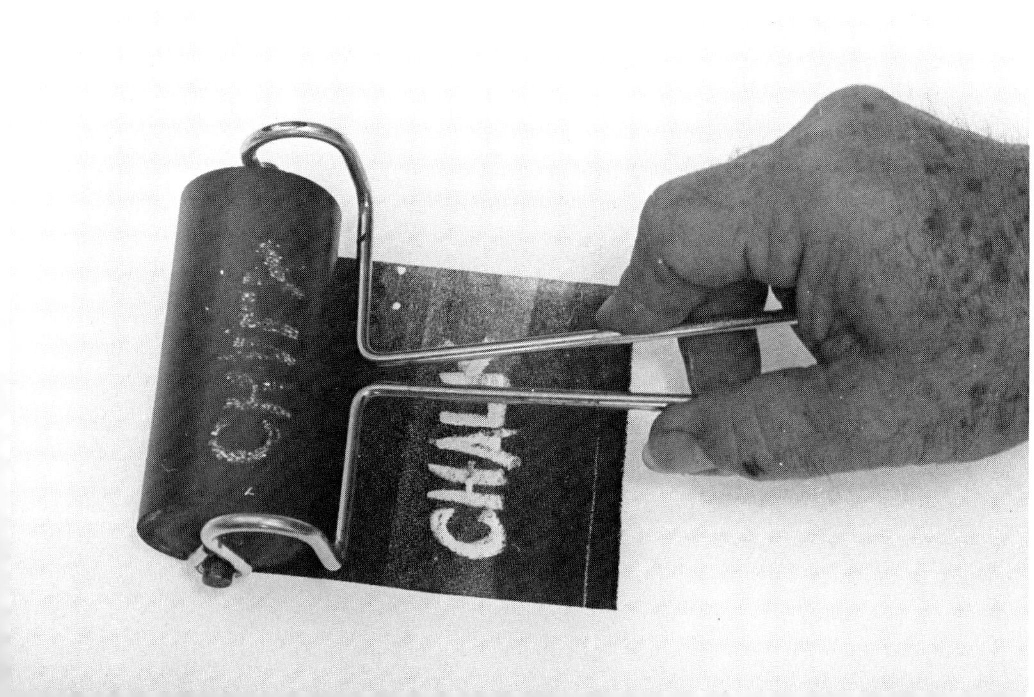

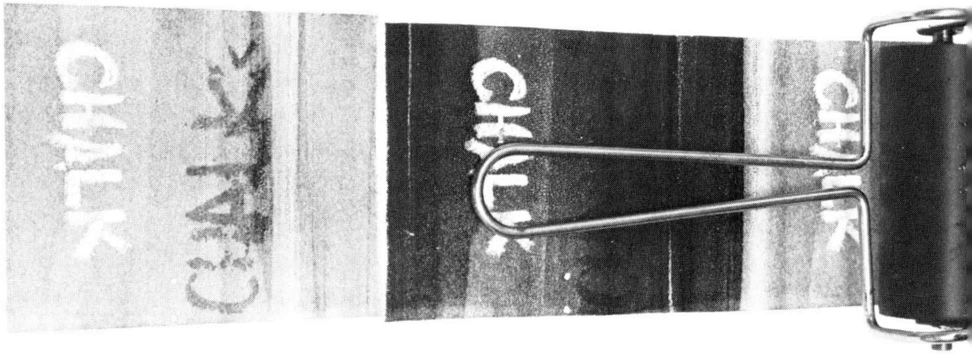


Achieved by continuing the roll of the brayer.

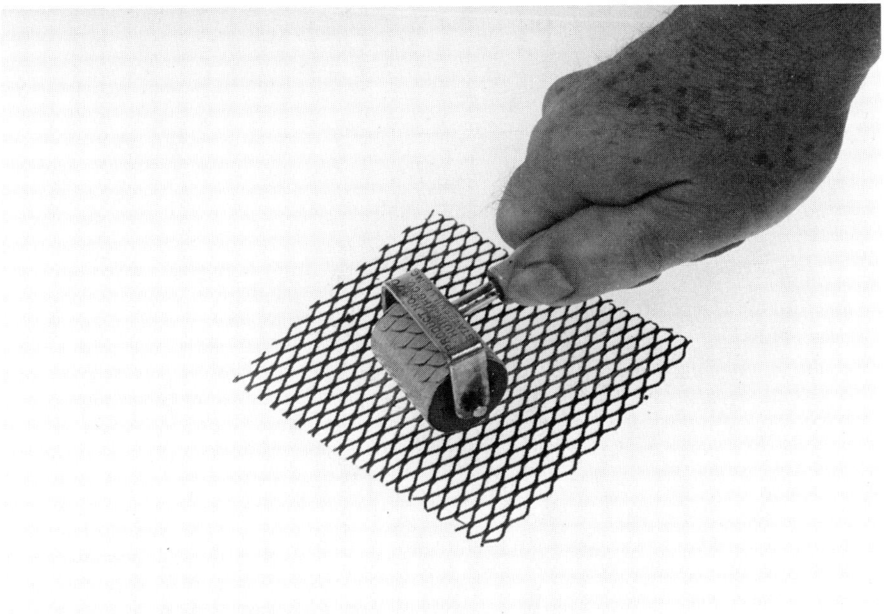

**the metal mesh impression technique**
Coat the roller with ink. Make a single pass across the metal mesh, leaving a reverse pattern on the roller itself.

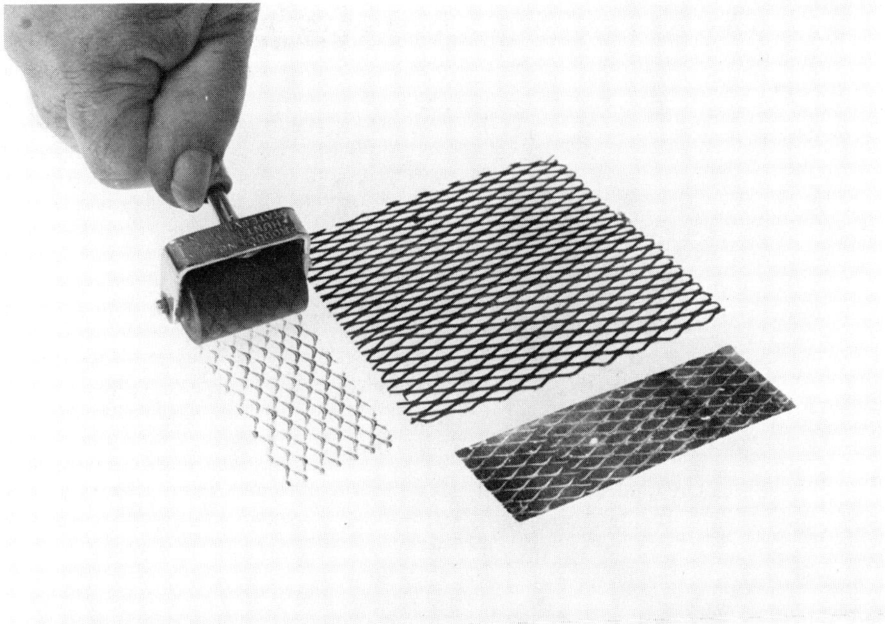

Shows the negative pattern when it is rolled on the paper.
The positive pattern is made when a clean brayer picks up the pattern from the inked metal mesh and it is rolled on the paper as illustrated.

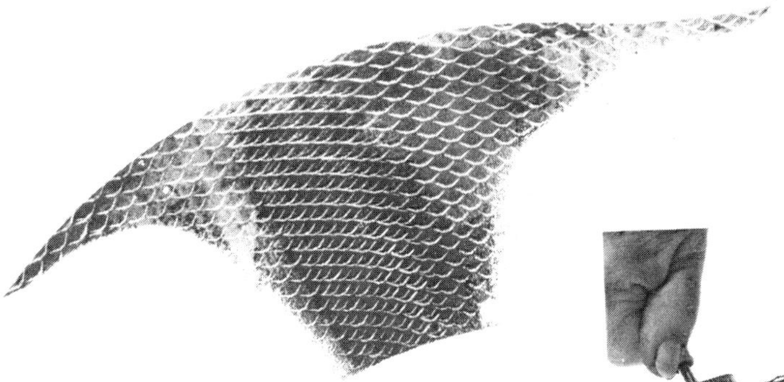

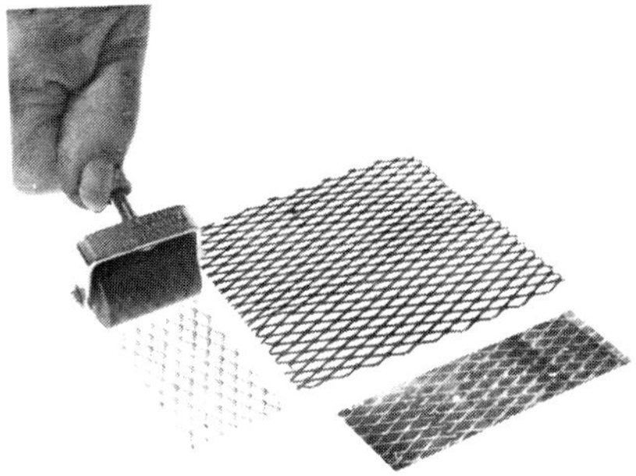

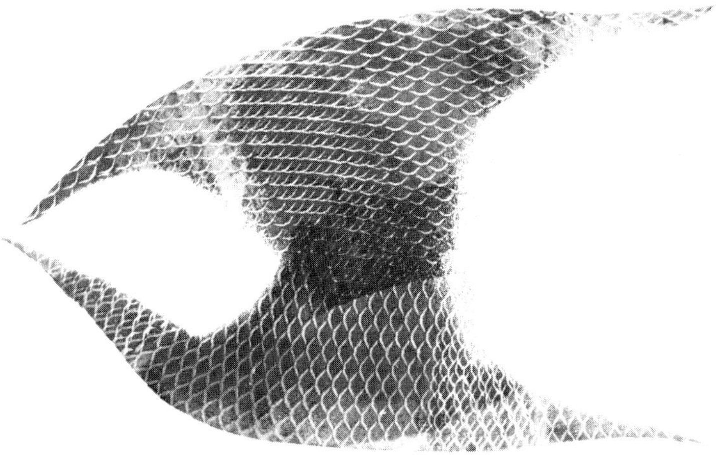

FISH IMAGE: A four-stage exercise build-up. Prepare the brayer for the design pattern as illustrated here and on page 33.

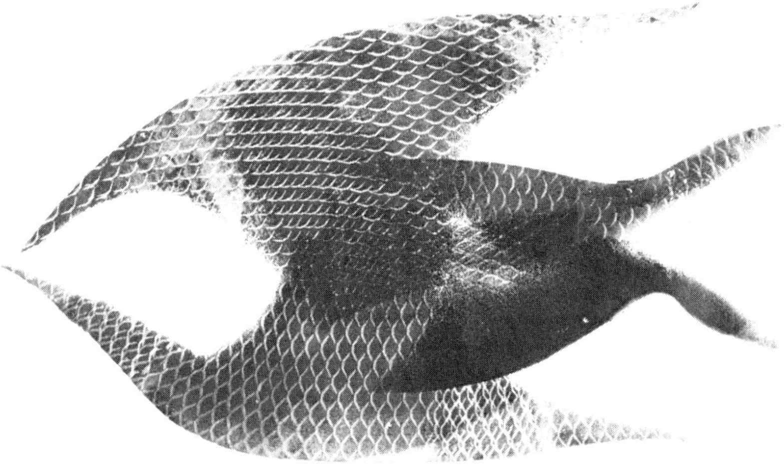

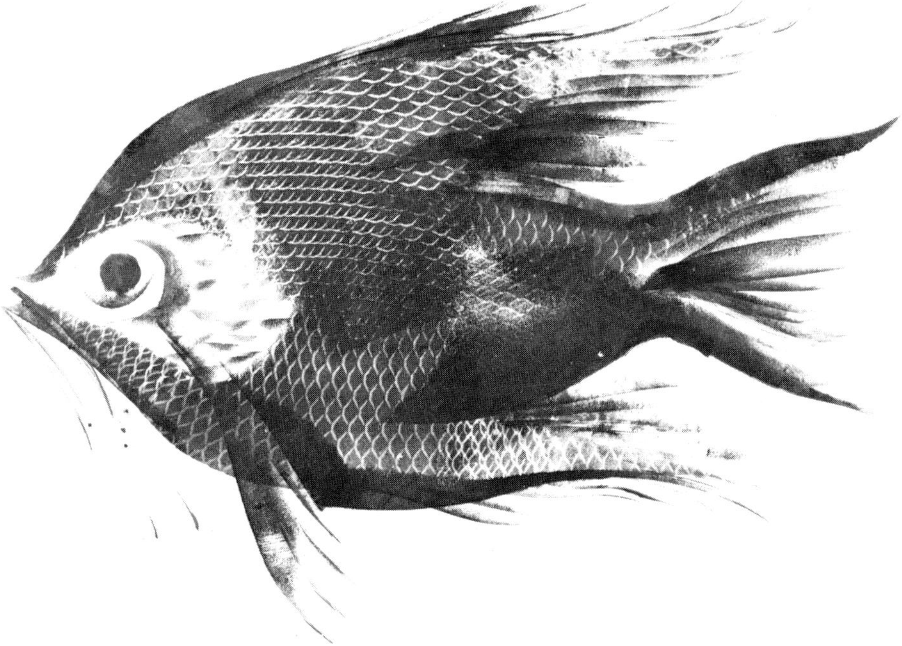

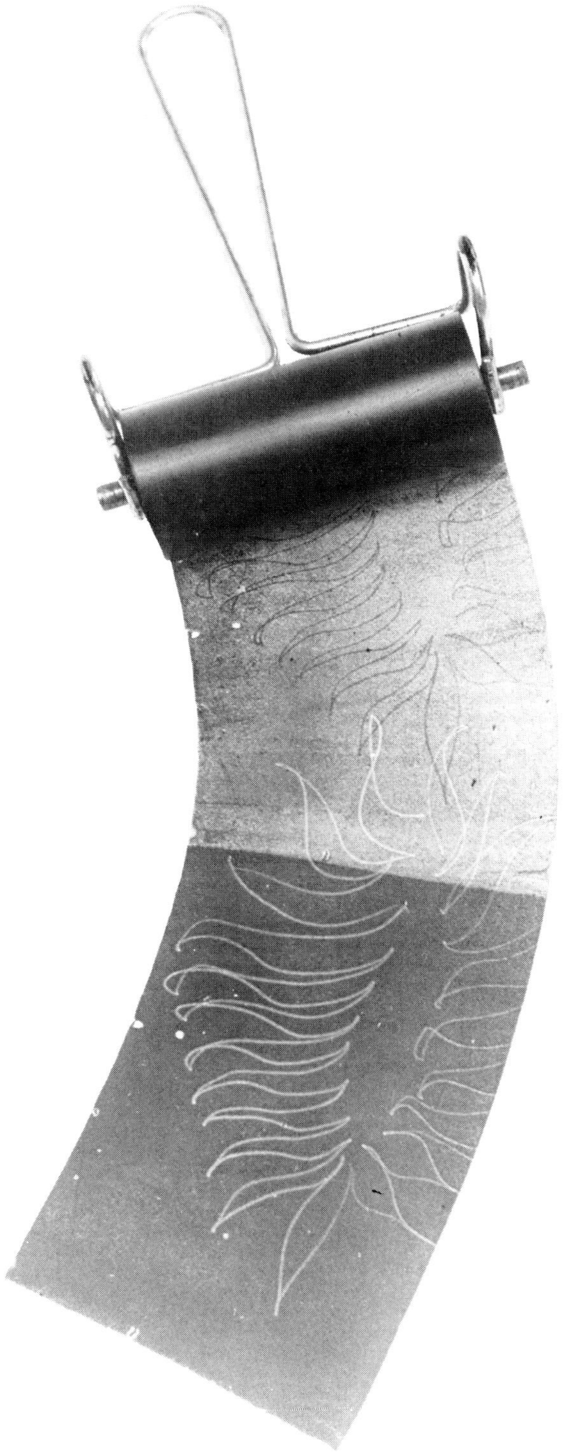

**the wax resist technique**
Using regular household waxed paper, draw your design through the waxed paper onto your art paper with a stylus or hard pencil.

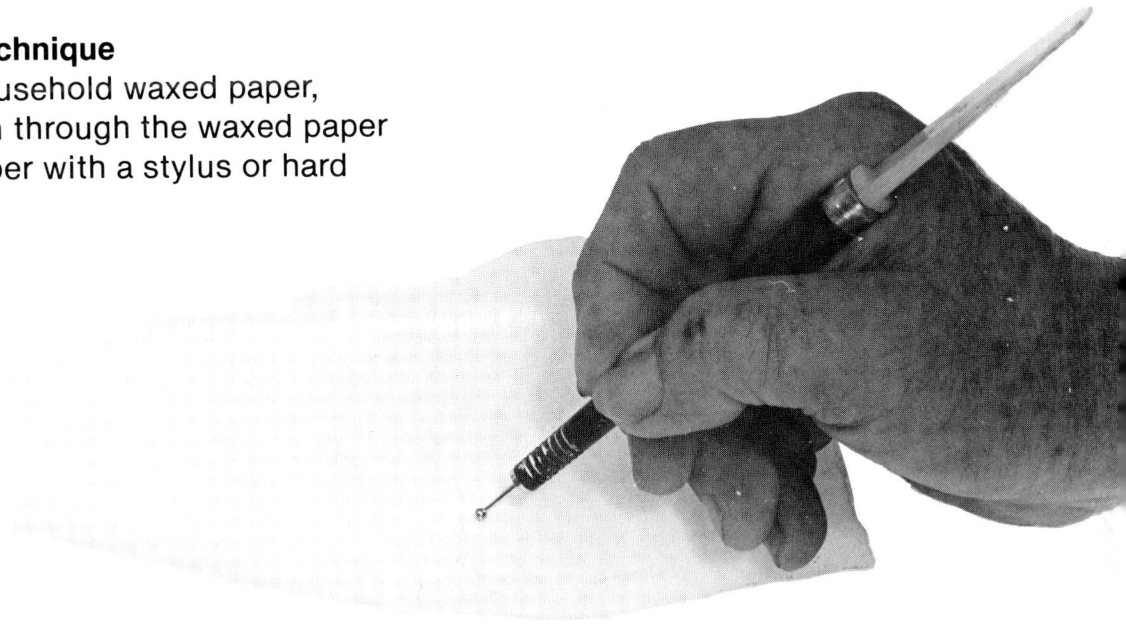

With the ink-coated brayer, roll across the waxed image on the paper. The resist in the wax is similar to the chalk resist technique. The difference is a finer, sharper line.

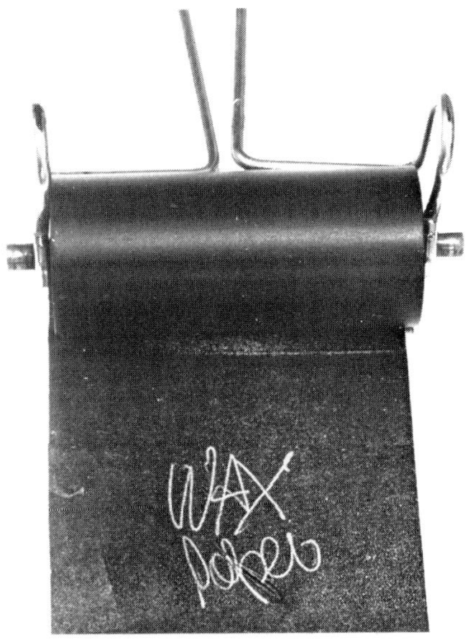

**the leaf of nature impression technique**
With an inked brayer, roll across the fern leaf once. Place the inked fern face down on the paper and, with a clean brayer, roll across the leaf. As you lift the leaf you have a reproduction image of the leaf on the paper.

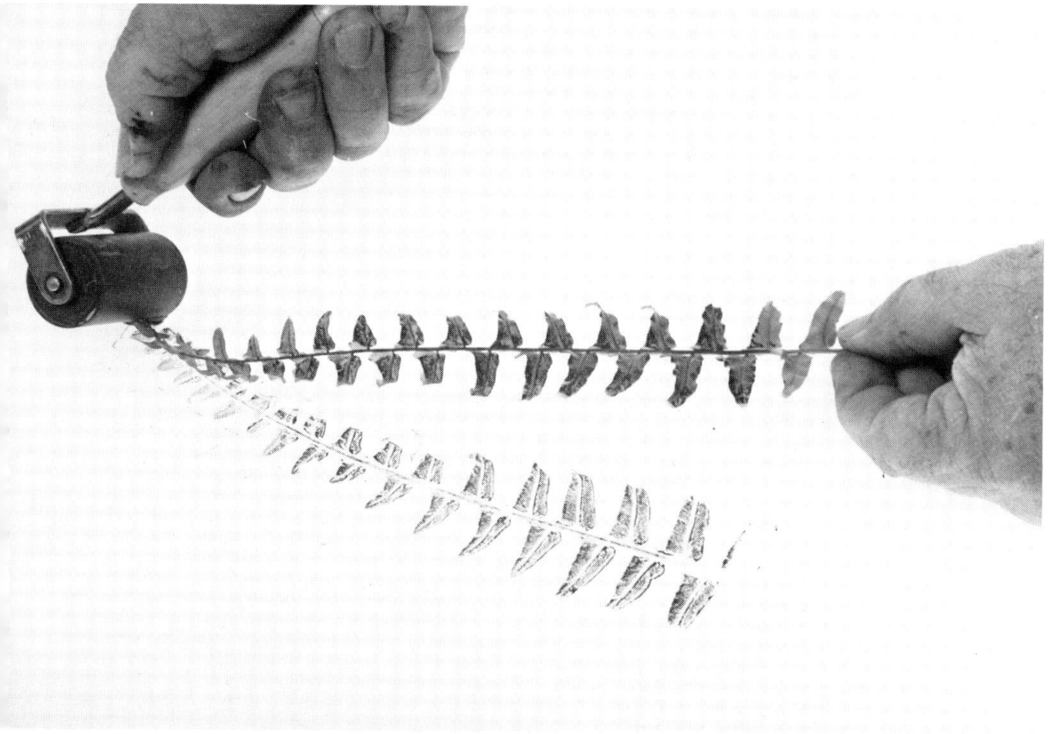

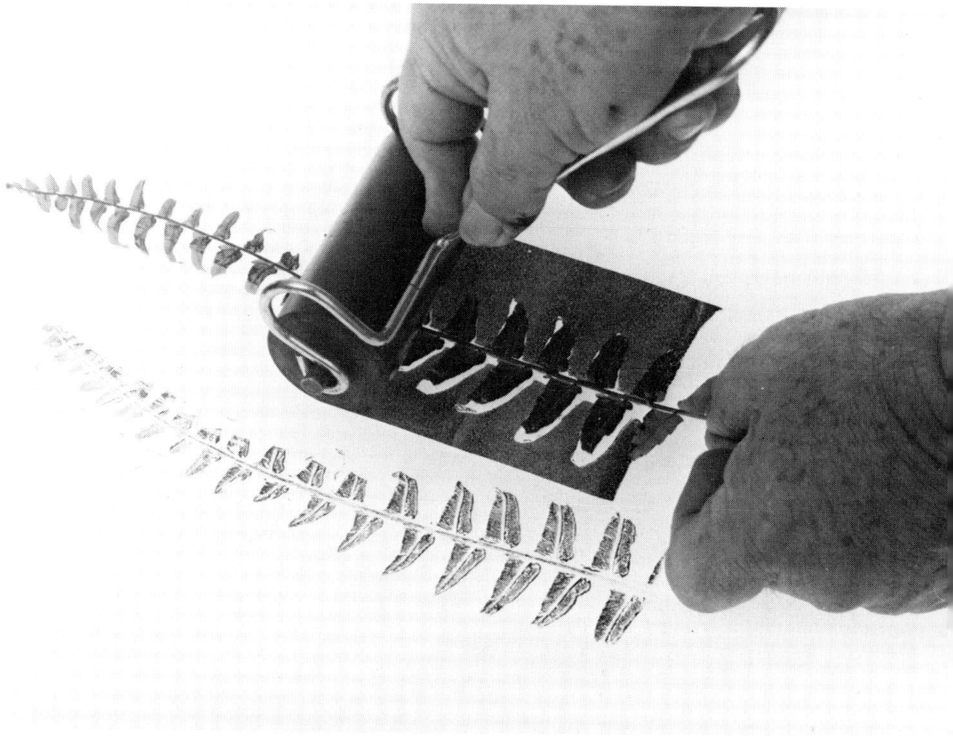

Place the inked fern leaf face up on the paper surface and roll across the leaf with a roller covered with ink. Keep the leaf steady with your other hand, then lift the leaf from the paper and you have a negative reproduction of the same leaf.

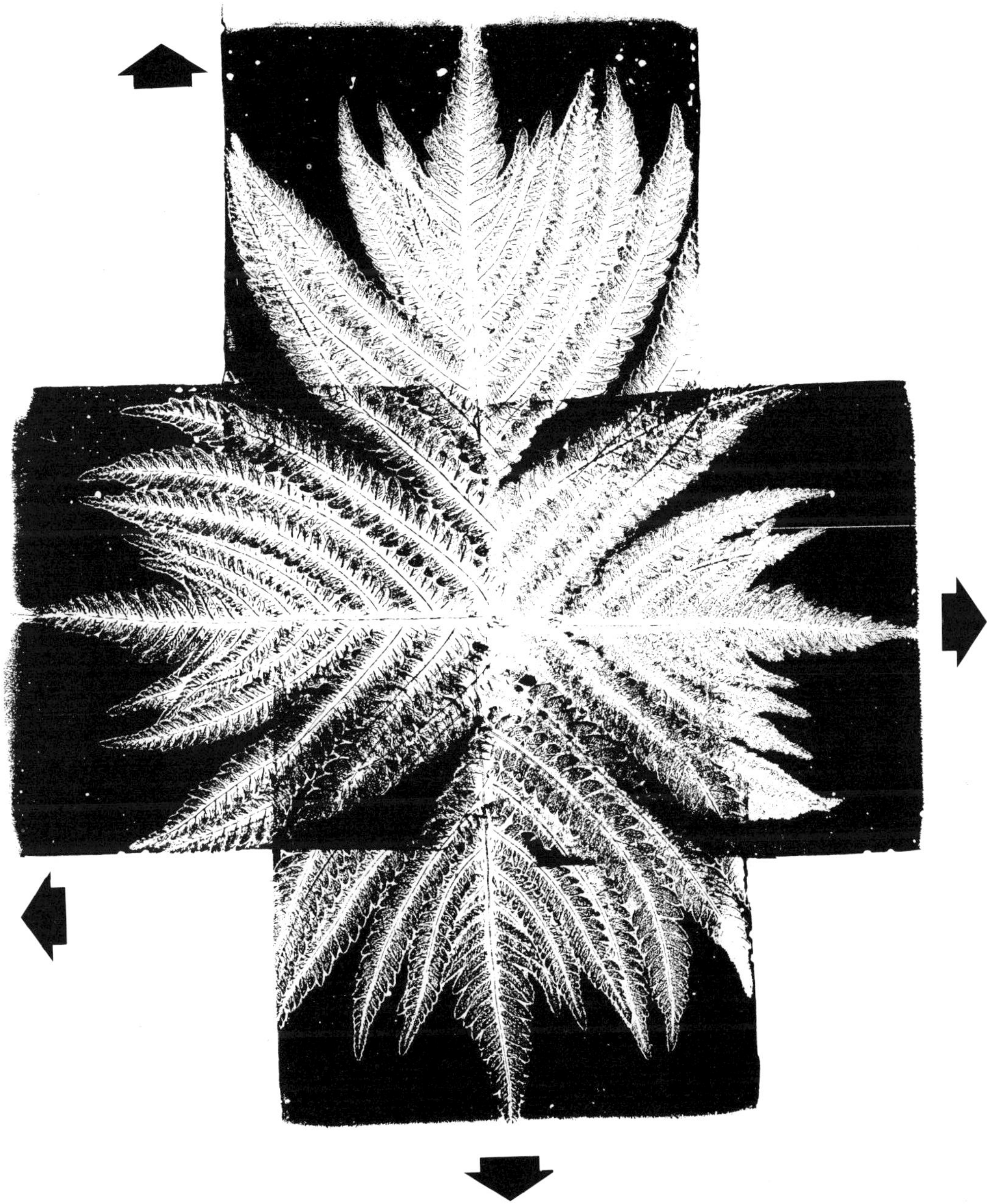

After placing the inked fern face down on the paper and rolling over its surface with an inked brayer, the above star-shaped design was developed.

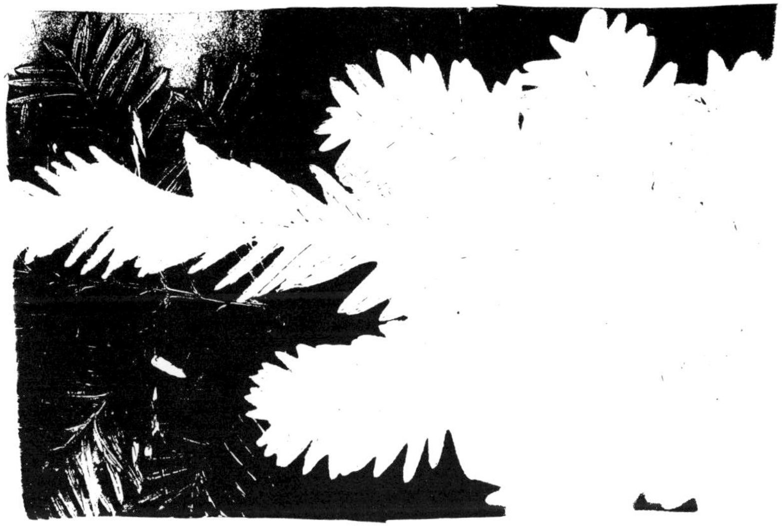

Negative image.

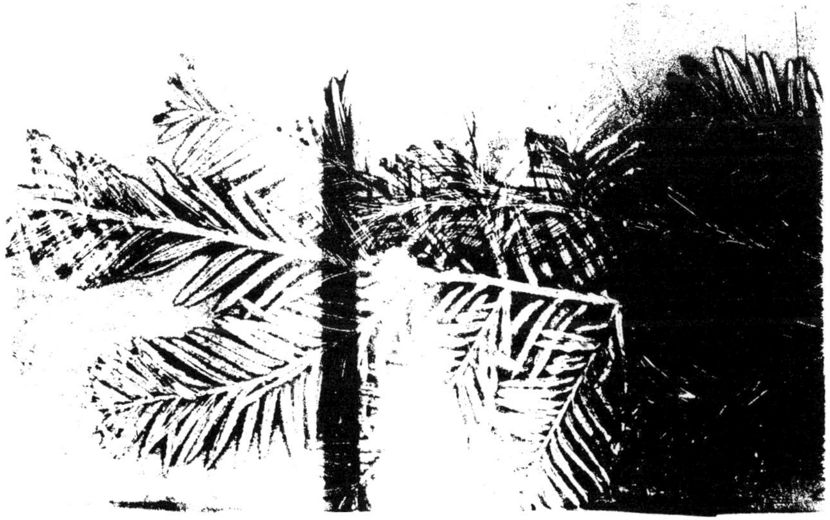

Positive image.

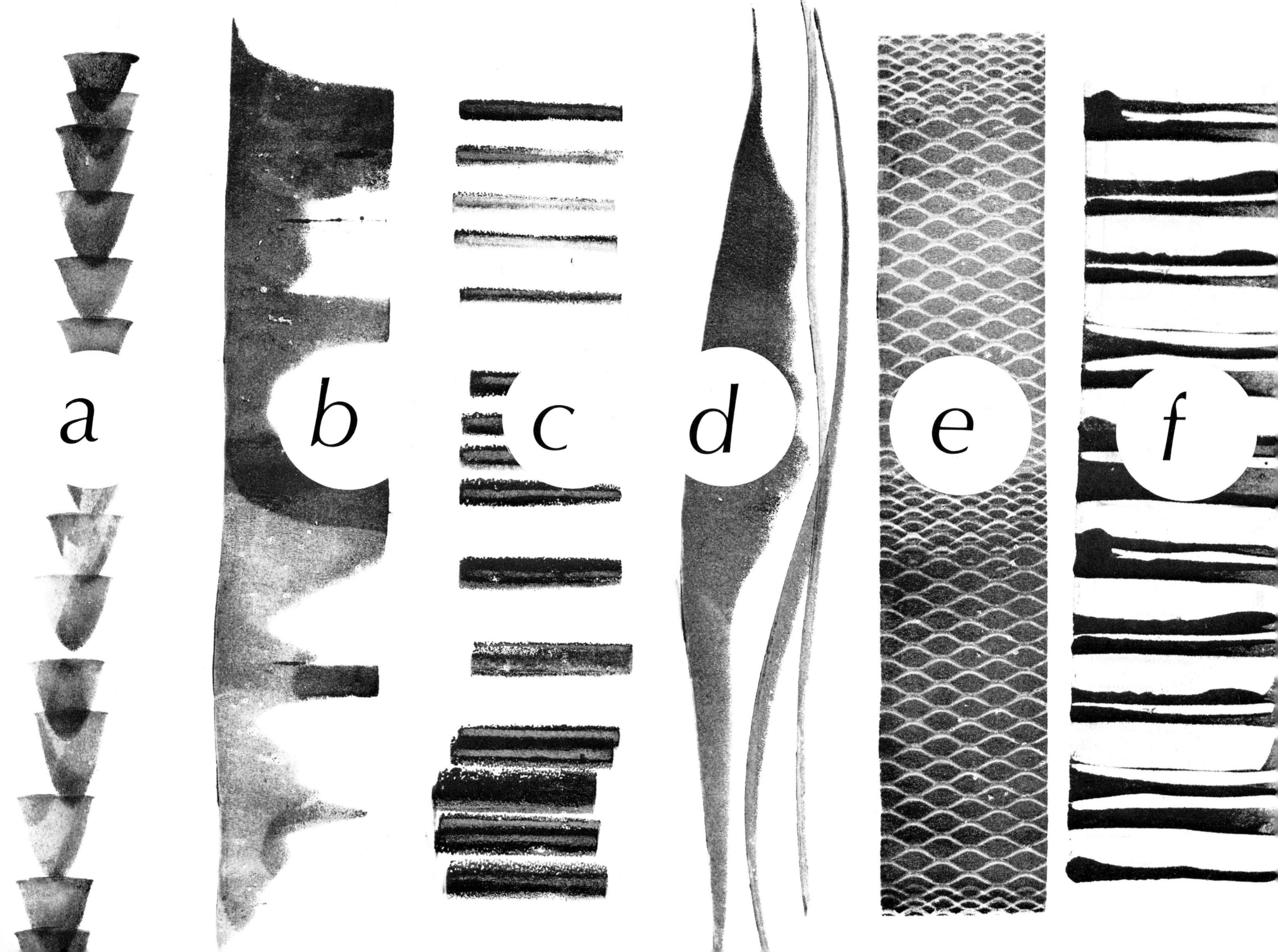
a
b
c
d
e
f

These strokes and rolls are coded alphabetically for quick reference to the types used to make up the frog and crayfish.

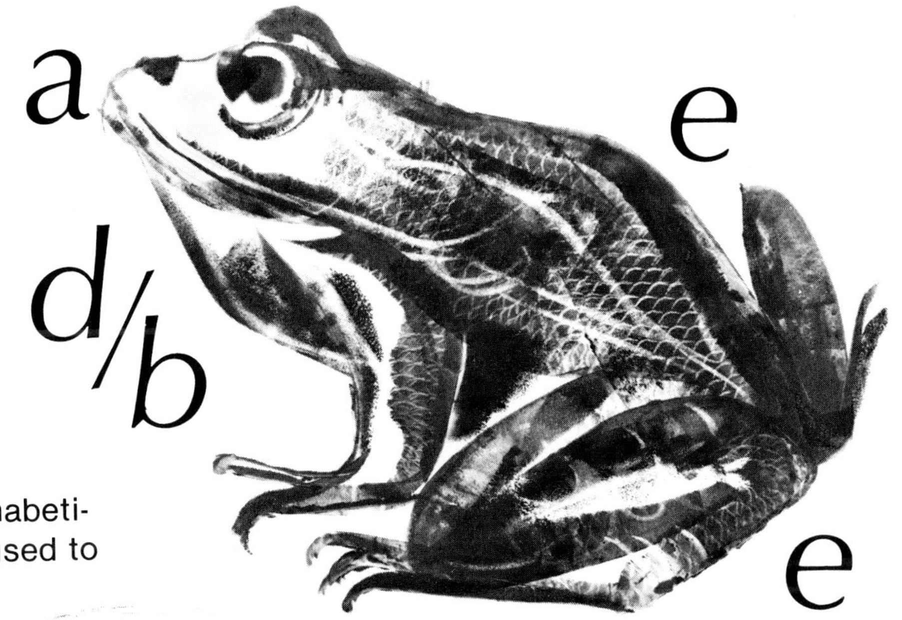


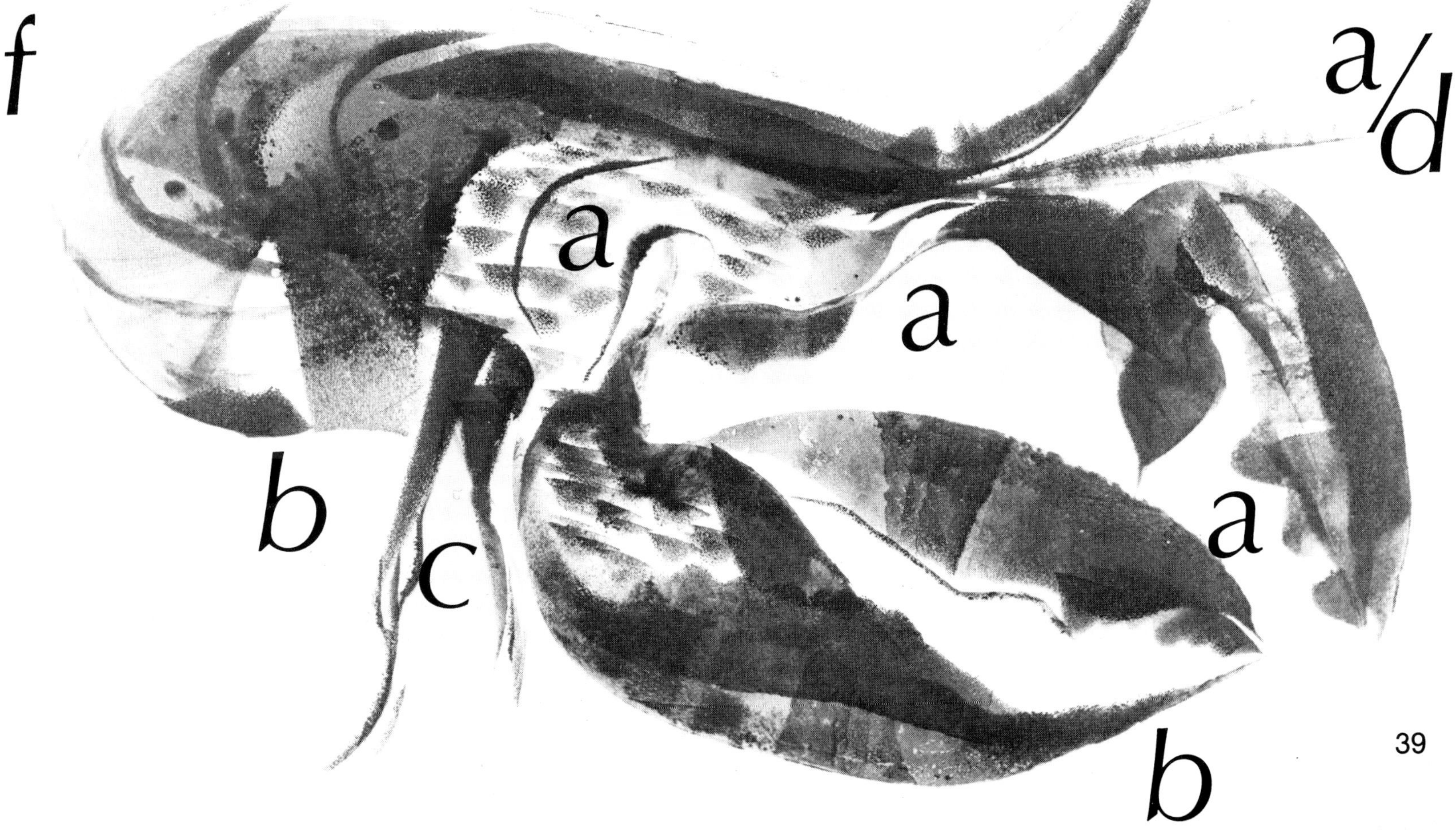

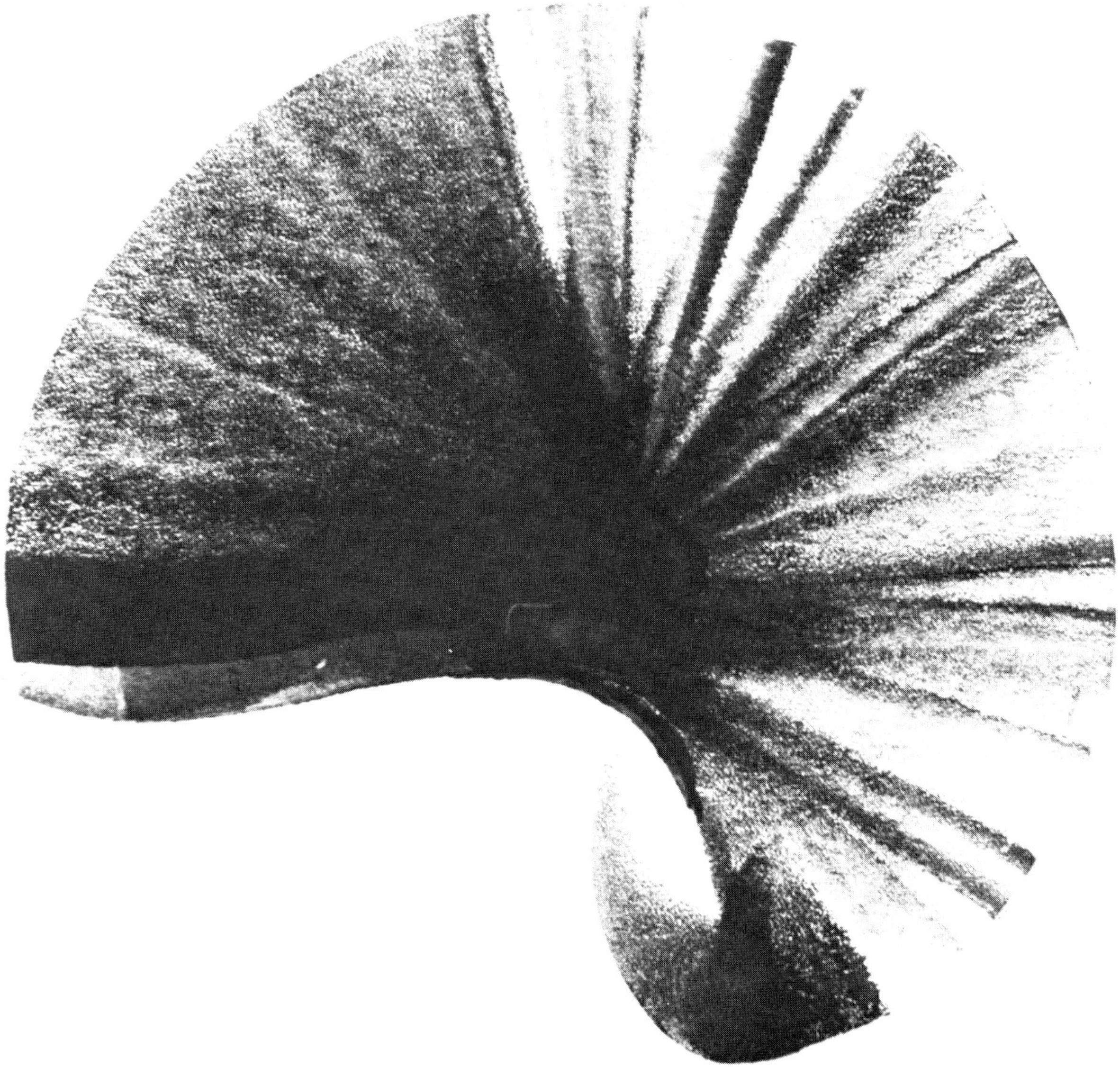

This handsome image was created with the swivel stroke. Additional data on page 20.

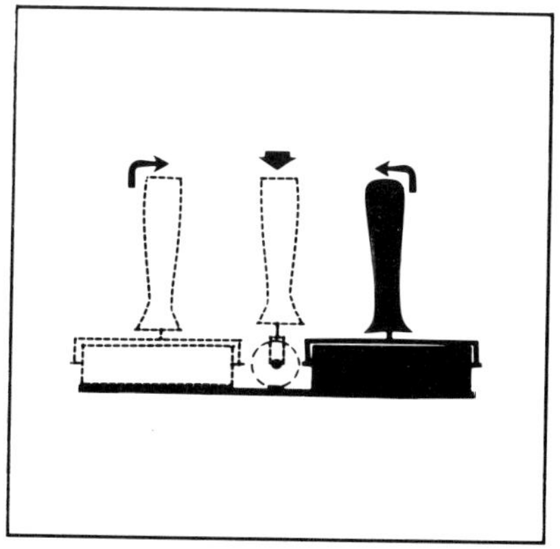

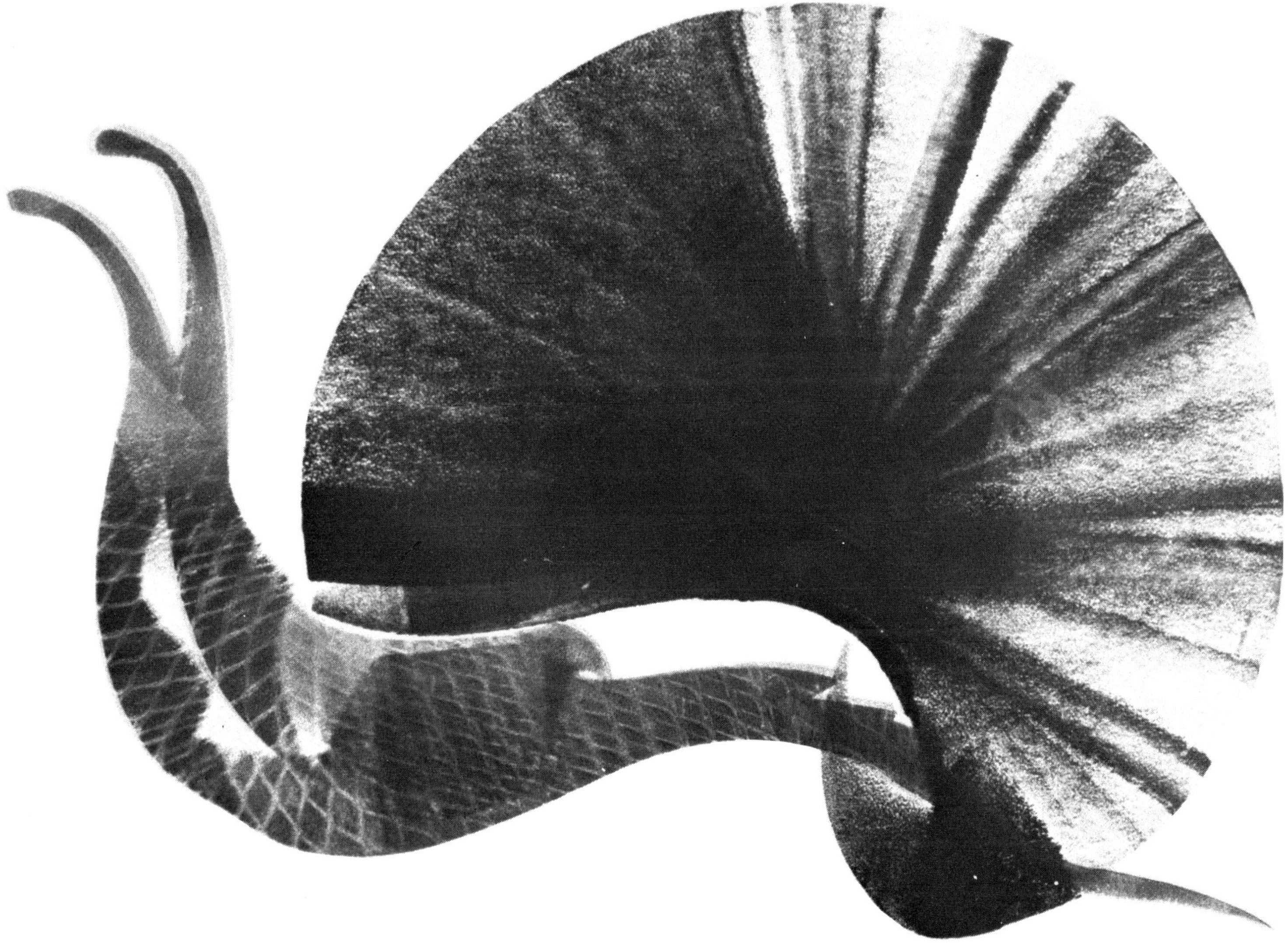

This snail drawing is the result of combining swivel and mesh impressions (see pages 20 and 33). Actual size image: using the #5 brayer, 4 x 1¾-inch diameter.

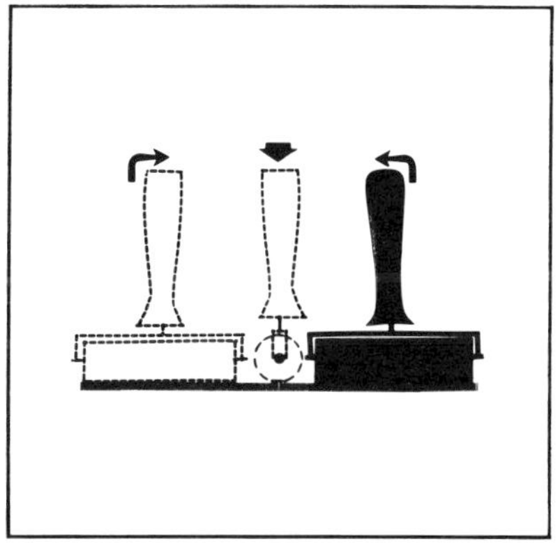

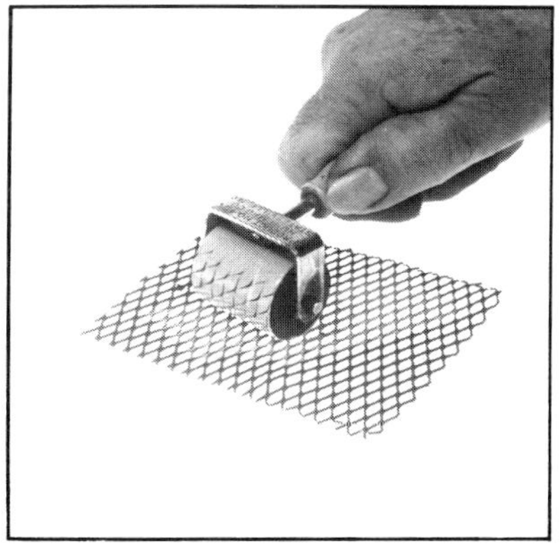

## spatter and blotting

**pick-up spatter methods — transparent or opaque**

In this same exercise, use the transparent light value spatter method to block out areas. First, load an old brush with clear water and flick the brush along the brayer handle onto the exposed area. Use paper masks cut to appropriate shapes and place in position to protect the other areas. While working with this method, be sure your work is lying flat and not at an angle.

Next, take a blotter or paper towel and blot the excess water carefully. Using a clean brayer, immediately roll over this same area vigorously several times. The rolling will soften the spatter spots and the color. Stop when you have the desired effect. Dark spatter-spotting can also be achieved in the same manner by first loading the brush with pigment instead of clear water.

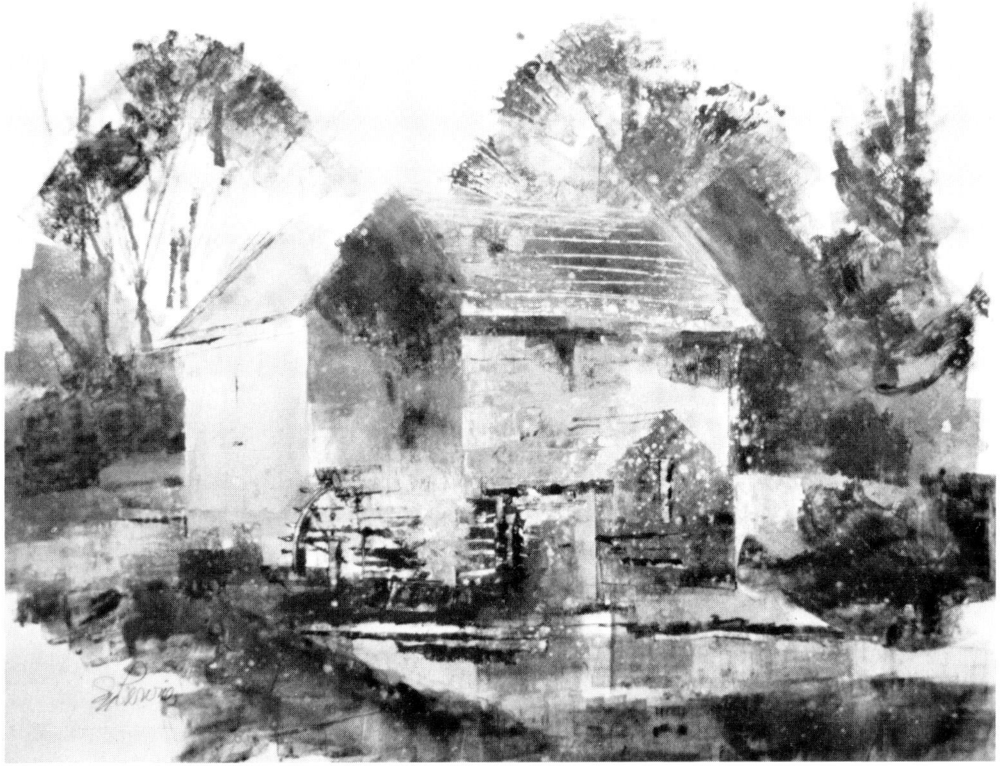

**working mill**

Size: 18 x 24 inches, watercolor.
Painted on location in Ireland.
The clear water spatter used in this sketch was a natural. An act of the gods, a sudden rainfall supplied from the heavens, and all I had to do was blot and roll.

**musca domestica**
Better known as the ordinary housefly, is an excellent subject for its amazing structural dynamics; a natural for the brayer. This subject was illustrated with water based inks on a gesso treated paper base.

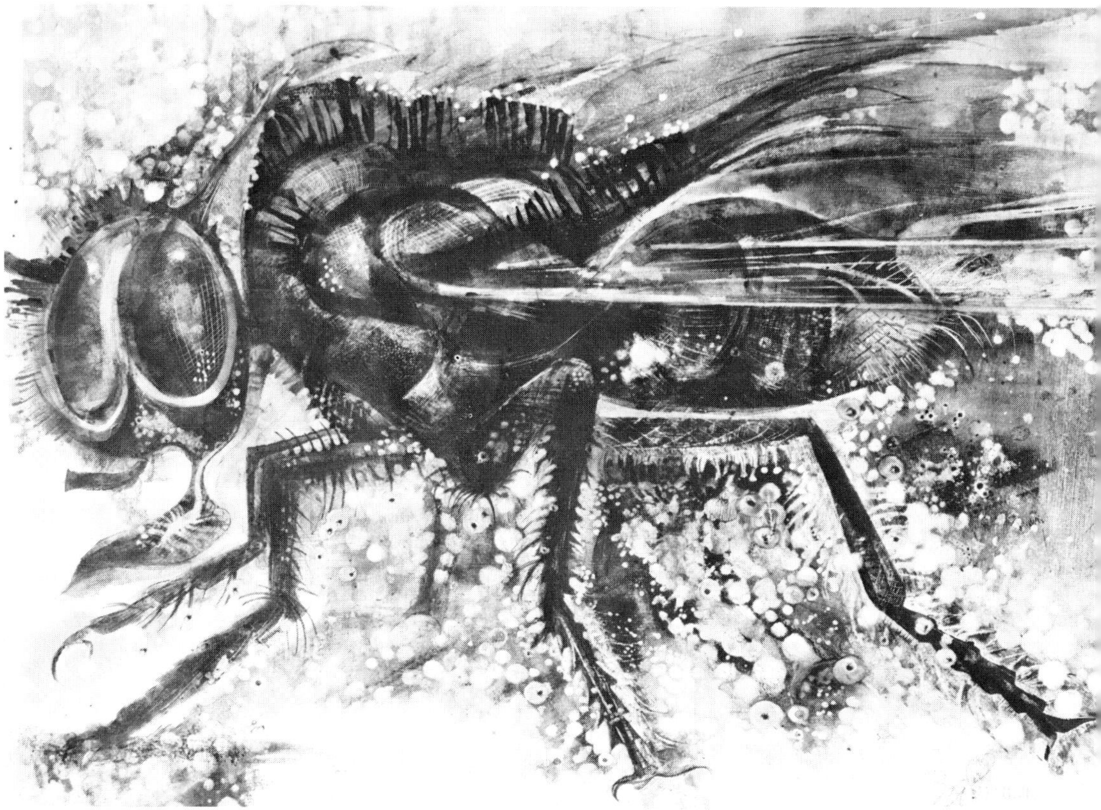

Size: 17 x 23 inches

I also used cotton swabs dipped in clear water to accent the background spatter areas.

Detail

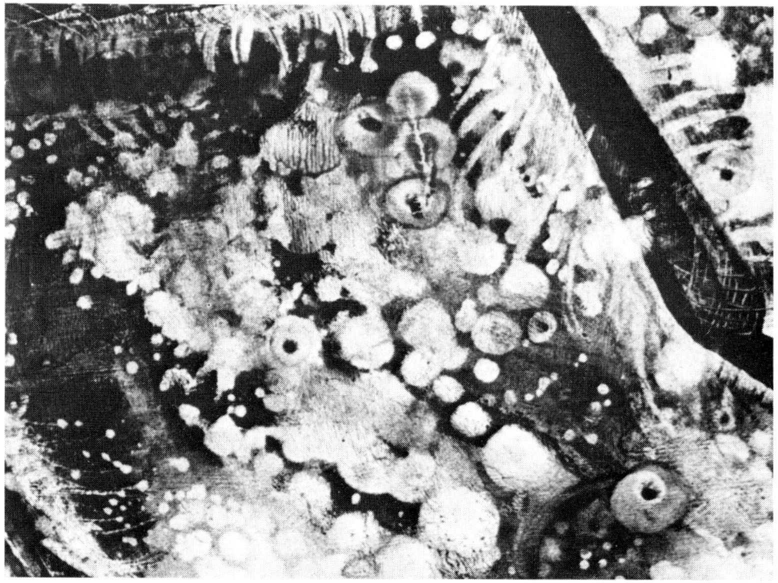

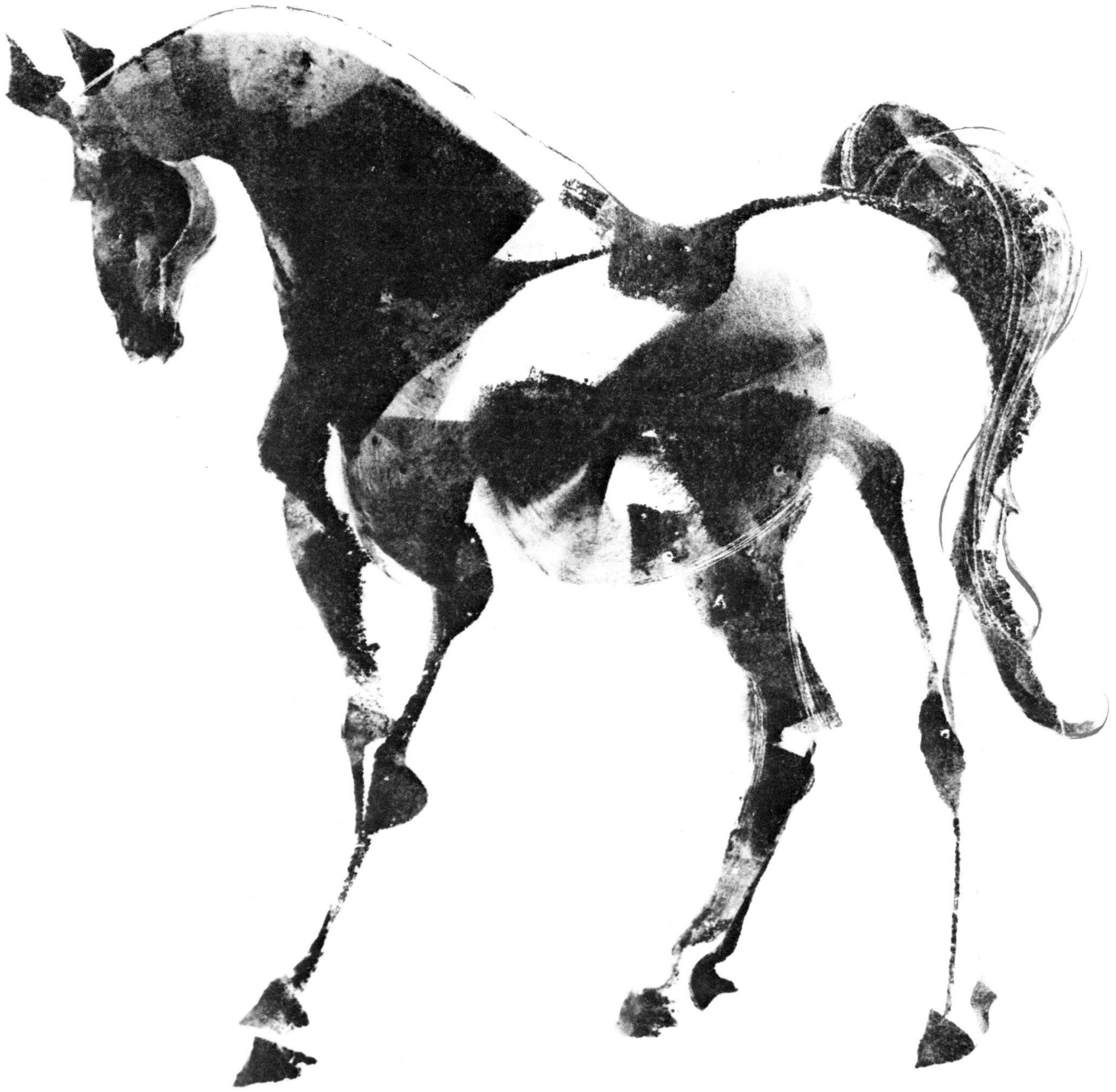

Horse image: One-third actual size.

These first basic strokes establish the action and character of the subject. Illustration 1.

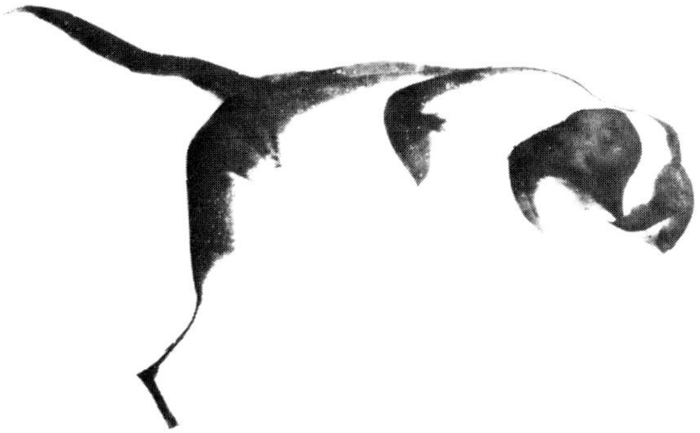

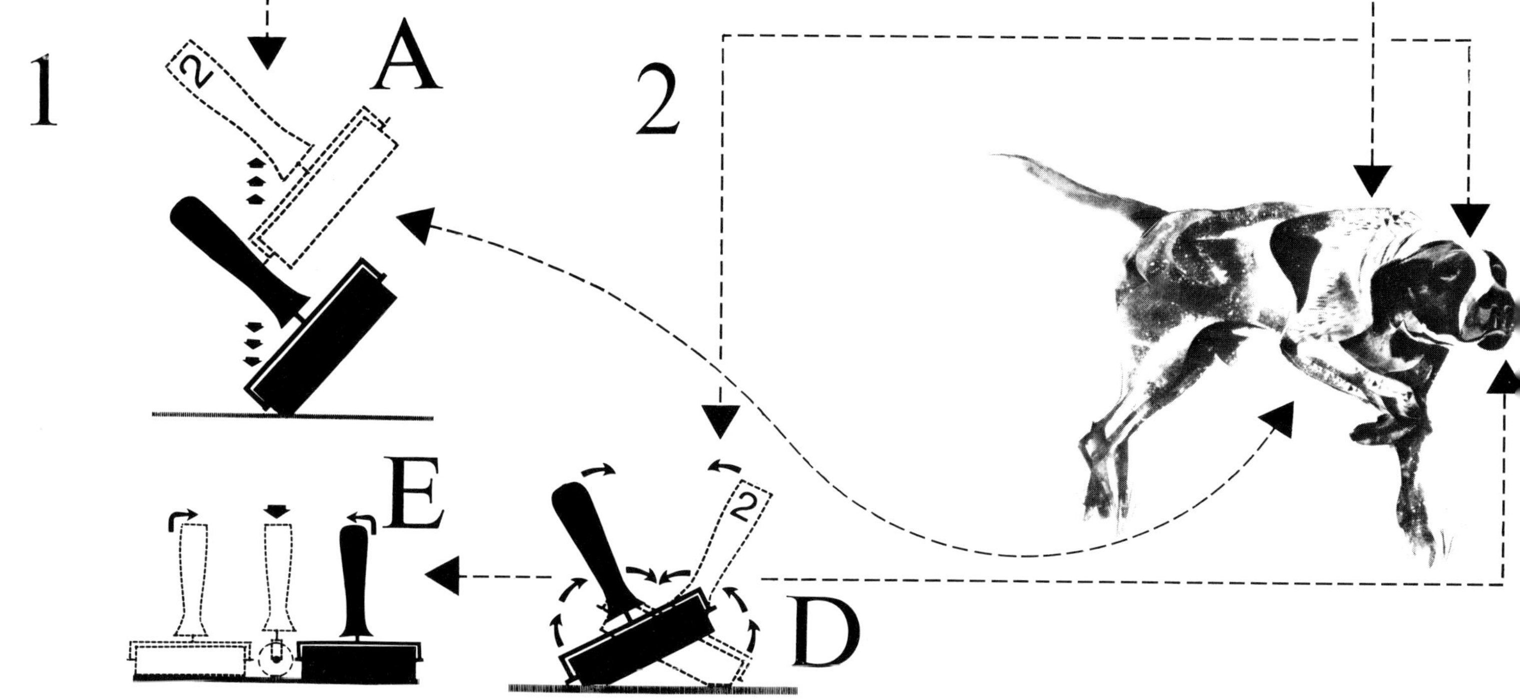


Diagrams A, E and D illustrate the proper placements and strokes of the brayer.

3

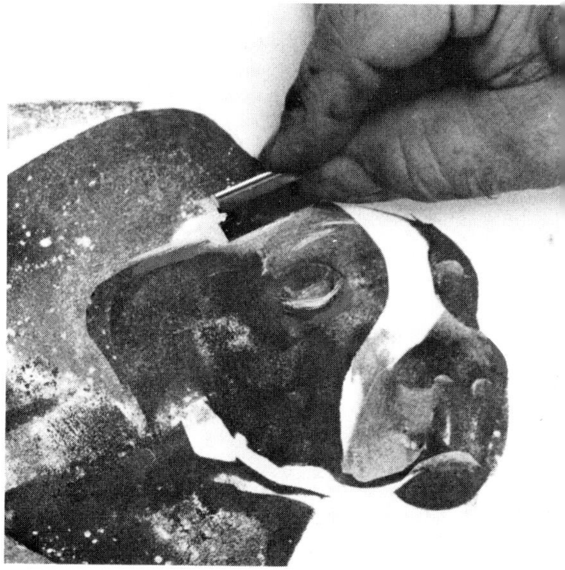

Image 3: illustrates how some of the detail can be achieved with the razor technique while the ink is wet.

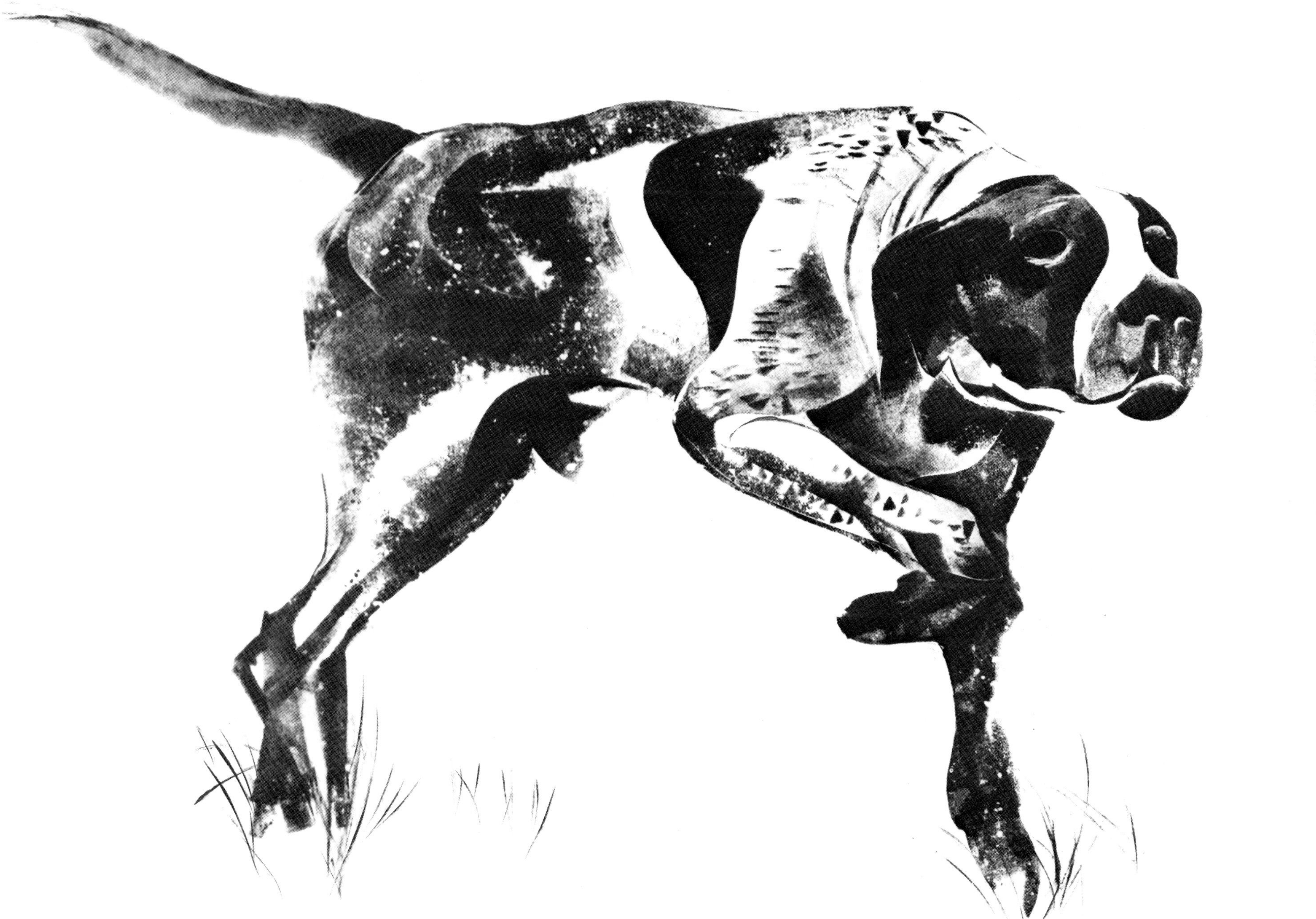

Dog one-half actual size.

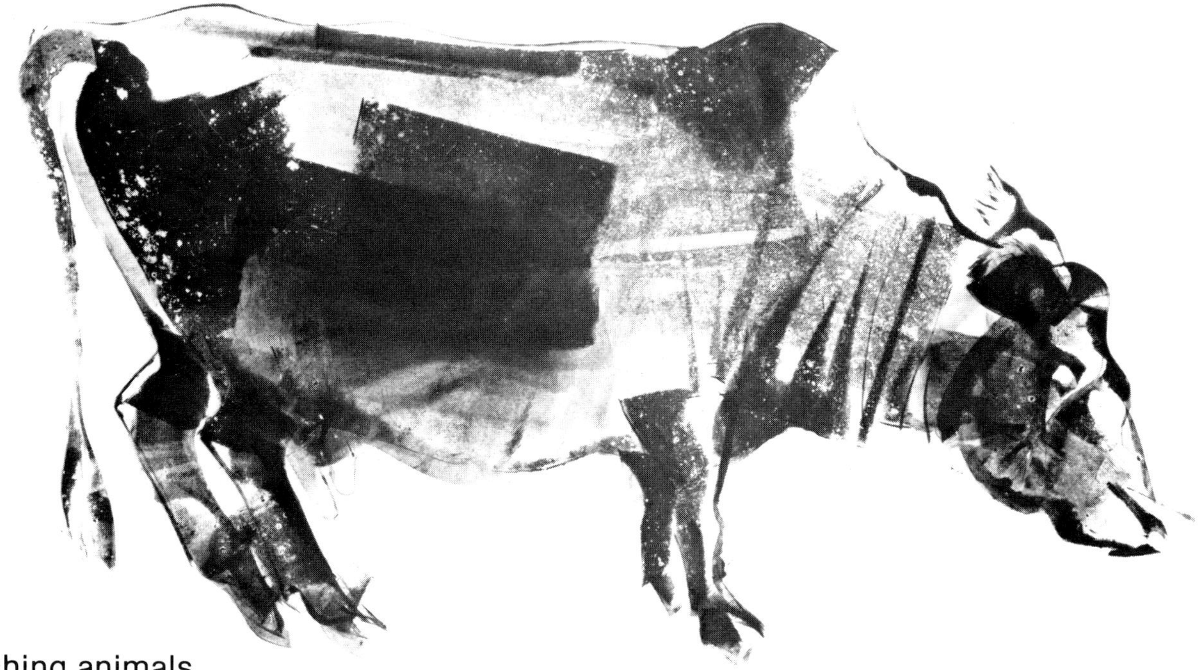

Another good location for sketching animals is in the country on a small farm. Subject matter is easy to find; ducks, chickens, horses, sheep and cows are usually available. Cows will pose reasonably well for hours at a time.

Size: 18 x 20 inches. One color, water based paint.

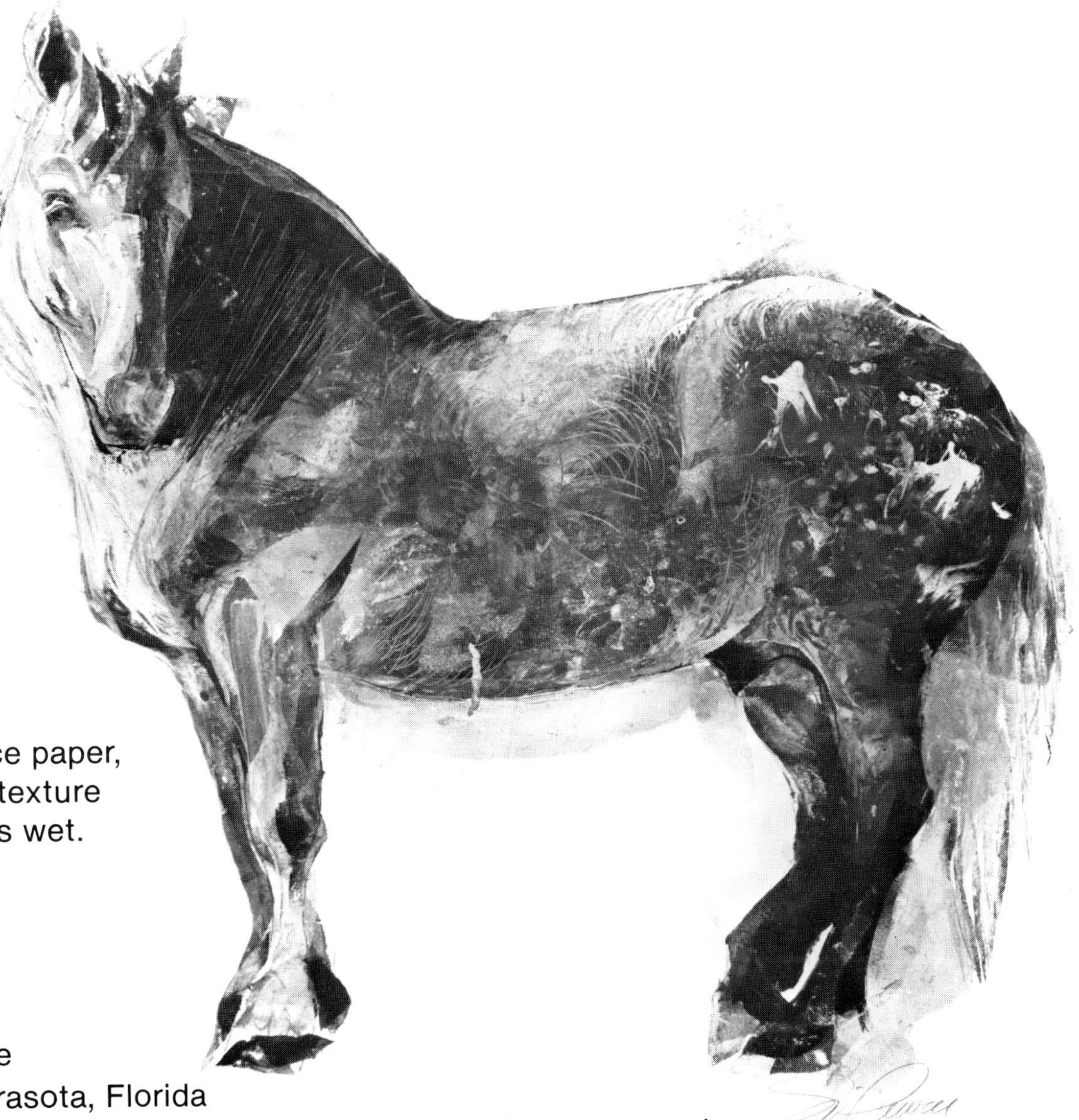

Sketched directly with a brayer on rice paper, using oil paint and scratching in the texture with a sharp knife while the paint was wet.

Old circus horse
On location: Sarasota, Florida

Size: 14 x 18 inches — two colors.

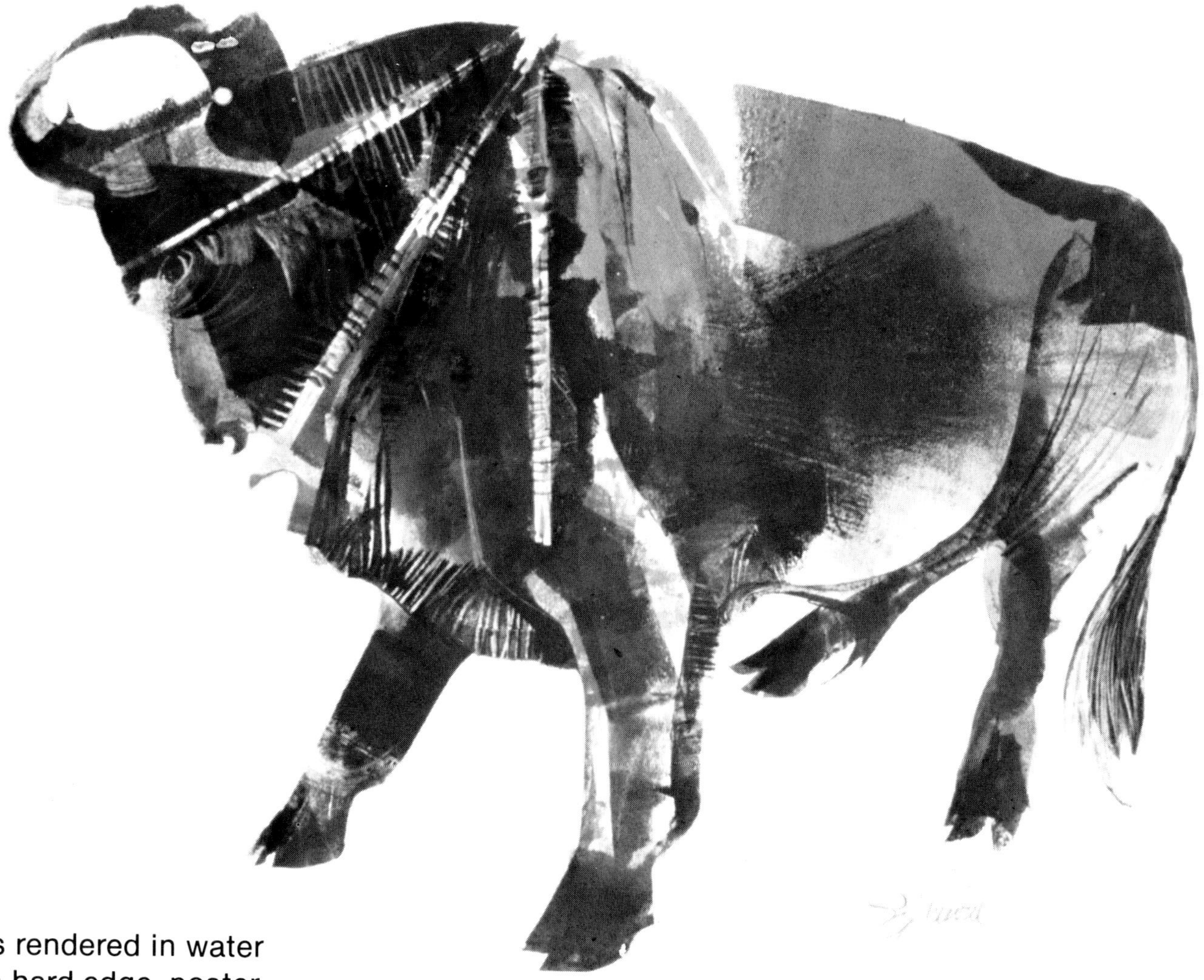

This painting of a bull was rendered in water based inks, full color. This hard-edge, poster-like treatment is a good example of brayer handling in its simplest form. Accents in the bandarillos were scratched in with razor blades.

Size: 26 x 30 inches.

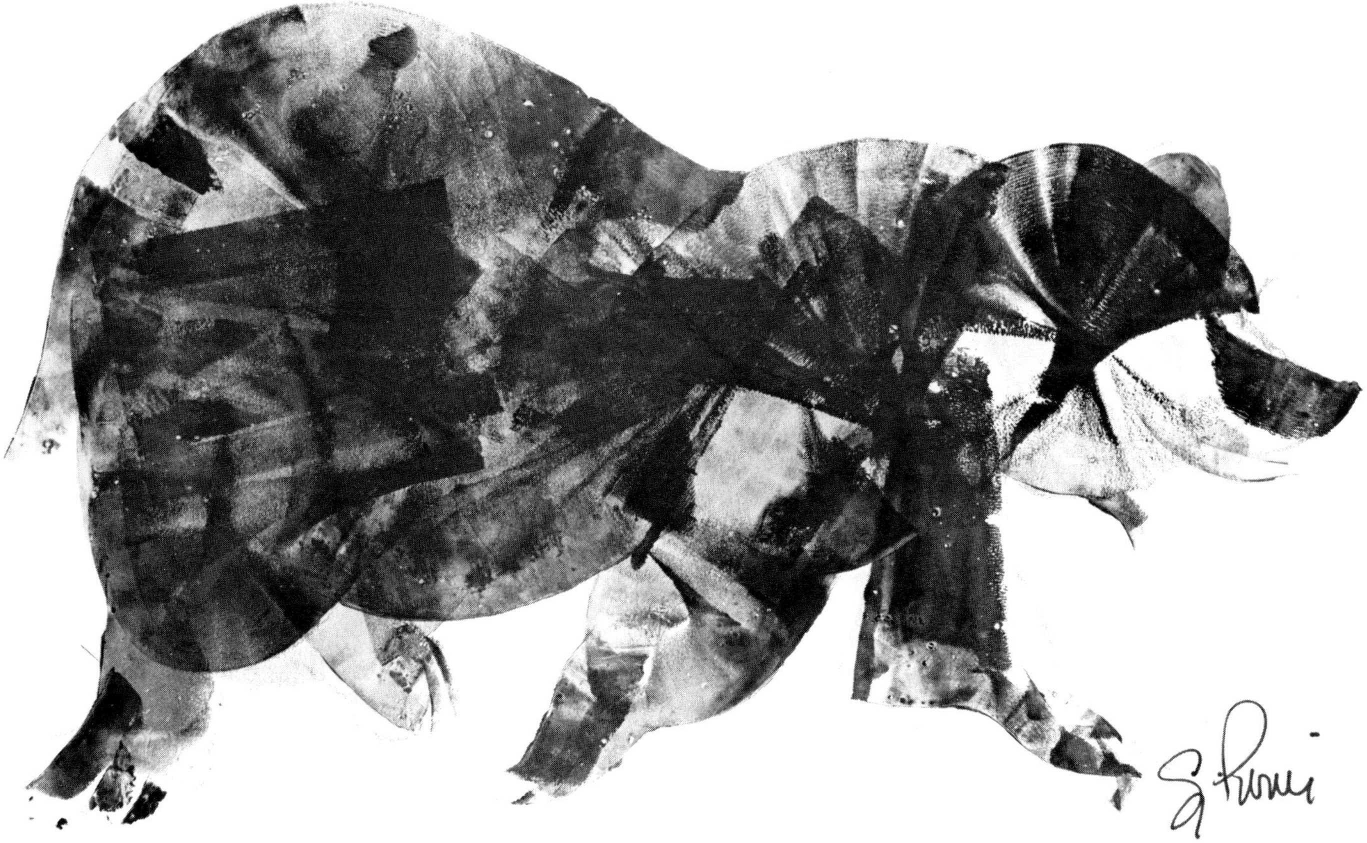

The zoo is a wonderful place to find subjects for action-sketching. With a brayer you can capture character, form and action, all in one sweep, like the bear in this sketch. I used a #6 roller and one color.

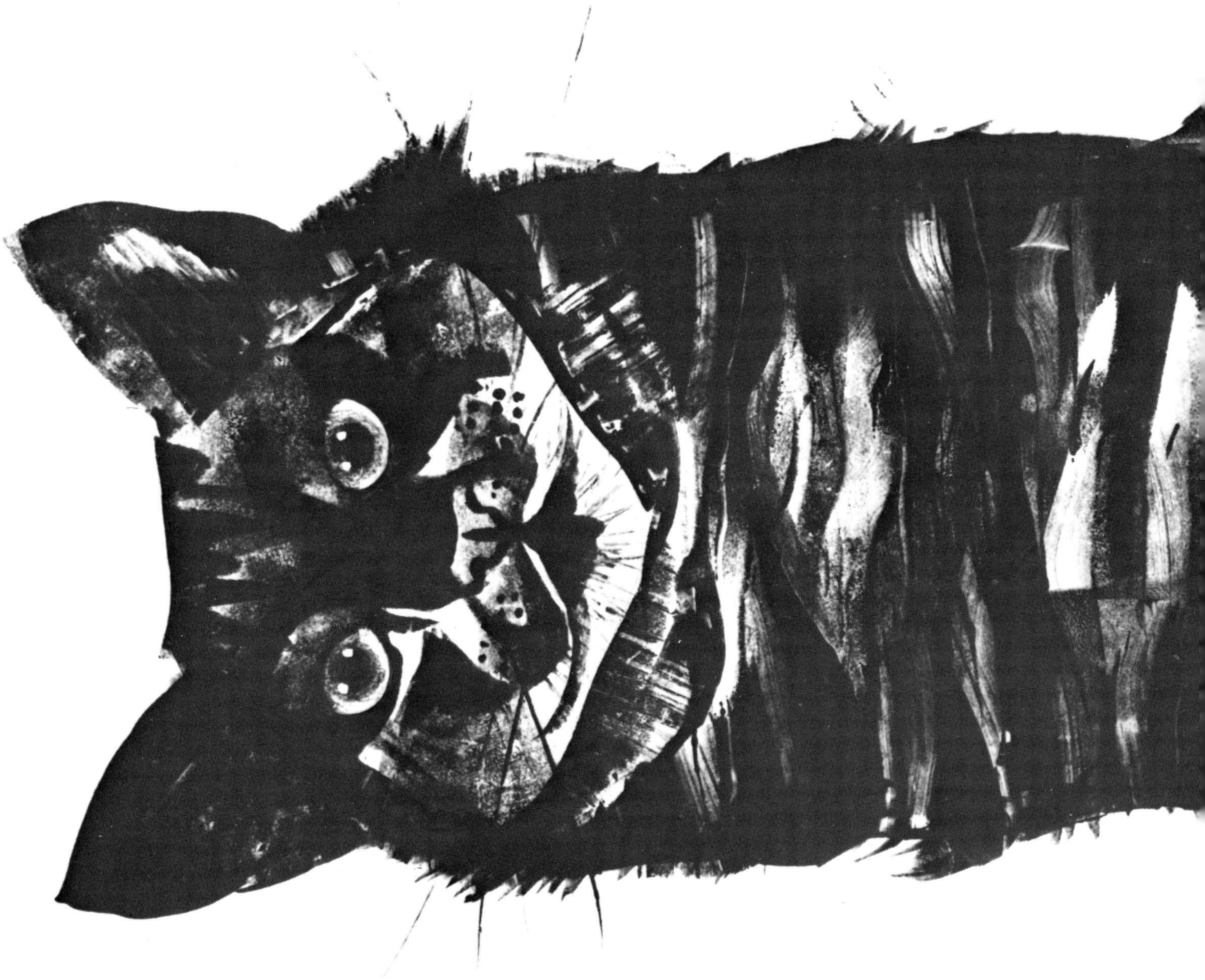

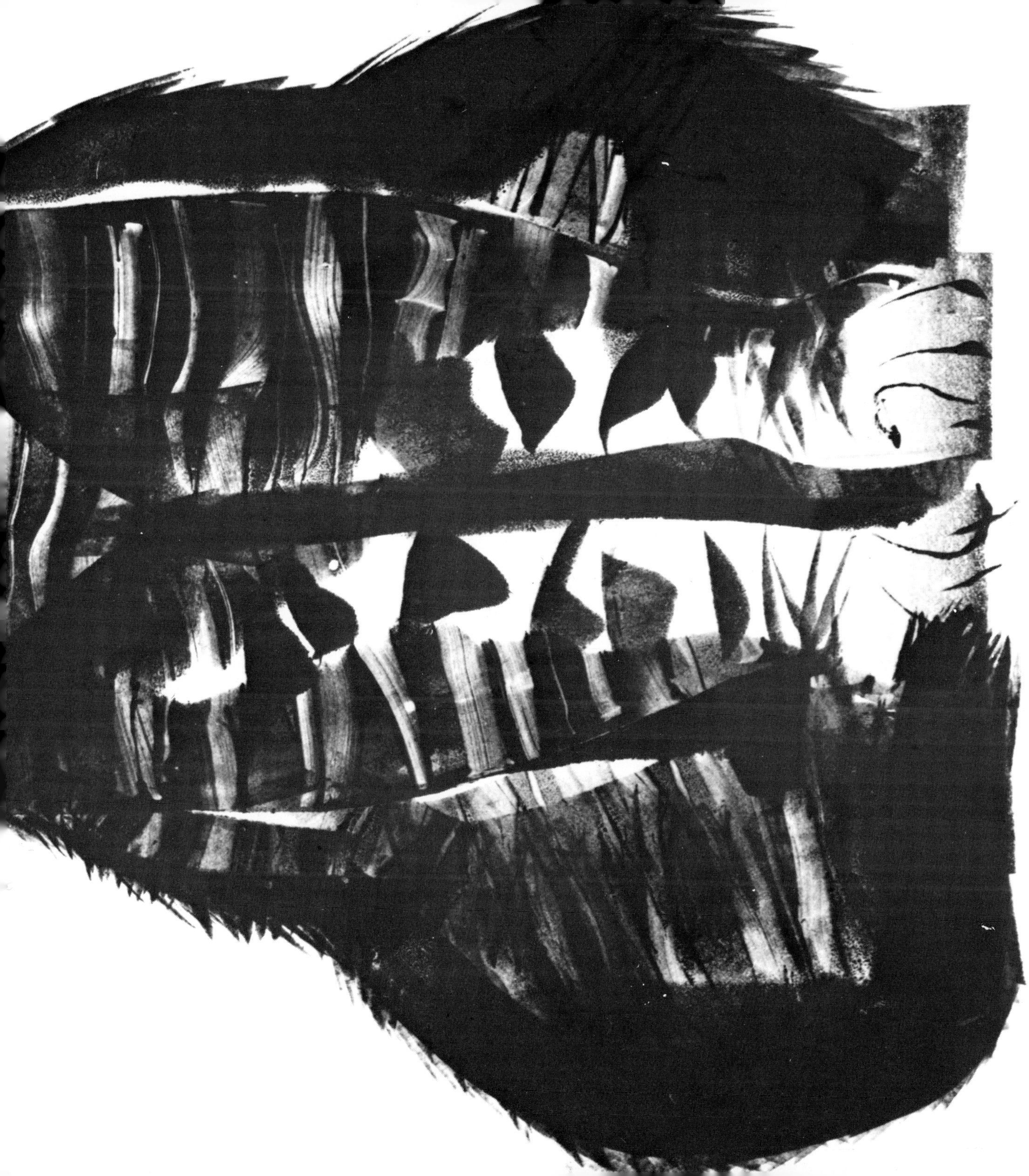

Reproduced same size as original art.

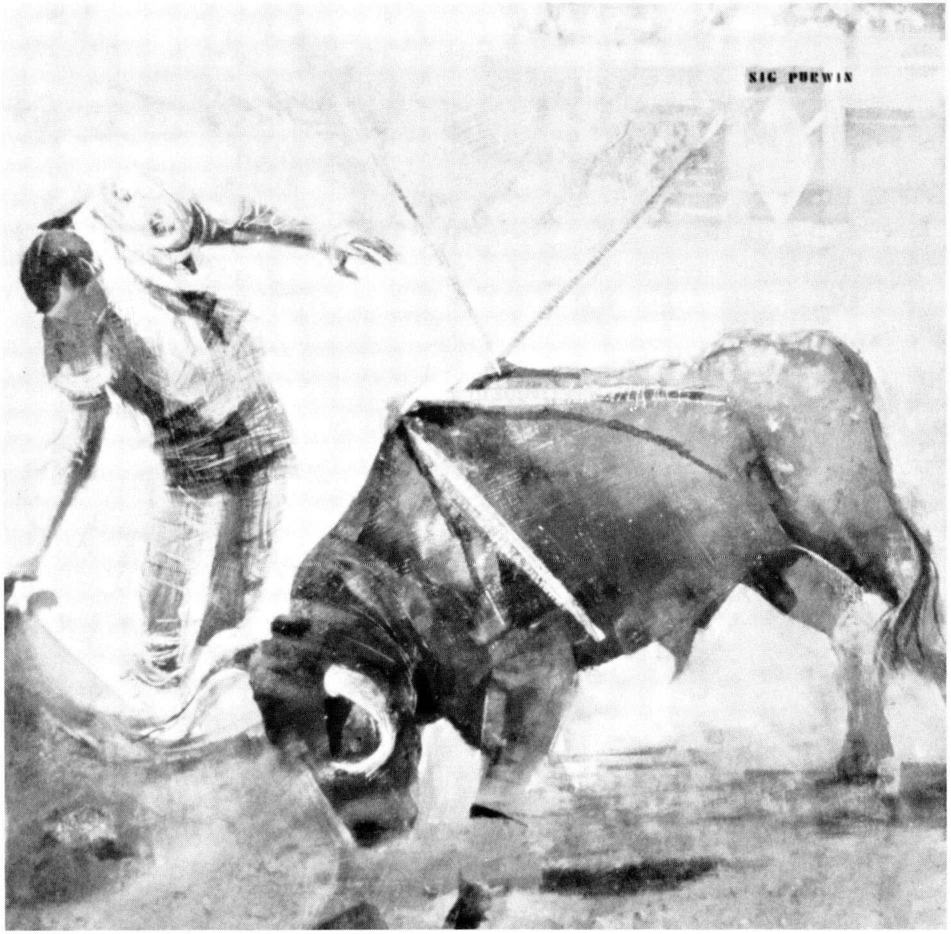


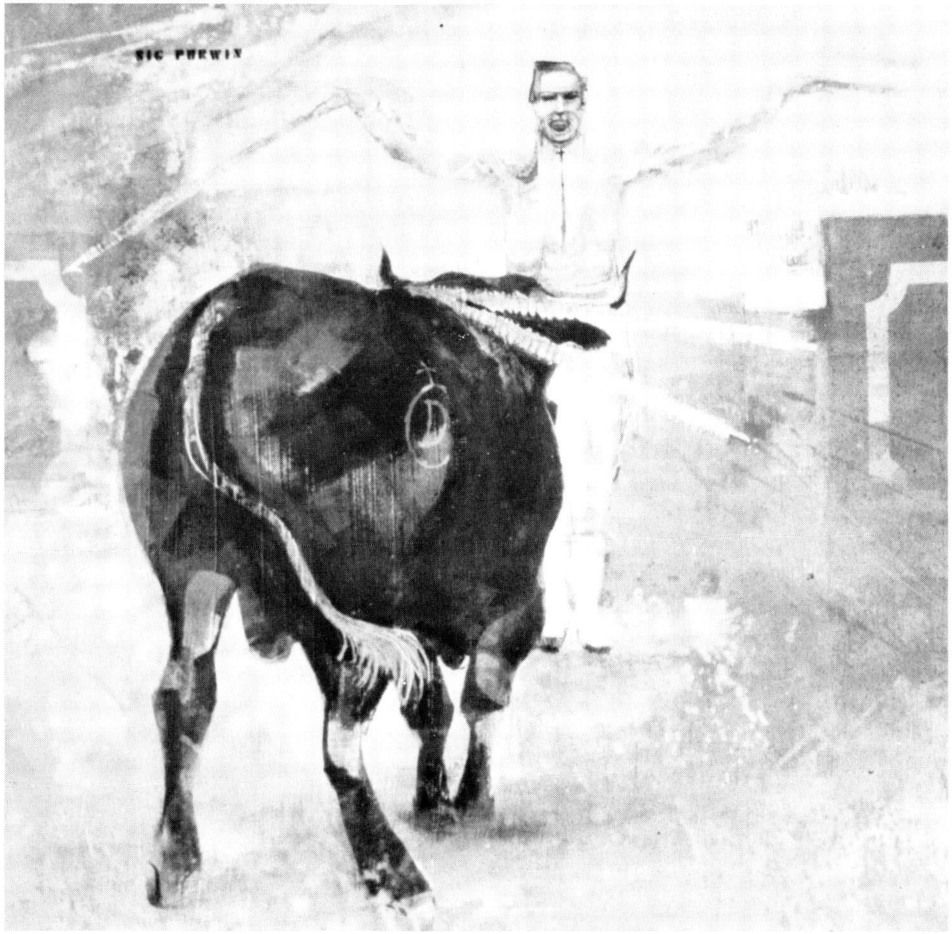


These two illustrations were rendered on 23 x 23 inch masonite panels with a gesso base. Water based inks were used with the brayer.

Drawings were in ink before starting and scribing with a sharp tool. The spatter technique was used extensively on the backgrounds.

## human figure

**figure drawing**

Drawing with a brayer is an experience in itself. Drawing with a brayer from the human figure can be a very exciting way to work.

Your interpretation of the pose and the action of the model is your number one objective. For quick, simple suggestions of movement, the brayer can be a worthy tool. Using the brayer will give you more time to study your model for good composition, form and line of action because of the incredible deftness of the brayer in transferring the pose to paper after thorough study. Spontaneous exaggeration forces you to ignore all detail. What you achieve is an emotional expression. Changing pressure on the roller gives you a varying character line.

Once you study and understand the relationship of the spine to the pelvis within the figure, the dynamics of the pose will be more easily controlled. The purpose in studying human anatomy is to *understand* the figure's function.

Put the anatomical detail on the back burner of your mind and concentrate on the immediate task of translating your concept to paper. Memorizing the names of all the bones and muscles is not pertinent to your understanding as an artist. If you acquaint yourself with the way the body moves, where and why it bends, the way you see it, you are halfway to a successful drawing of the figure. You can work boldly or with deft, sensitive touches. The brayer will follow the will of the hand.

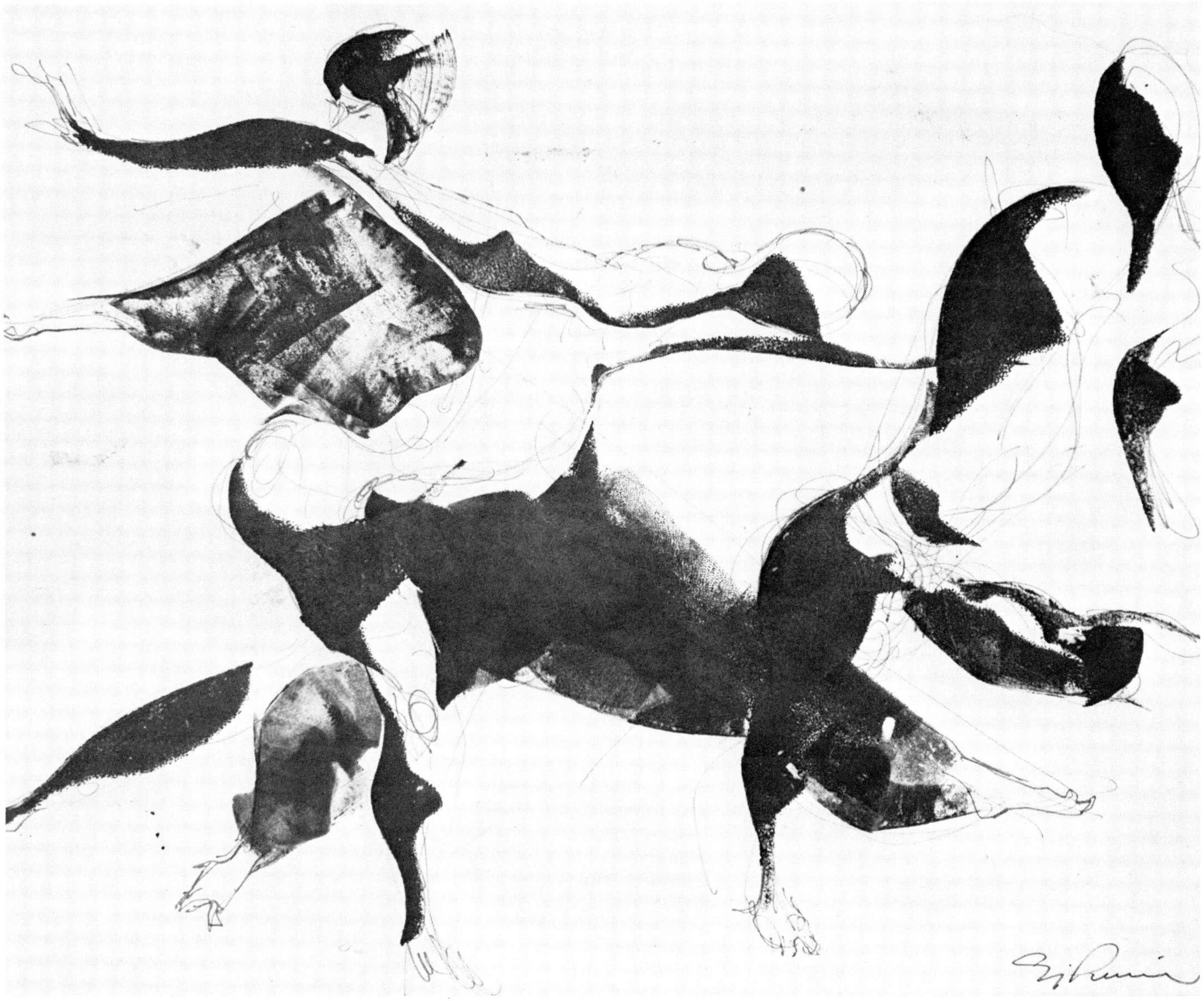

Action sketch with the brayer while the dancer performed before the class. I used a felt tip pen for contour definition, while the brayer was used for the massive structural forms. Size: 24 x 36 inches.

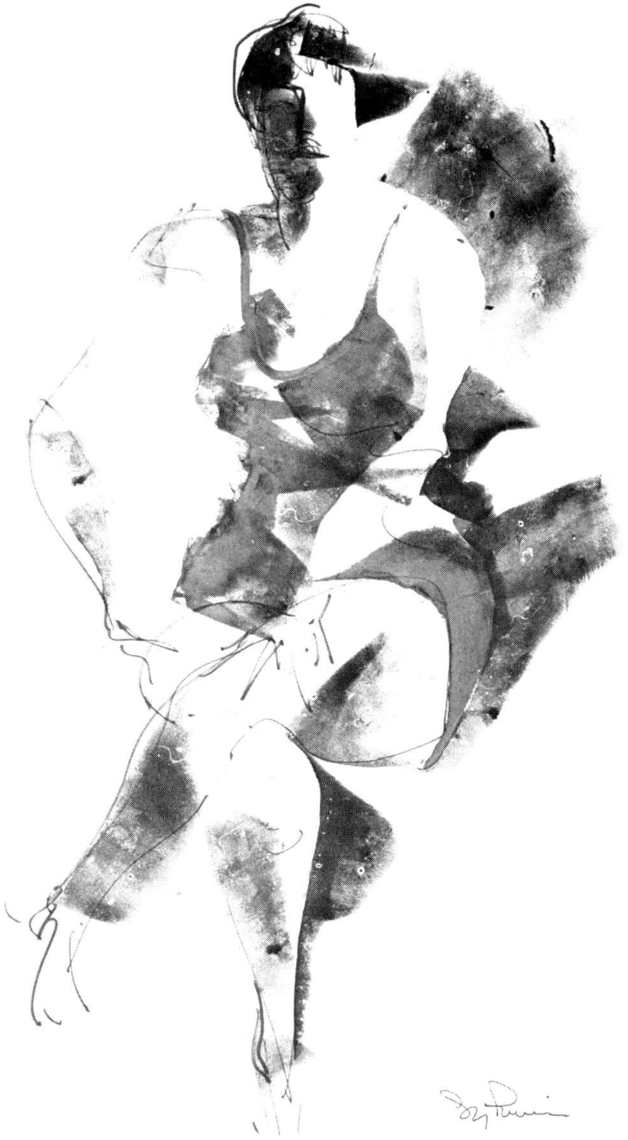

Draped figure, brayer and felt pen.
Size: 36 x 30 inches, two colors, orange & black.

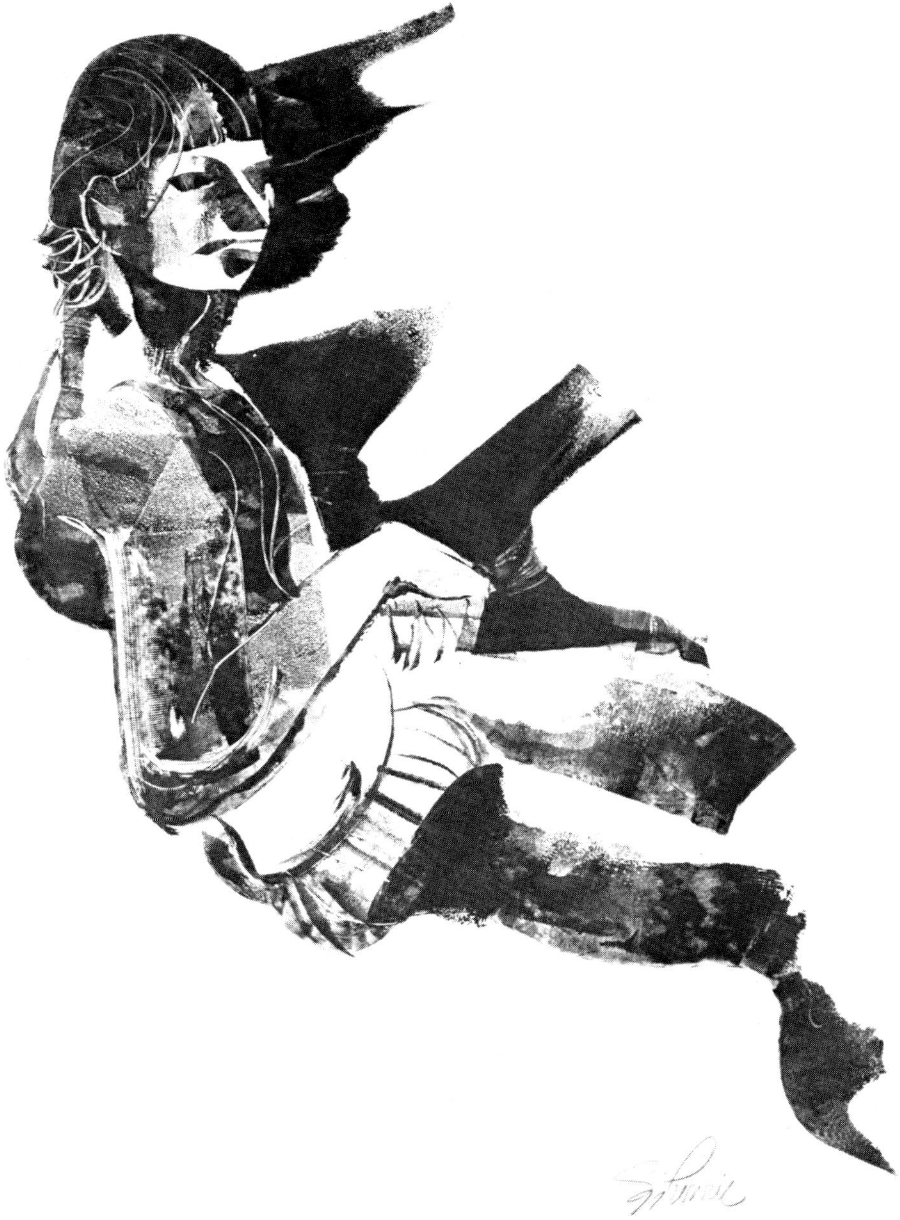

Brayer & scratch blade lines.
Size: 32 x 24 inches.

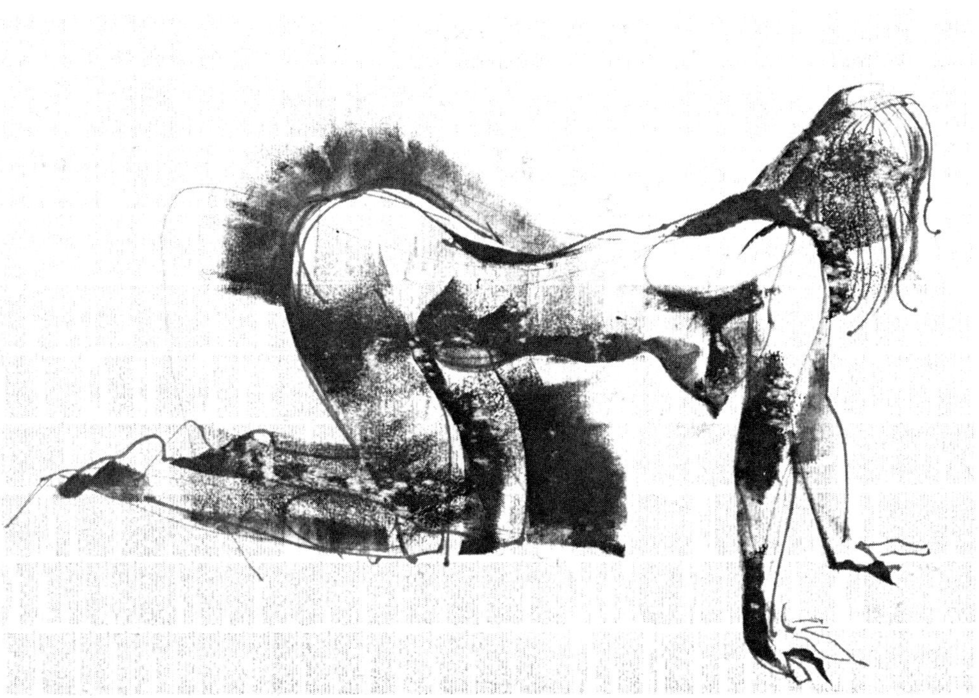

Brayer drawing on newspaper with the print matter in the background.
Size: 14 x 22 inches.

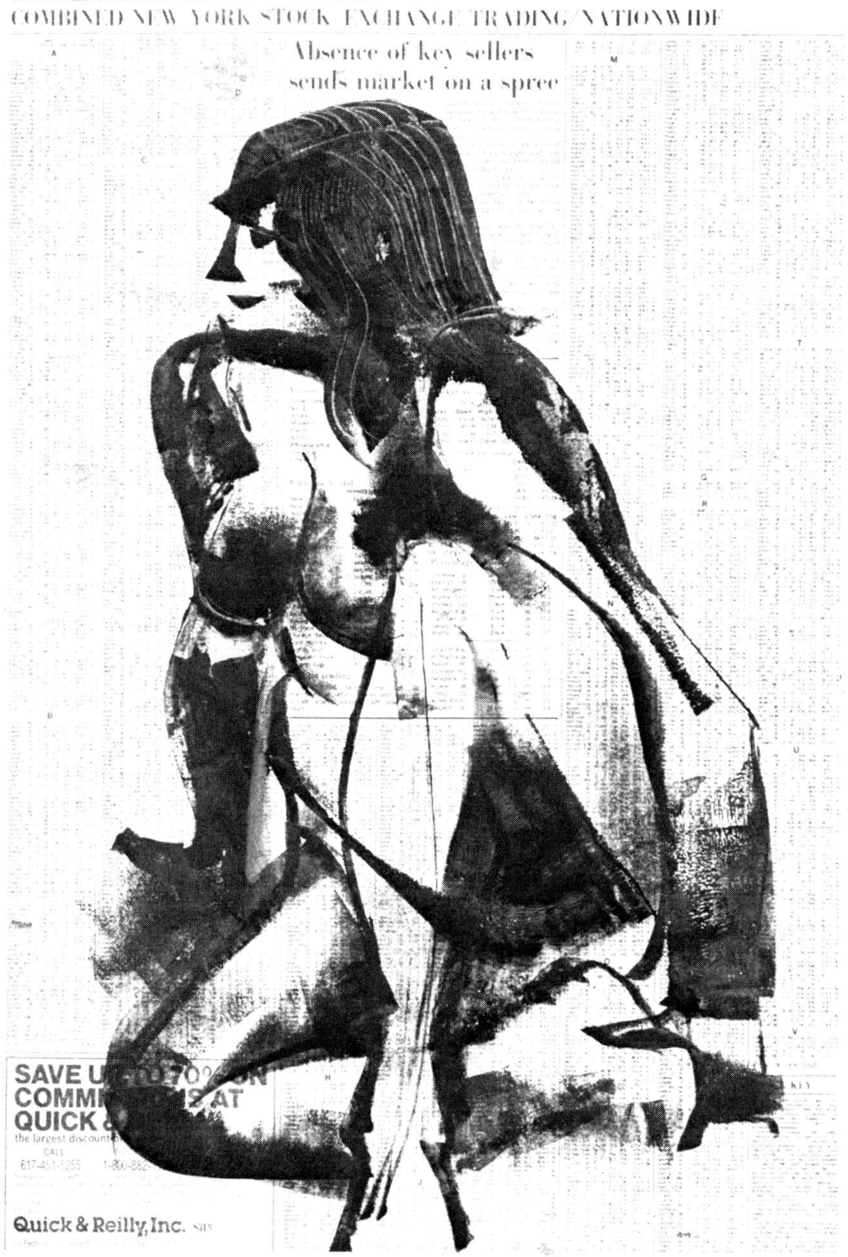


Size: 24 x 18 inches.

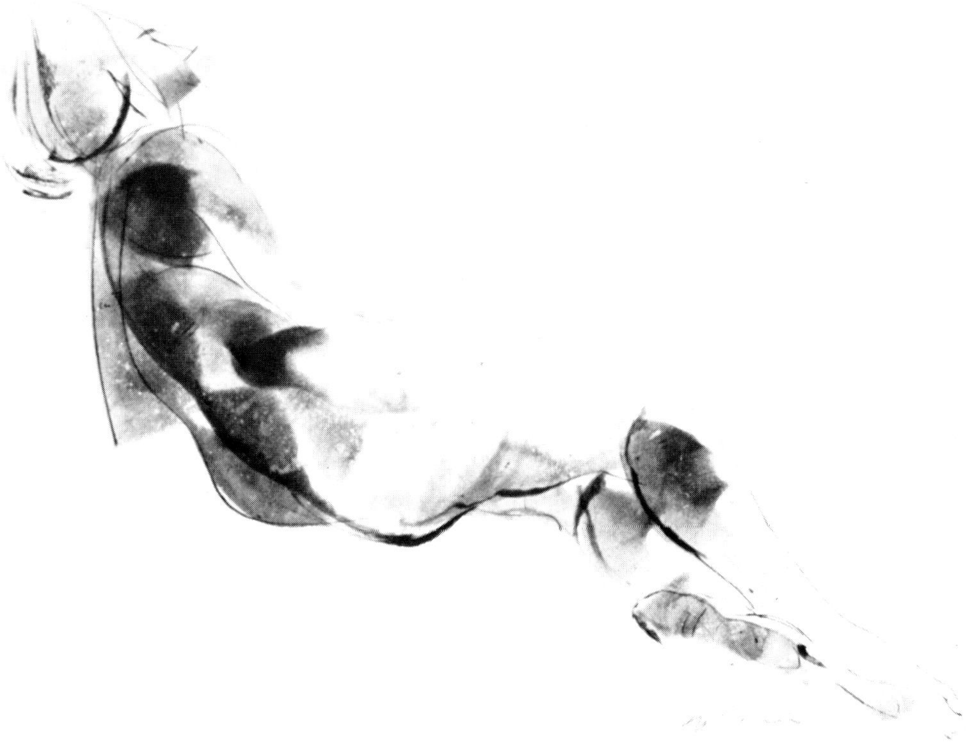

The subtle treatment of the forms, both in value and shape, as in the above drawing, illustrates the deftness in brayer handling of this subject.

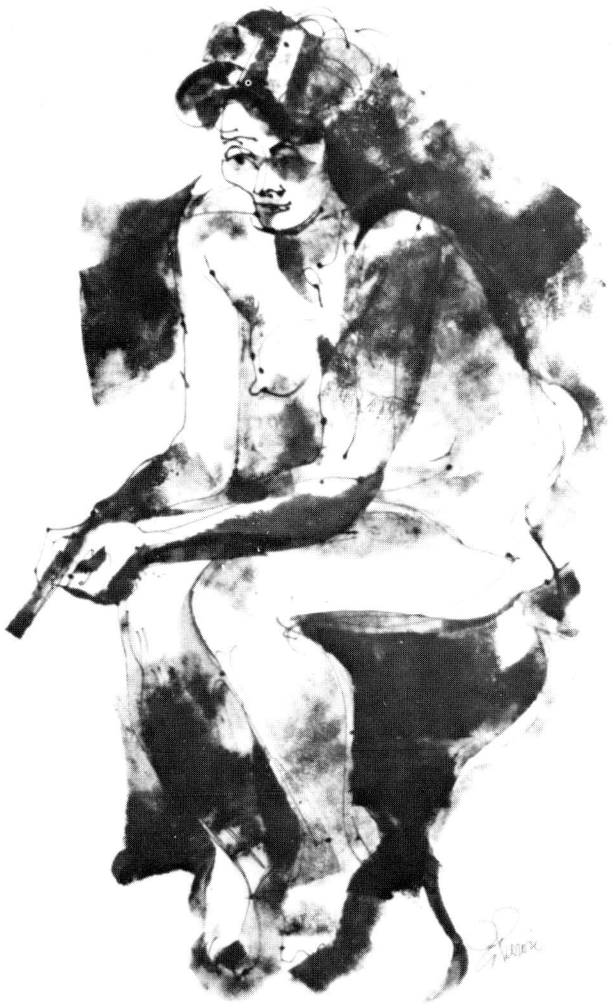

The bolder treatment of the figure was accomplished using pen line in combination with rapid brayer strokes to grasp the character of the pose. These were quick sketches of five to ten minutes each.
Size: 18 inches high, blotting type paper, two colors.

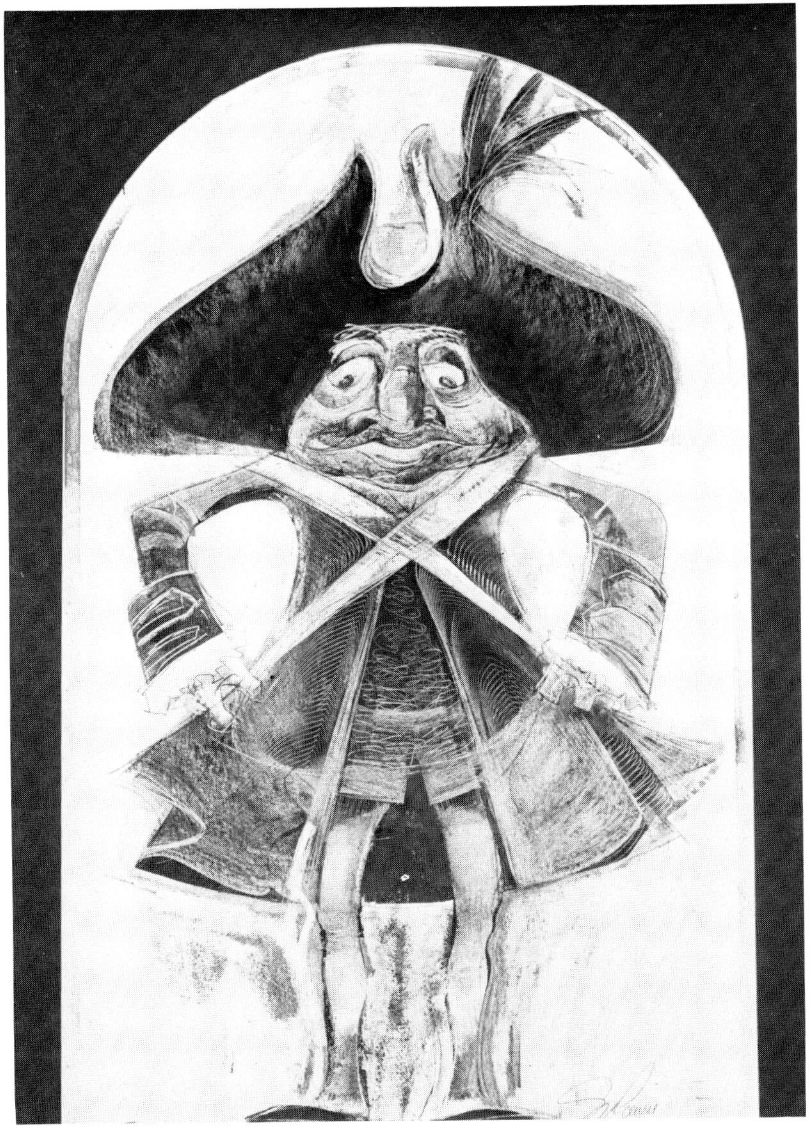

Revolutionary American

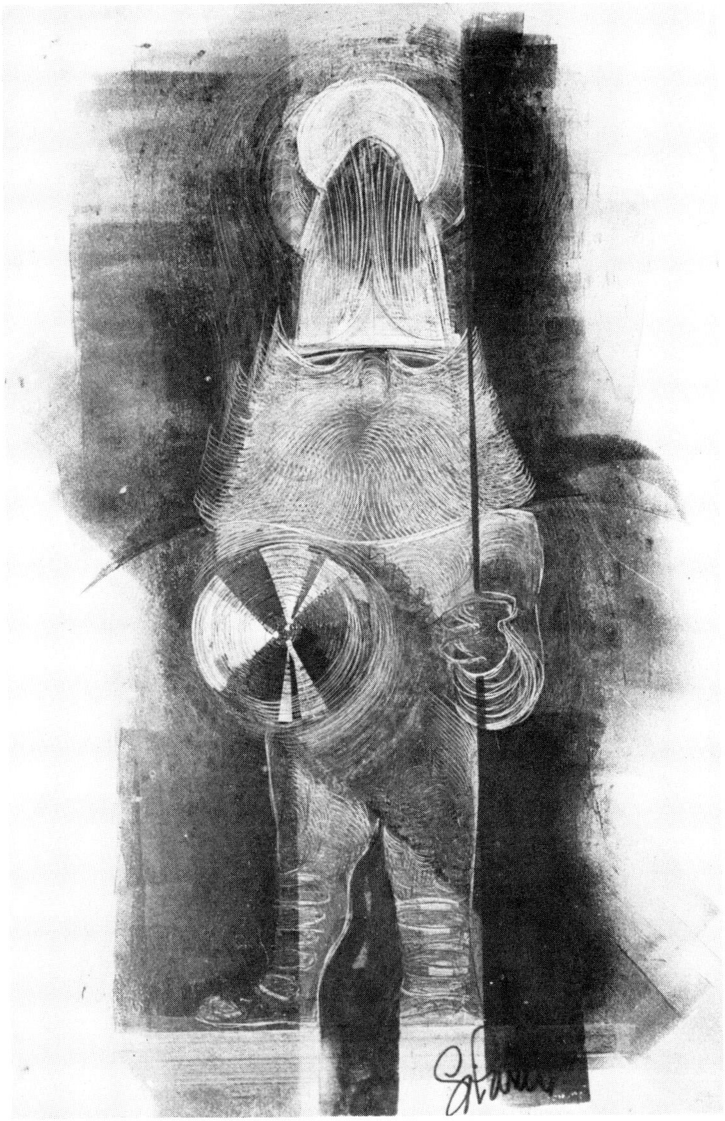

Hairy Viking

After finishing the rendering of these two characters, I literally combed patterns into the wet paint of each figure with a hair comb.

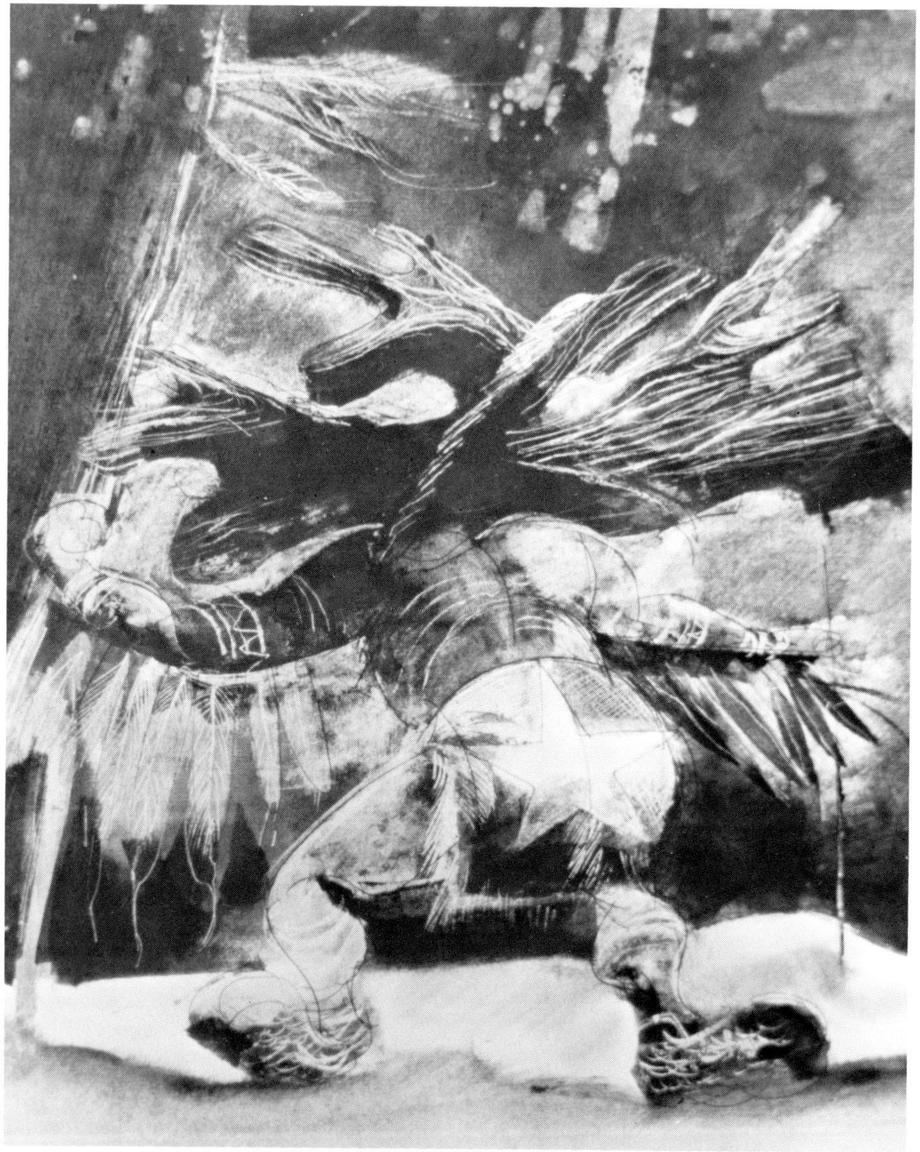

These are preliminary color drawings of Indian folklore for children's books. They were done in full color with oil crayon and oil paints thinned with glaze on paper.

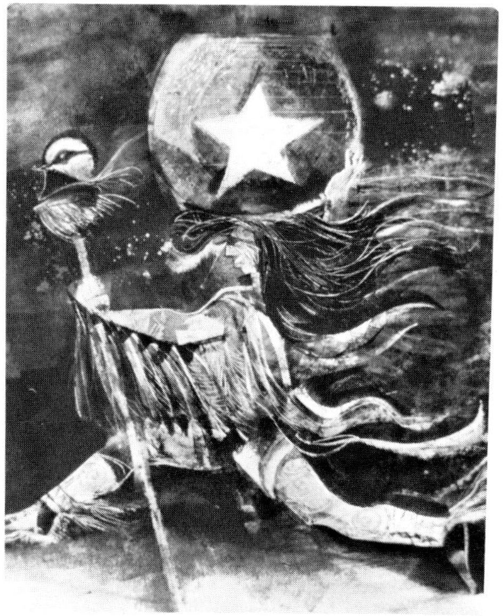

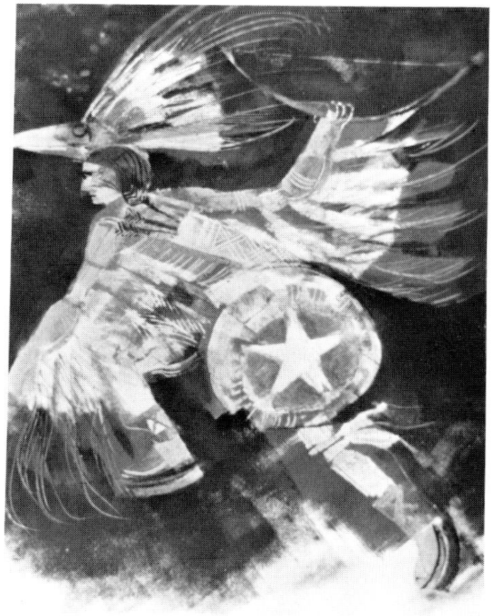

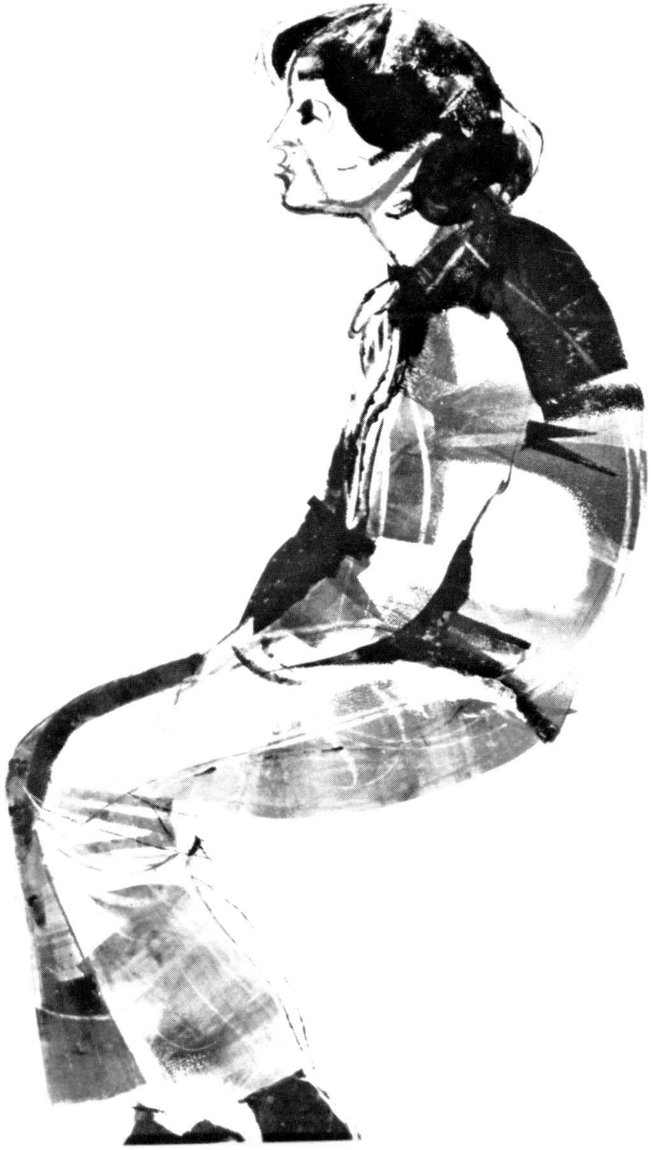

Simple, direct study of seated, clothed figure.

Size: 28 x 24 inches, two colors.

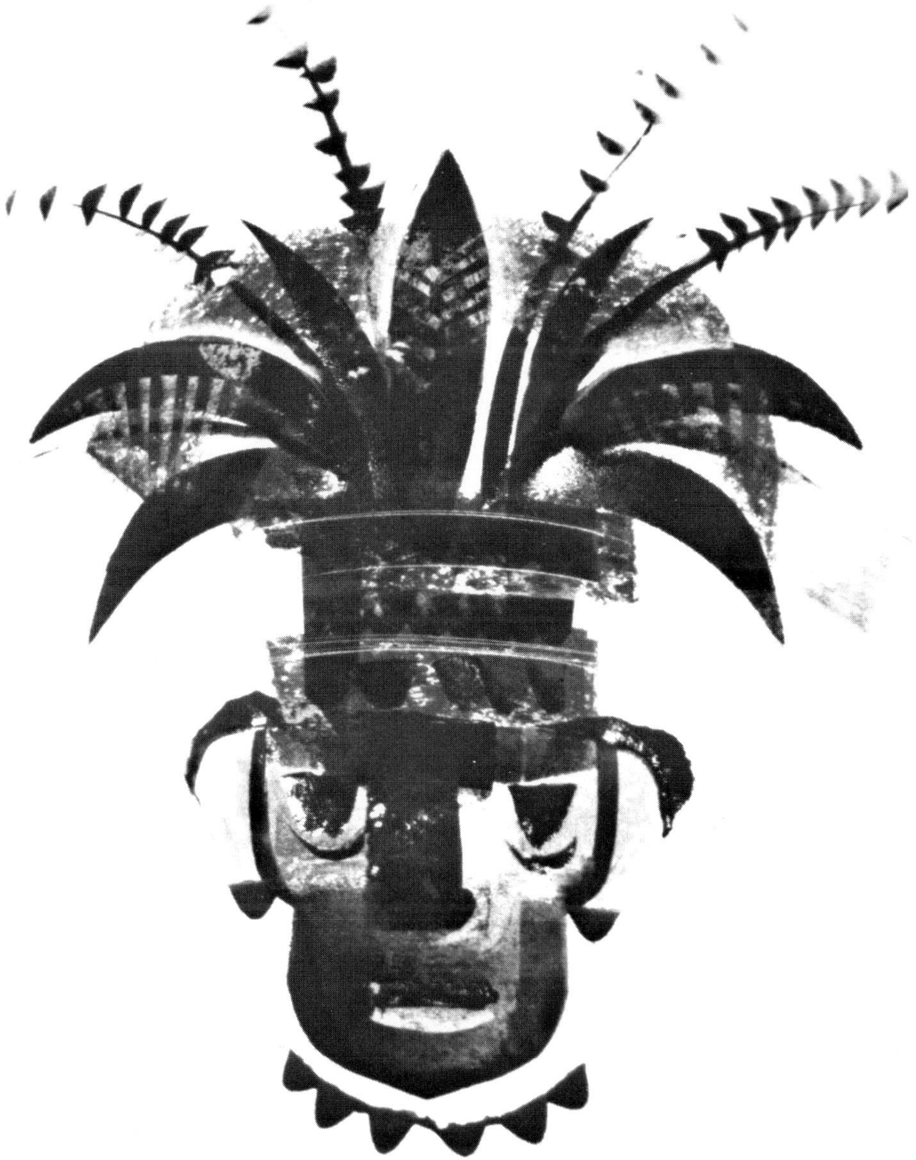

Full color decorative mask.

Size: 22 x 14 inches.

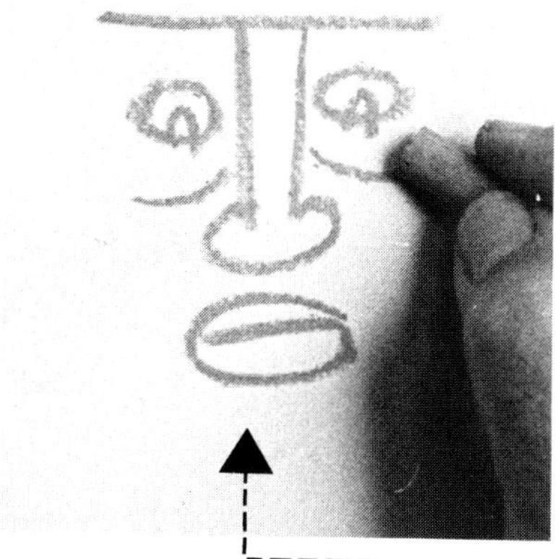

E

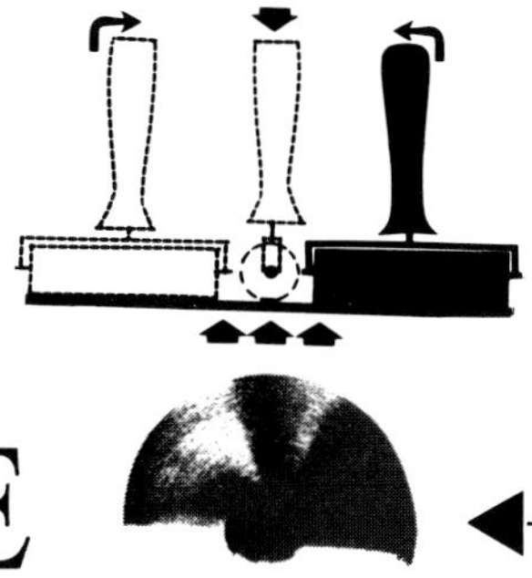

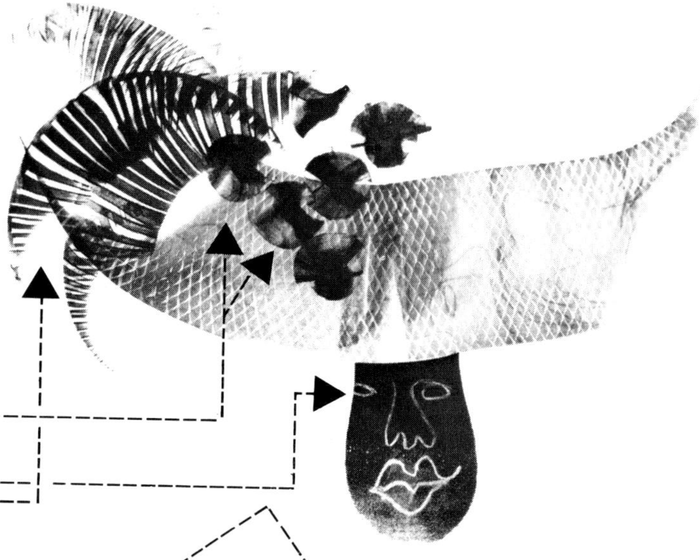

Native figure image.

Reference pages:

| | |
|---|---|
| Chalk and metal mesh | page 32 and 33 |
| Diagram E | page 20 |
| Scrape method | page 23 |
| Diagram D | page 19 |

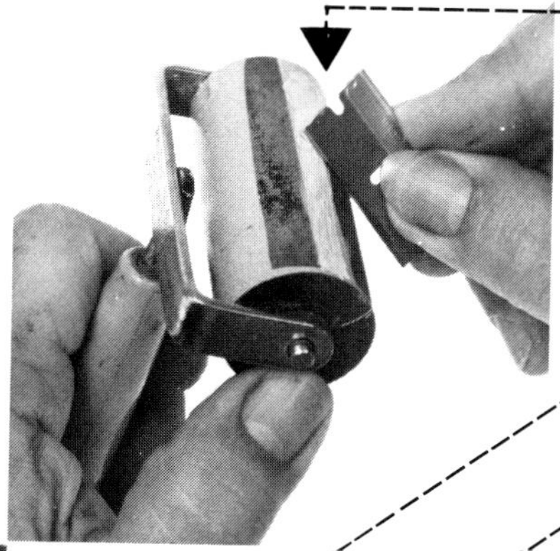

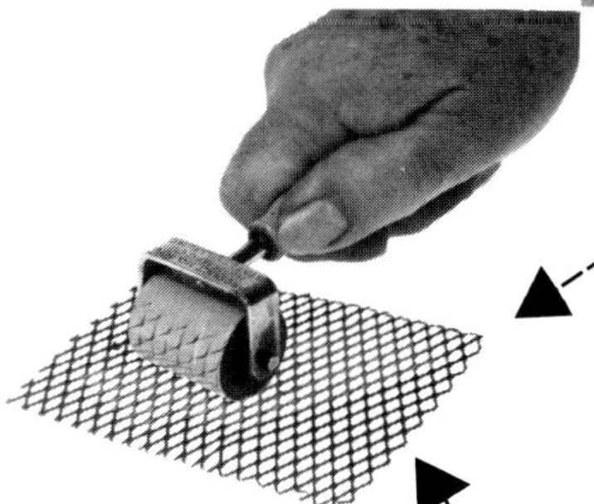

D

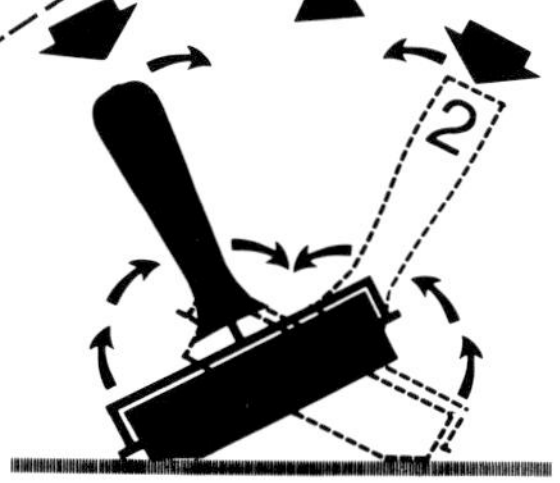

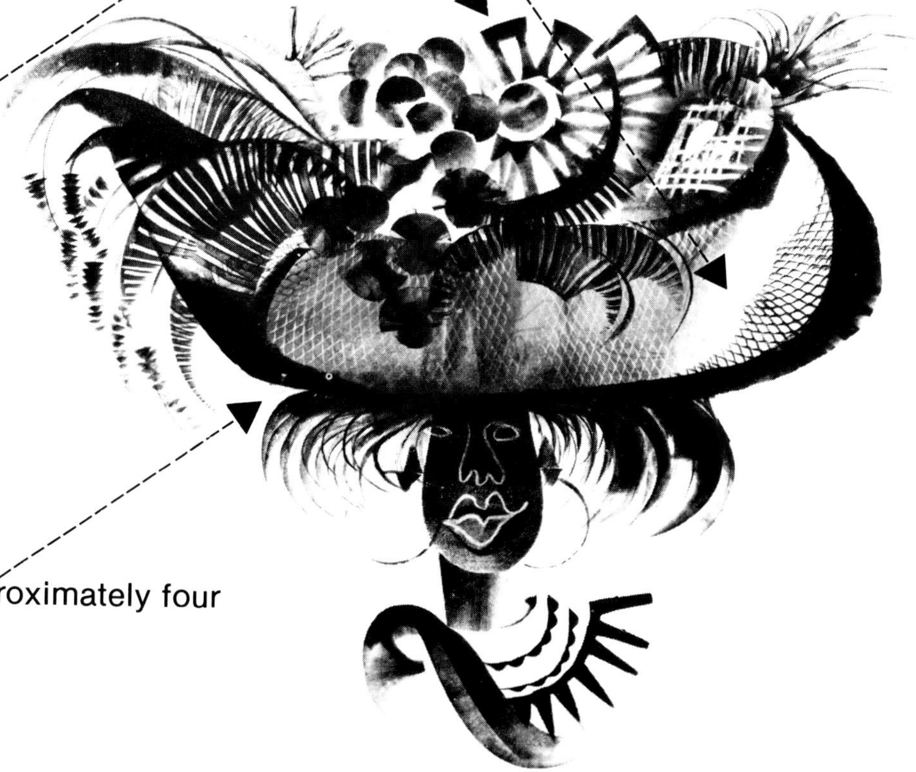

The completed image is approximately four times larger than shown.

Cast metal type plate

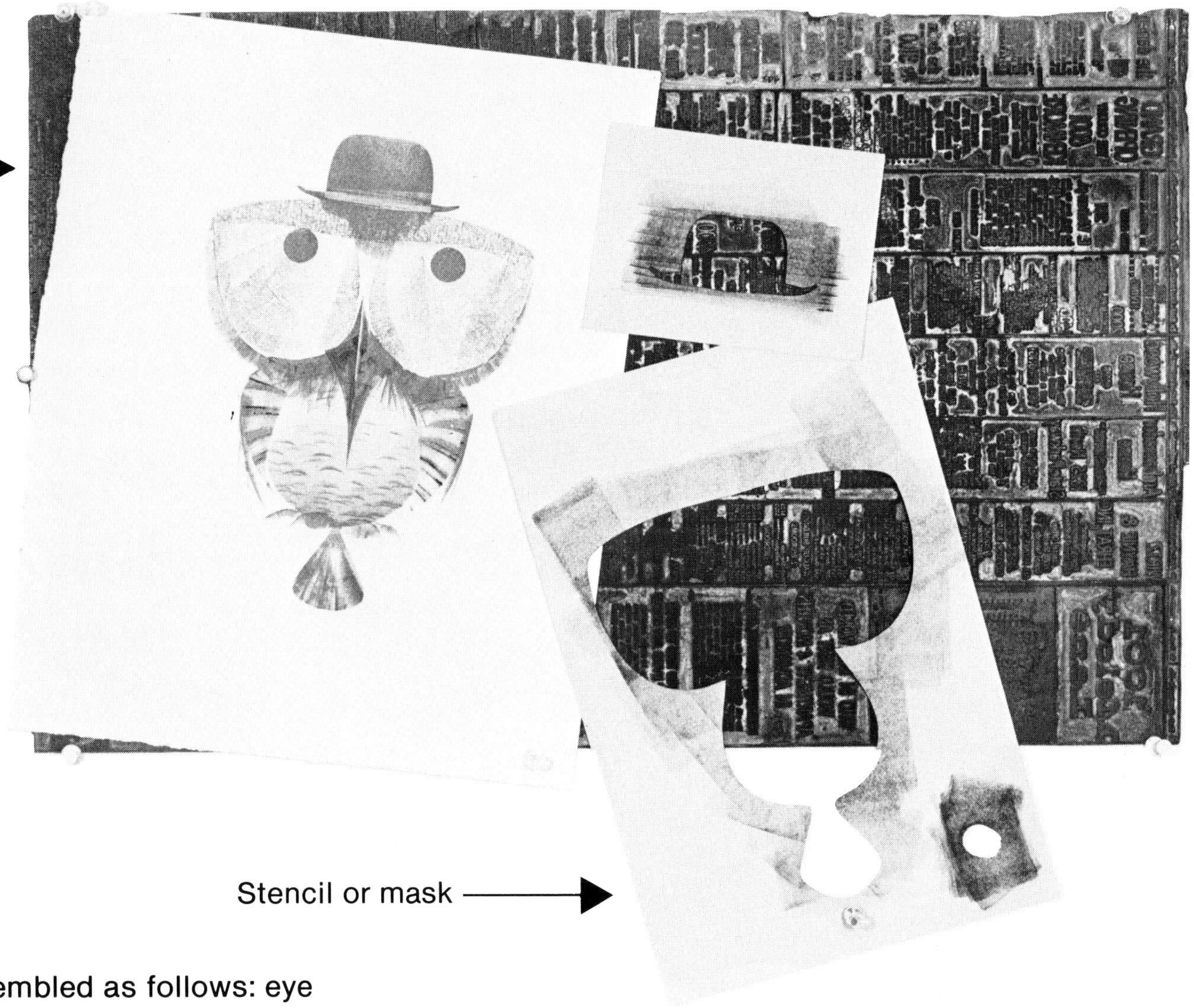

Stencil or mask

This character was assembled as follows: eye glasses from a metal type plate impression; wings and feet by scraping method strokes; the edge bounce strokes on its breast; a paper stencil was used to retain the clean edge silhouette of the bird.

## motivity

This was a simple, direct drawing done at a demonstration in response to a request by a youngster. In brilliant colors of red, purple and brown, the stick figure handling fulfilled his wish to know how to use his skills with the brayer.

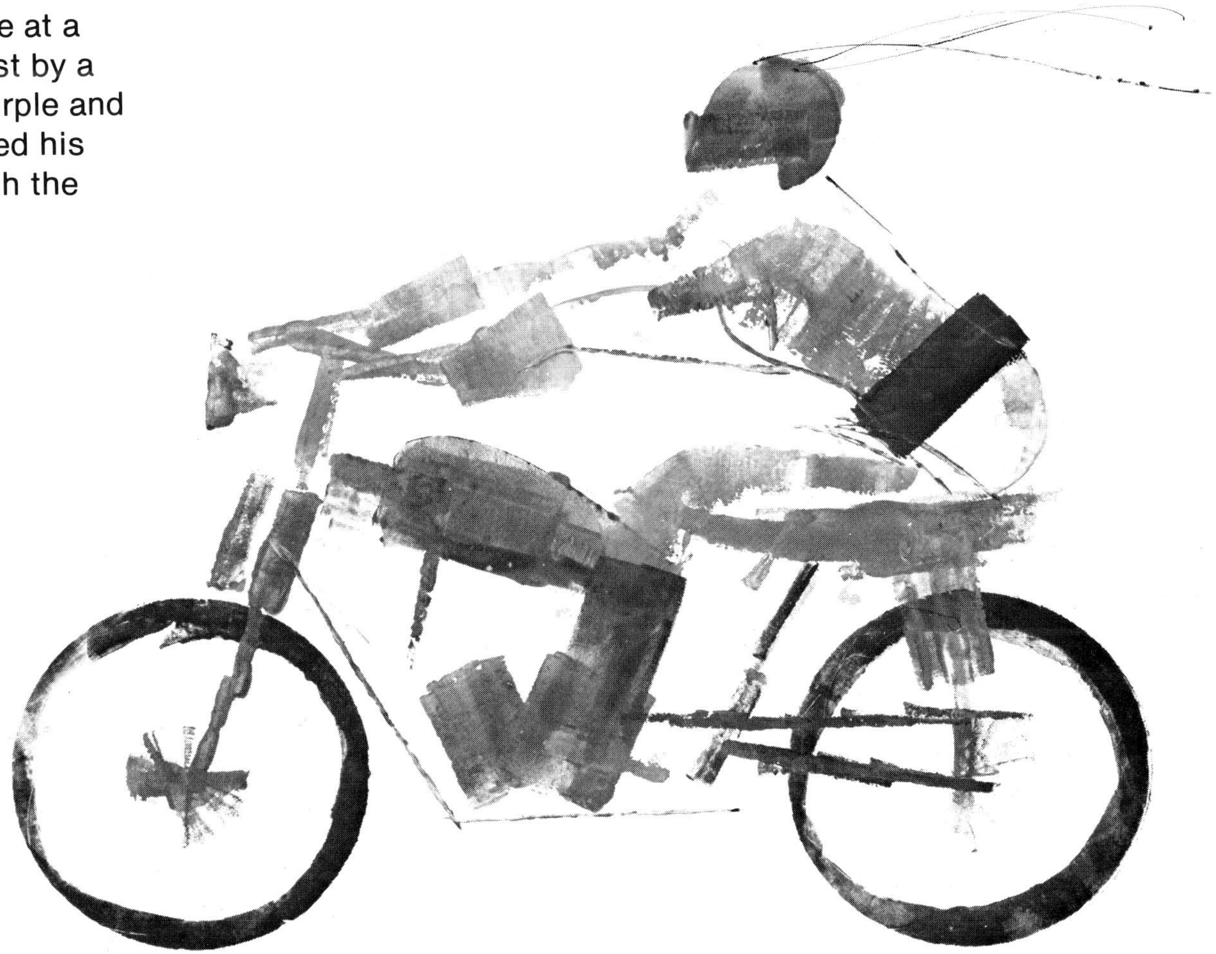

Size: 8 x 12 inches.

These classic car drawings are illustrated and reproduced in black and white. Original art is approximately four times larger.

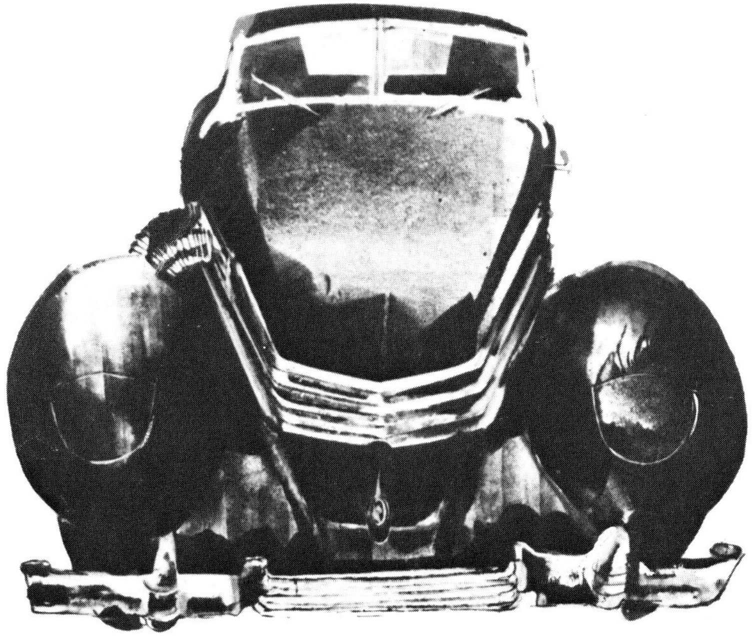

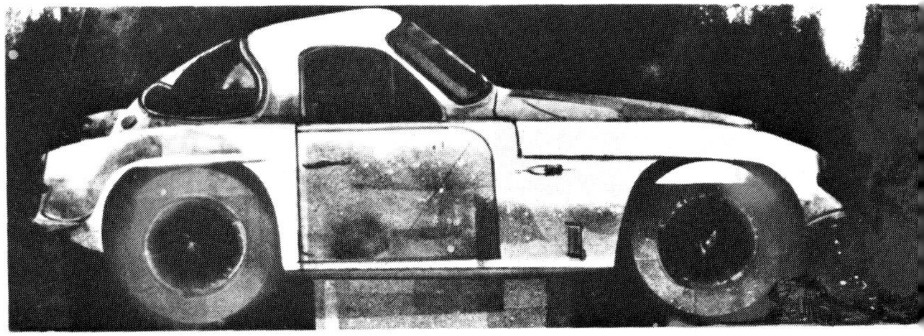

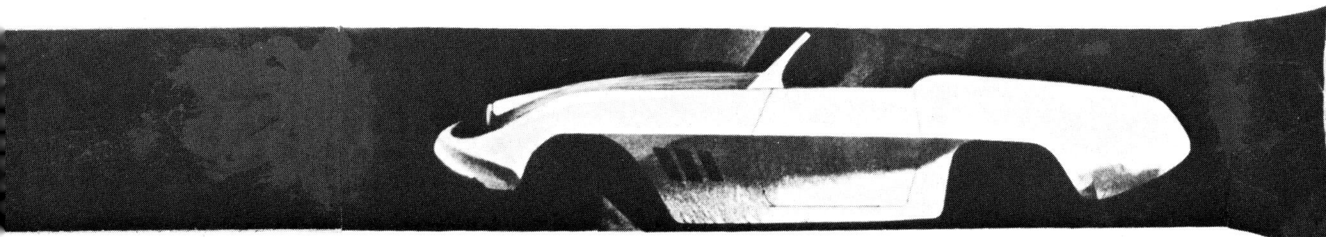

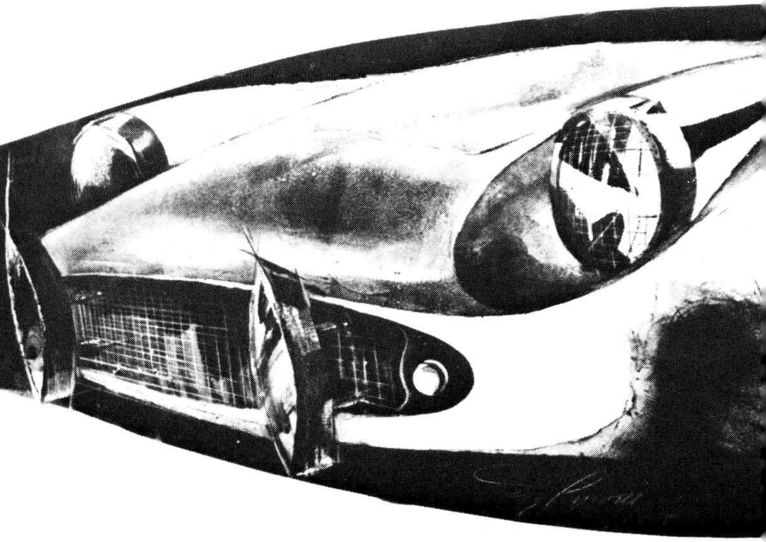

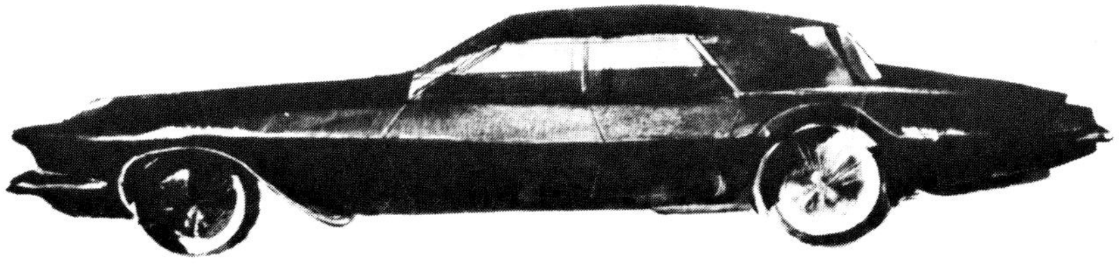

My participation in the sport of motor racing was short and on a very modest scale, but the firsthand acquaintance with the people, experiences with the cars and race locations gave me an insight into the subject.

I sketched and used a camera extensively at these events when not involved otherwise. Motoring machinery can be a fascinating subject for an artist.

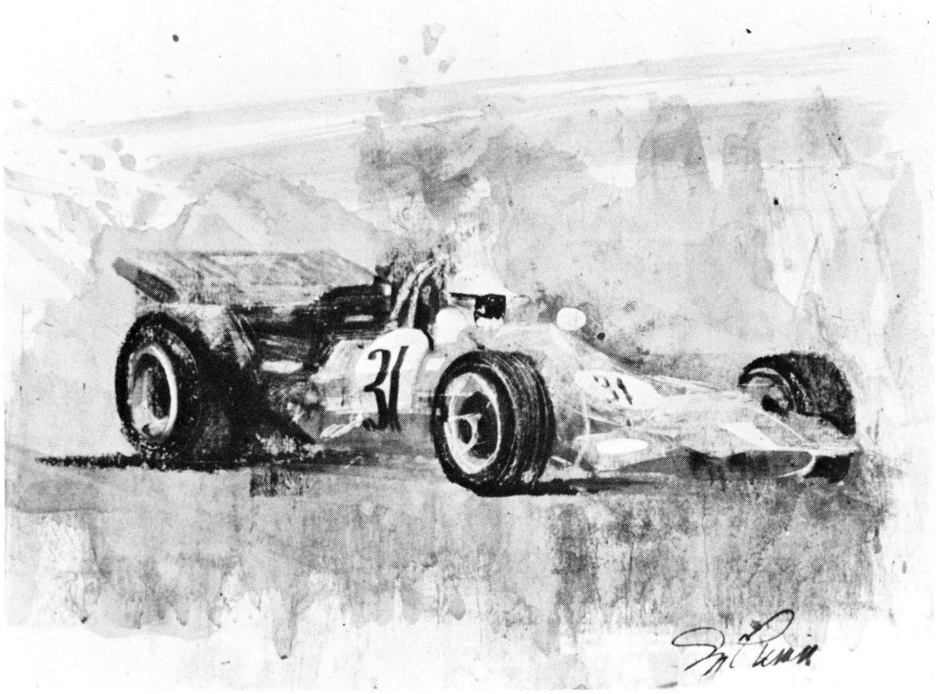

Size: 24 x 28 inches. Oil crayon base with a thin turpentine color rolled across the surface. Detail drawing scratches with razor.

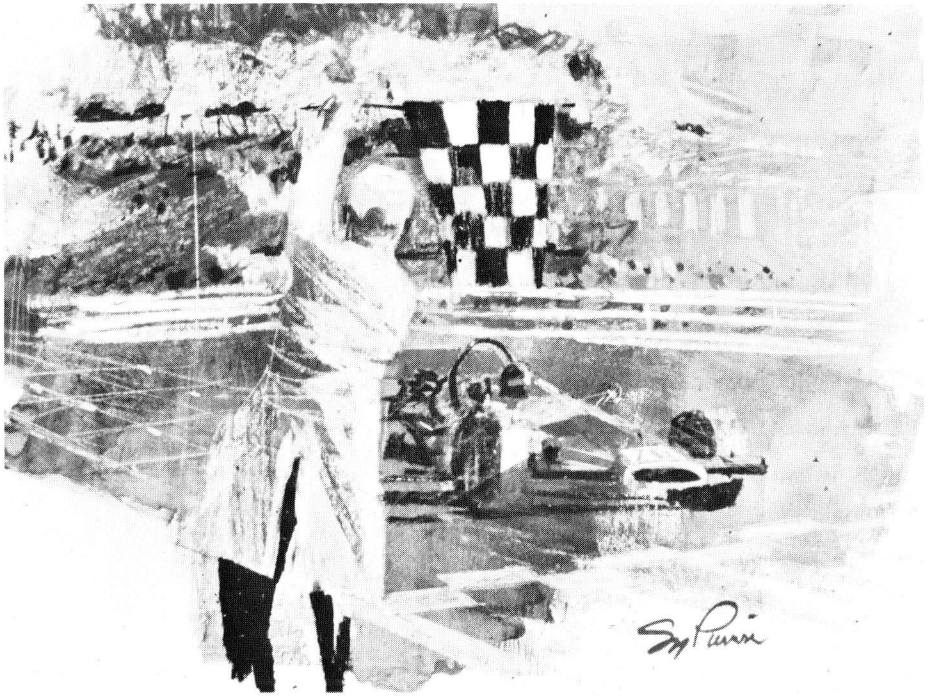

Size: 24 x 28 inches. Oil crayon drawing base with thin oil color wash rolled with brayer. Details scratched and accents highlighted with razor blade.

These illustrations were developed from sketches and candid camera shots. Although only suggested details, they had to be correct; therefore the camera reference. The use of photography should not inhibit or restrict the personal style or flair that gives this type of rendering its special punch.

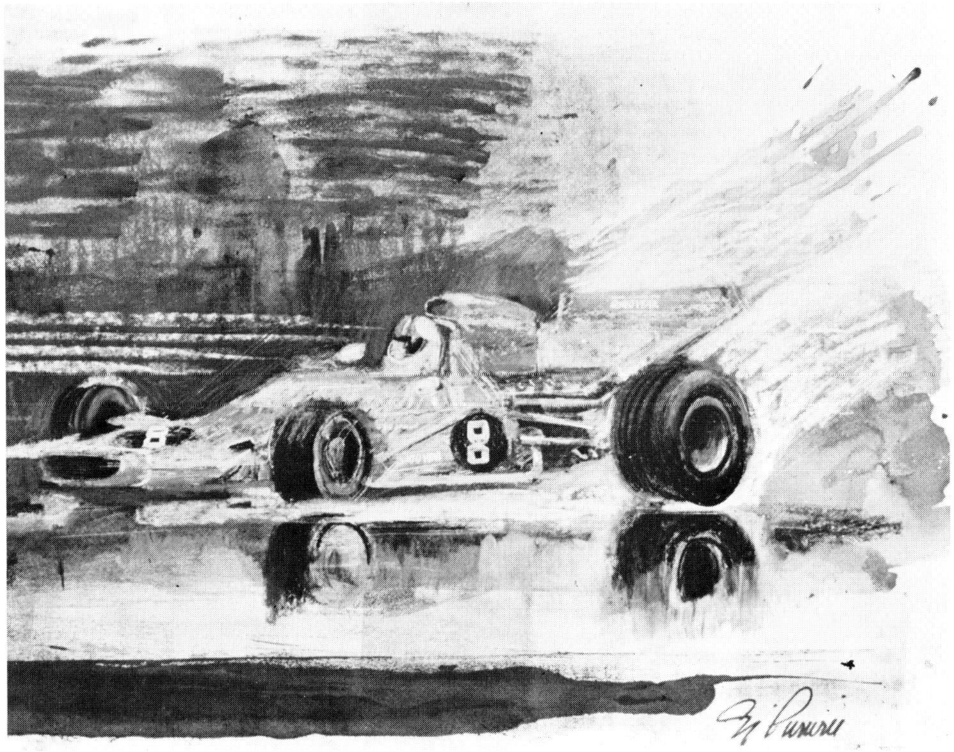

Size: 24 x 28 inches. Oil crayon base, turpentine and oil paint wash with brayer.

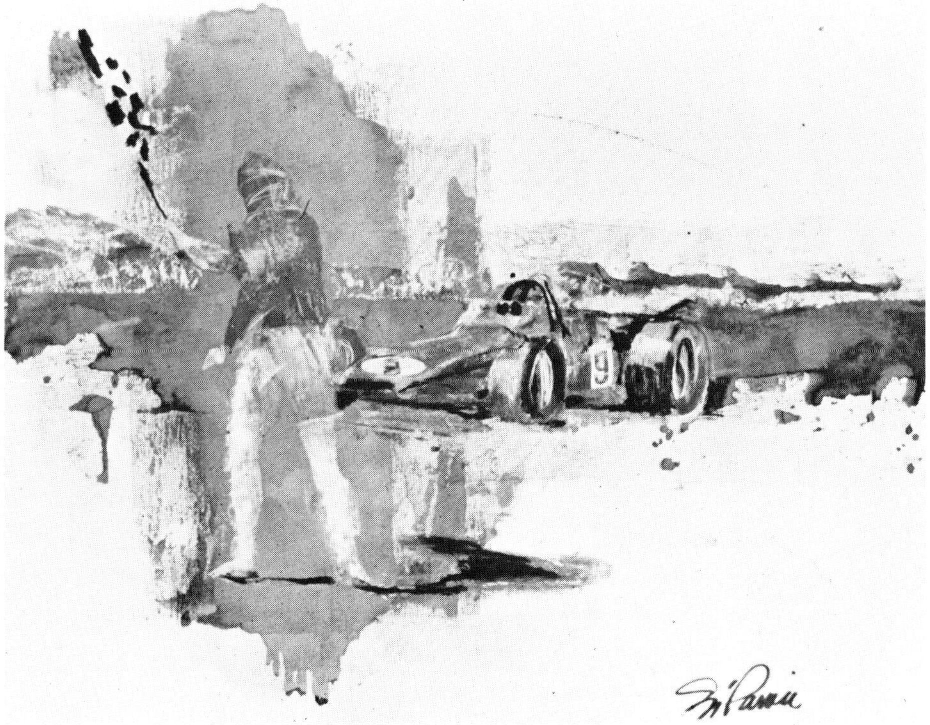

Size: 24 x 28 inches. Oil crayon base, turpentine and oil paint wash on paper. Brayer detailing overlay and scratch art.

These big, burly, double-deck buses sway from side to side in their usual stop-and-go journey through the streets of London.

From a quick sketch, I painted this pair of red "elephants" one evening in my hotel room.

Since then I have made several versions in various media, but I favor the simple, massive treatment that the character of the brayer conveys.

Size: 24 x 20 inches. Full color on offset stock.

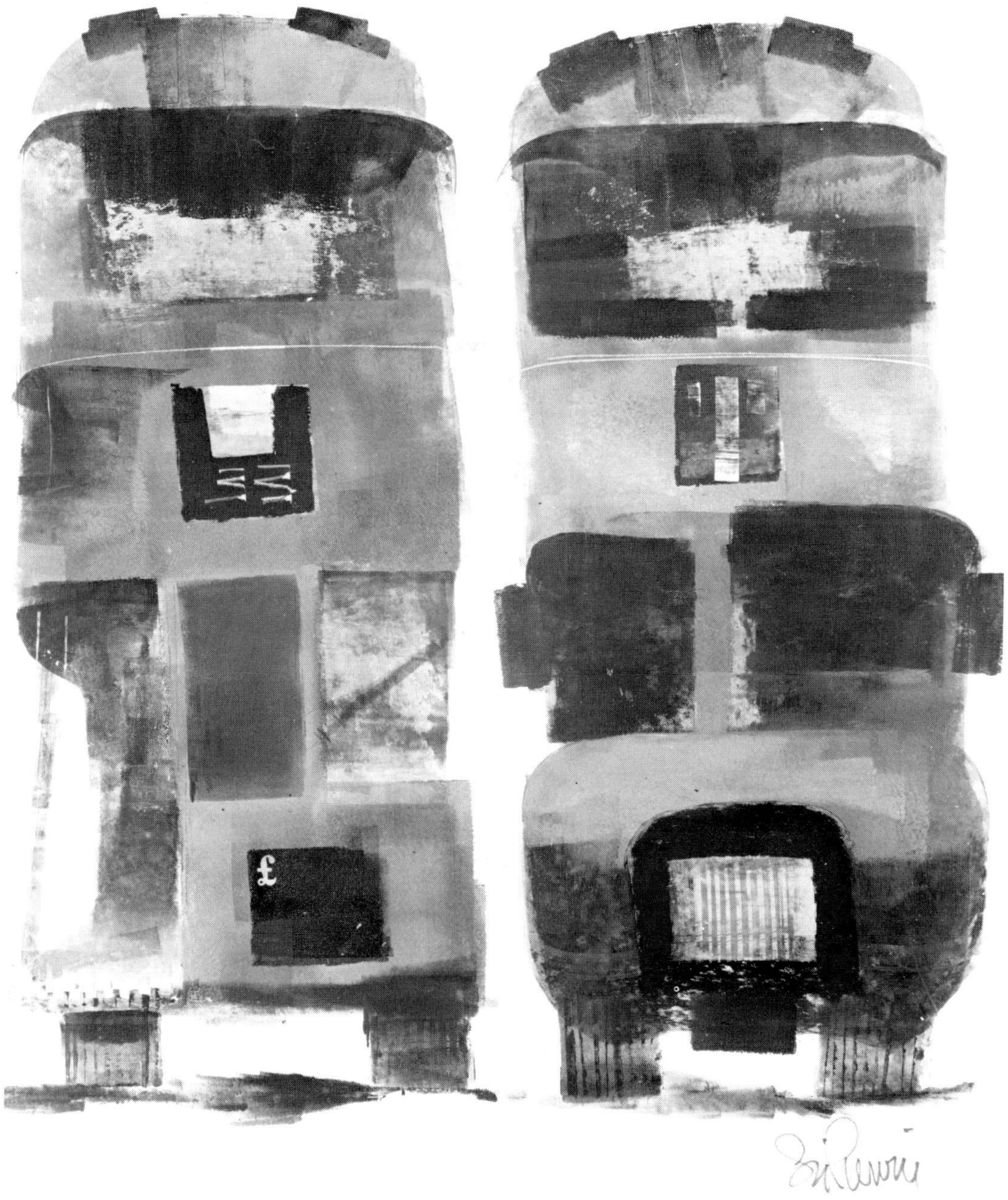

## indoor painting

When working indoors, the convenience of your materials makes for comfortable working conditions. The list of materials at the front of the book is a good start for your brayer painting needs. As you progress in your work, you will likely want to add to your material.

## Working surfaces

A 20 x 20-inch paper size is a good choice for practicing strokes and rolls. Working surfaces can be anything from heavy wrapping paper, newsprint, actual newspaper (the financial pages and want ads are best for a constant grey tone), trim cuts from production paper, rice papers, coated stock in various colors, smooth or textured stock. Gesso-coated masonite panels make excellent surfaces for permanent work.

While working indoors, I like working on two or three pictures at the same time and on the same subject.

When painting I try to retain: freshness, spontaneity, controlled stimulation, impasse awareness, and progress stages for comparison.

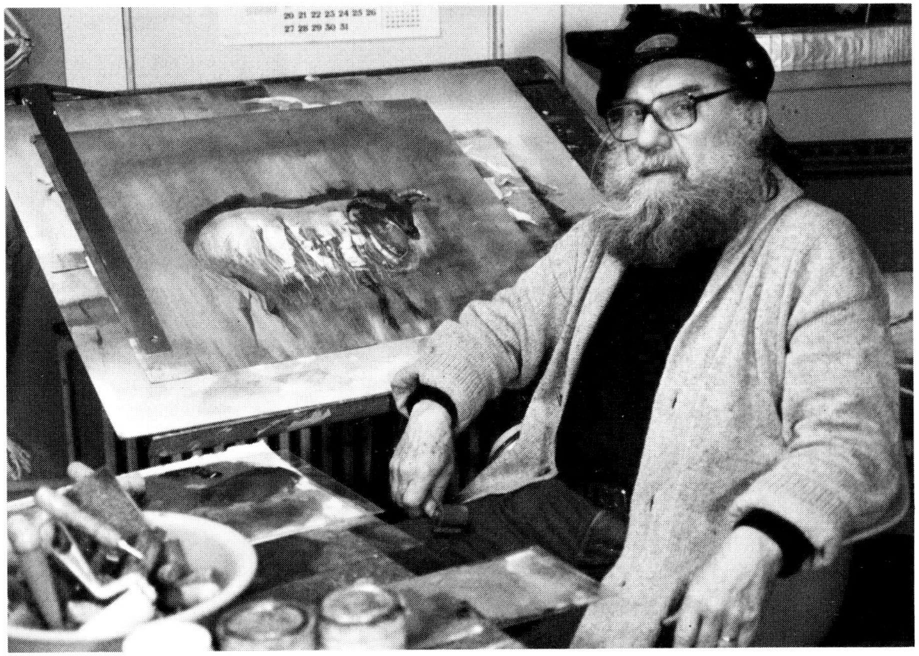

I then complete the work on the painting I have selected from this group, filing the others away to review at a later date.

I often use a mirror to check the color and tonal variations in progress. Seeing my work in reverse refreshes my mind's eye to a startling view of my progress at that stage. It helps relieve eye fatigue from an accustomed concept. It wakes me up to what is actually there. I prefer the use of a mirror to that of another artifact called a diminishing glass, which tends to flatter your work more then to help.

While painting indoors always try to retain the original spirit of intent in your work. Especially while using reference material such as photographs or clippings as aids. Use this material for recollection or reference only in need, or you're likely to lose the original reason for painting the subject.

Whatever thoughts you want to convey, be sure to keep them *intact.* Make simple, direct statements. Don't look for pat answers to all your painting problems; there may be none.

Gut feelings and self-confidence are your best guides. Before you start, get a good mental picture of what you want out of the painting. Then put away your reference materials and use them sparingly for clarification of detail as needed.

## picture building

This small sketch is the first step in preparing to paint a larger version.

Research on the subject was completed before starting any work. Reading on sailing twelve-meter boats, photography and my sketches of boating were my sources. Most of my composition problems can be resolved at this time, allowing me to concentrate on the painting and rendering.

The 30 x 24-inch paper is coated with several layers of gesso. When dry, I carefully draw in the subject with pencil ready as a start for the underpainting.

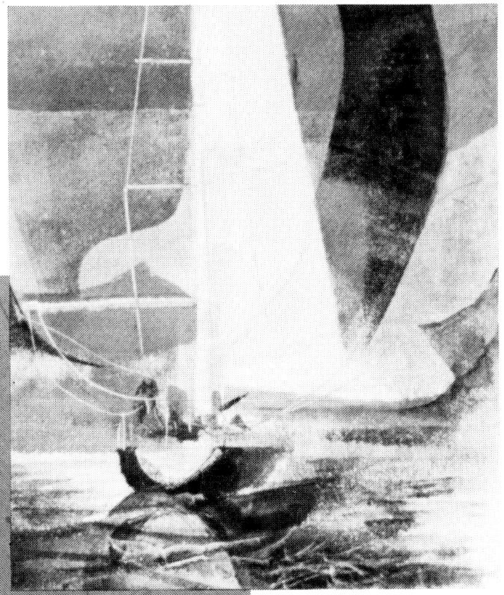

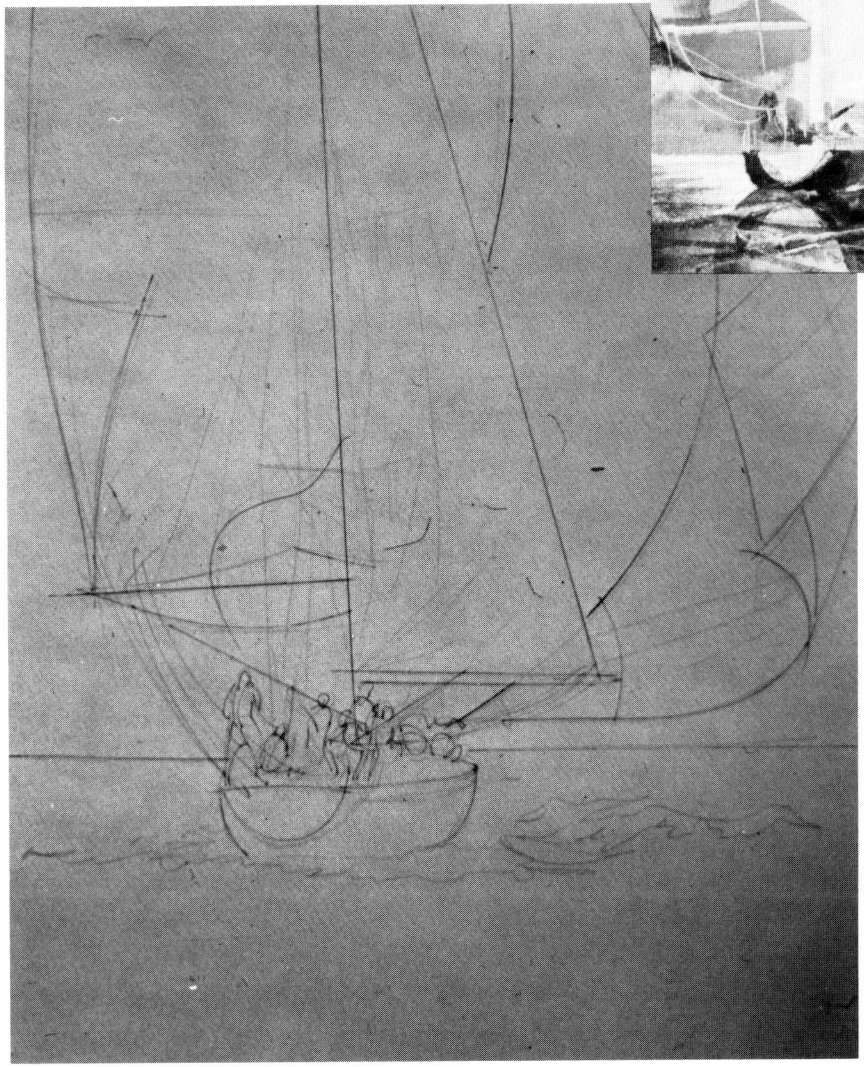

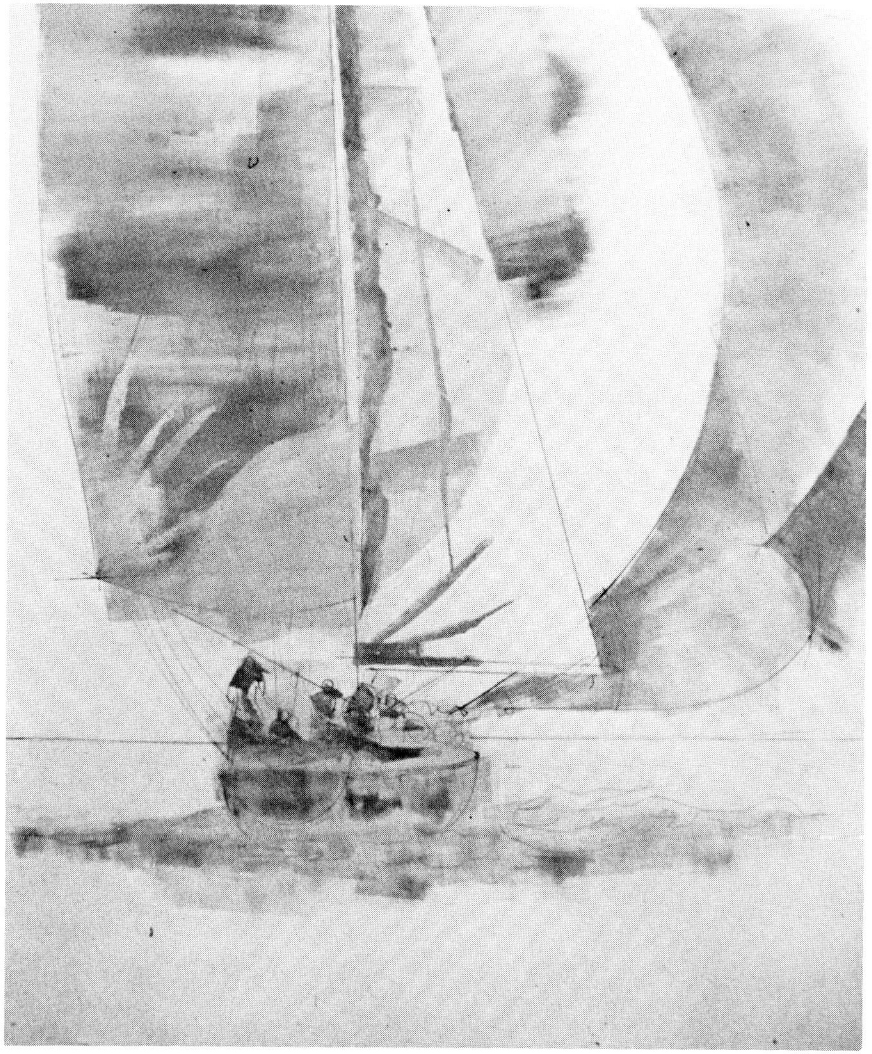

The long triangular mainsail (foreshortened) will remain predominant as the middle values around it begin to take shape. I prefer to retain an abstract quality to the painting as long as I can. The brayer varies my values simply by the changing of pressures on the roller itself.

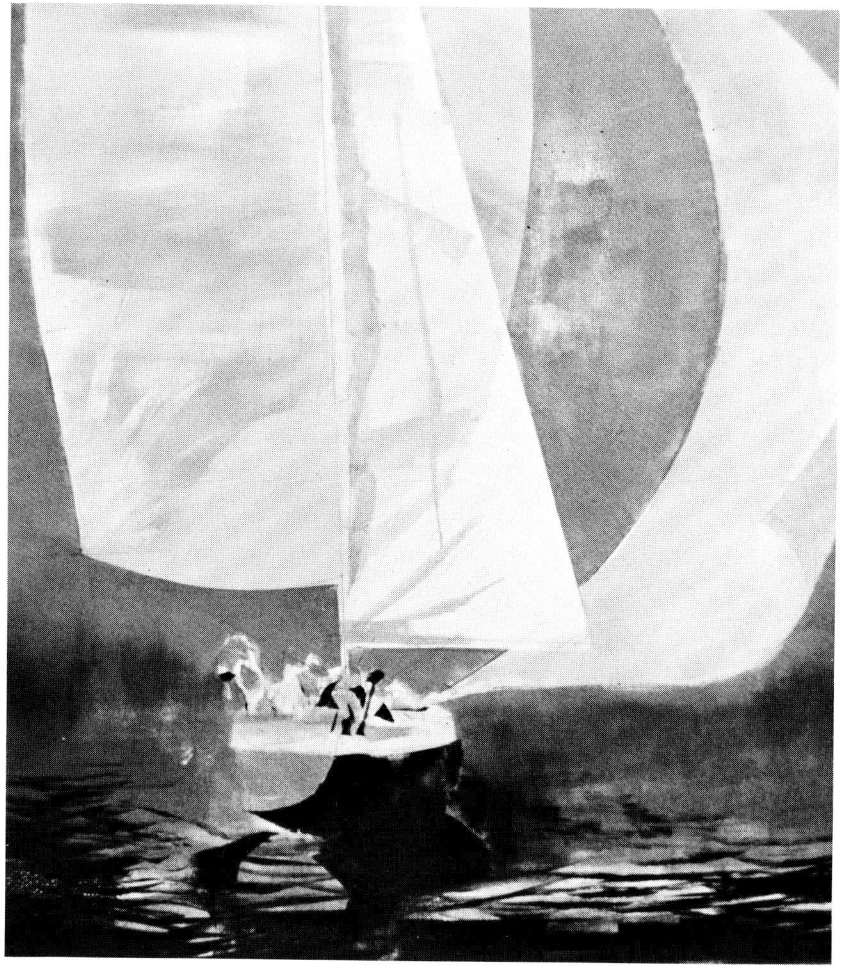

The experienced watercolorist will note this feature at once, for it is not necessary to dilute the paint with water to vary or change tones as in the conventional manner of transparent painting.

A poster-style handling of sky, water and the boat's hull is used in the follow-up series of strokes.

I now incorporate the bold, dark or strong colors for emphasis and contrast. In this final stage, the razor blade is used again to pick up pigment from the palette and spot in the rigging and structured details. Scratching in the white accents is done while the painting is still damp.

Many areas should remain inconspicuous and quiet by keeping detail to a minimum.

Size: 28 x 22 inches, water based inks on chrome coat stock.

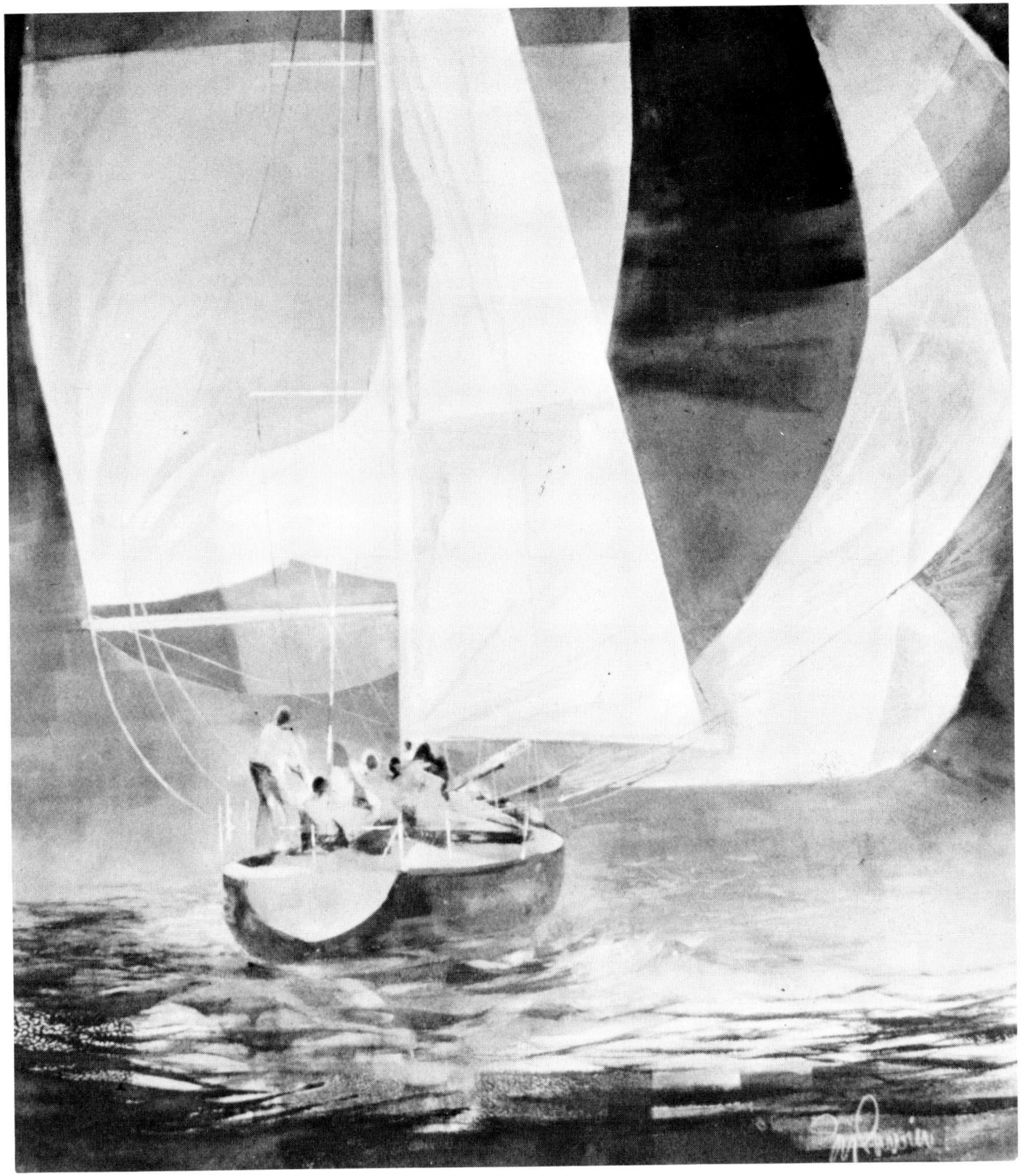

## brayer painting
## combination oil paint/oil crayon

Assuming you have selected your subject and have transferred the drawing to the paper surface, you are ready for *Step 1.* Using the side of the oil crayon, work in a broad manner with plenty of wrist action. These crayons come in a wide variety of colors. Usually when I get a new box of oil sticks, I peel off all the paper labels so I can work in broader strokes. I also separate the warm colors from the cool colors into separate containers, making them easily accessible.

Apply the crayon liberally, building up a continuous layer of color surface, working from light to dark. Wherever yellow and blue overlap you will get a green cast. Such overlapping keeps hard edges to a minimum. A certain percentage of white paper will show through, which will eventually be stained directly when the oil paint on the brayer is used. The rougher the paper surface, the more white paper will be exposed.

Painting with a brayer allows you a lot of flexibility, both in thought and action. Note how the characteristics of the brayer enhance your technical efforts.

*Step 2*
In brayer painting I mix gel with oil colors before starting, leaving ample space on the palette for rolling. Coat the roller surface with a thin layer of the selected color and begin the *up/down and drag* method as described on page 21. The values will vary according to the pressure of the roller and the density of the paint. The number of times that you roll the brayer across a given area will also vary the tone. You will note, the harder the pressure and repeat rolls, the lighter the value. Stop when you are satisfied with the tonal quality. This is the manner in which you formalize your shapes and forms and prepare for the next step.

*Step 3*
Accent and detail calls for more mental planing than the actual execution time involved. You will be using other tools such as a scraper (razor), screens, sponges, etc., in addition to the brayers. Try to stay loose and be bold during this stage. Remember you can resurface any area or vary any part of your painting you may wish to change, so don't be timid.

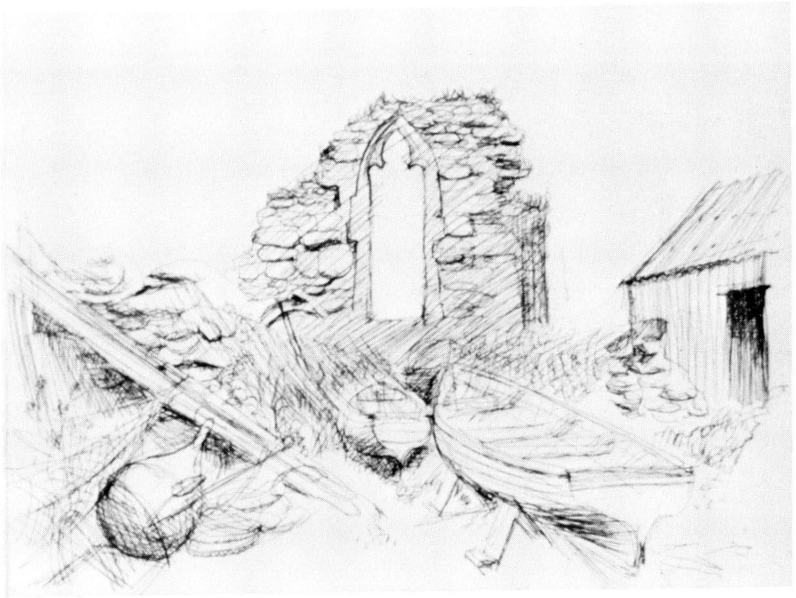

Pen drawing at site.

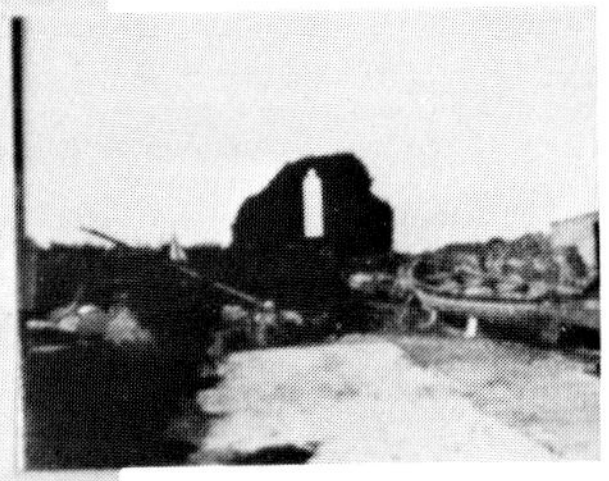

Photograph at site.

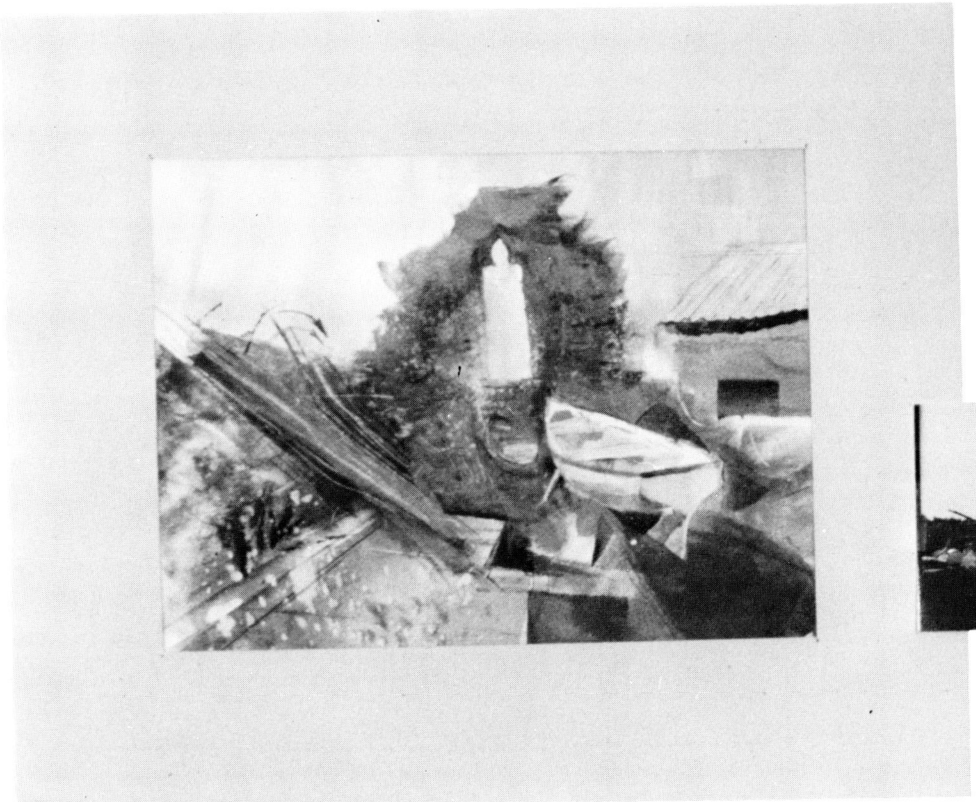

Full color brayer sketch at studio.

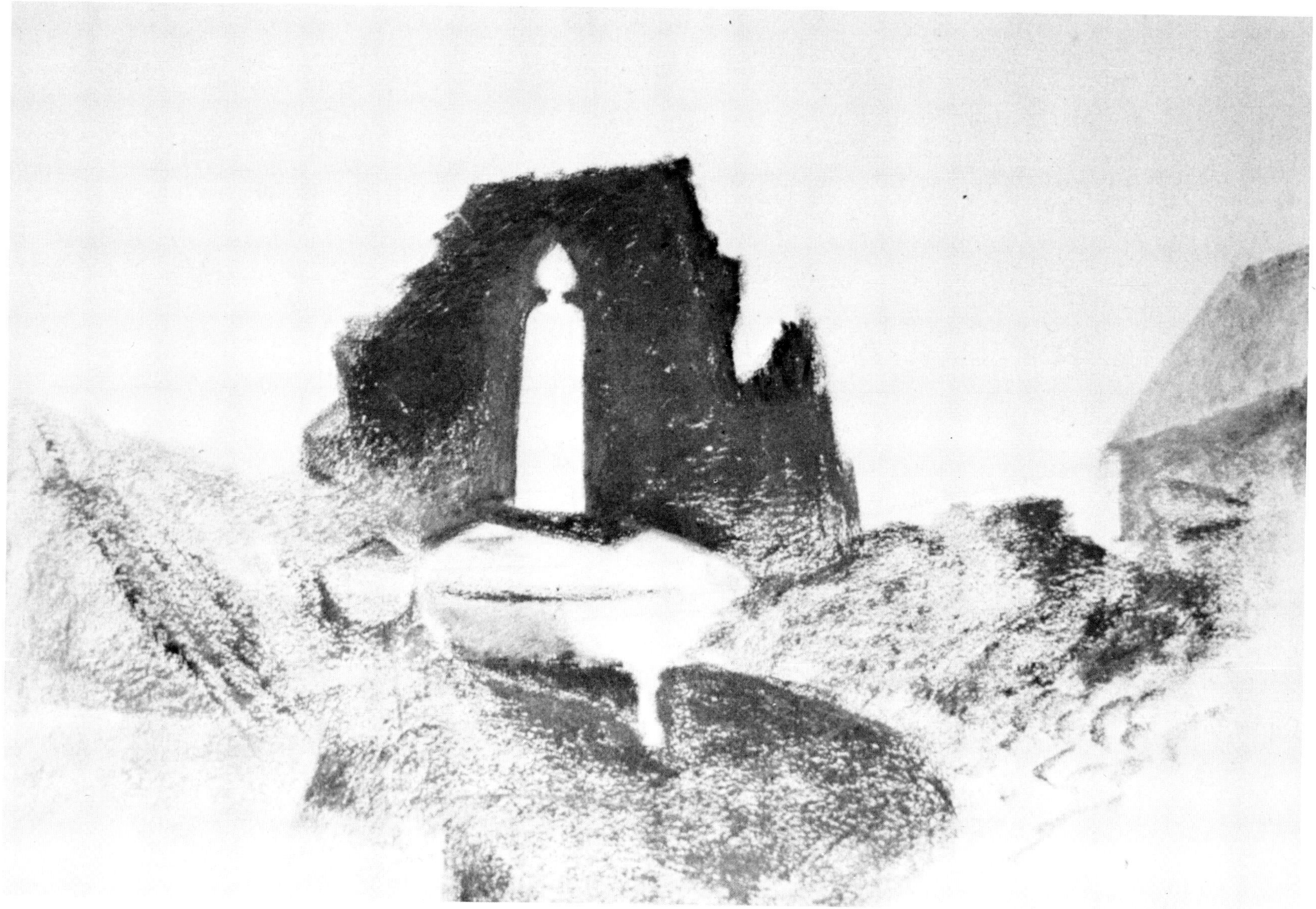

Stage 1
With the middle tones roughly indicated in crayon, I take the brayer, using a mixture of alizarin crimson and ultramarine blue and establish the darkest areas. Then, using the *up/down and drag* strokes with a thin gel mixed with paint, I glaze and blend the colors into the crayon undertones. At this time I put in the sky with diagonal drag strokes. The overall tonal concept is finished.

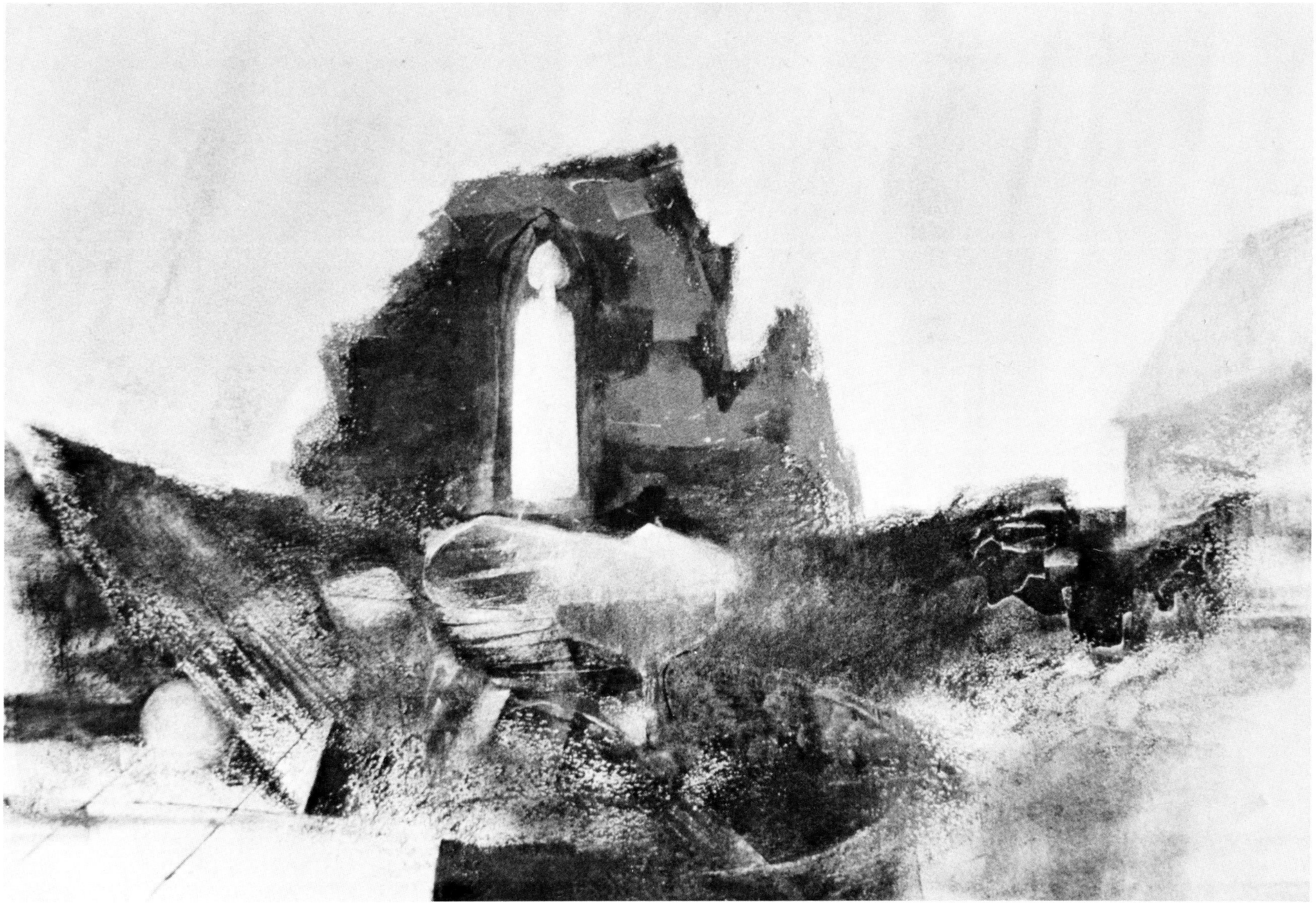

Stage 2
Using the information from the small sketches as a guide, I roughly sketched in the scene on a gesso-coated paper stock. Then I proceeded with bold vertical and diagonal oil crayon strokes.

With the side of the crayons I use a varied mix of yellow ochre, cerulean blue and alizarin crimson. The rough gesso texture gives a dry brush effect to the undertones.

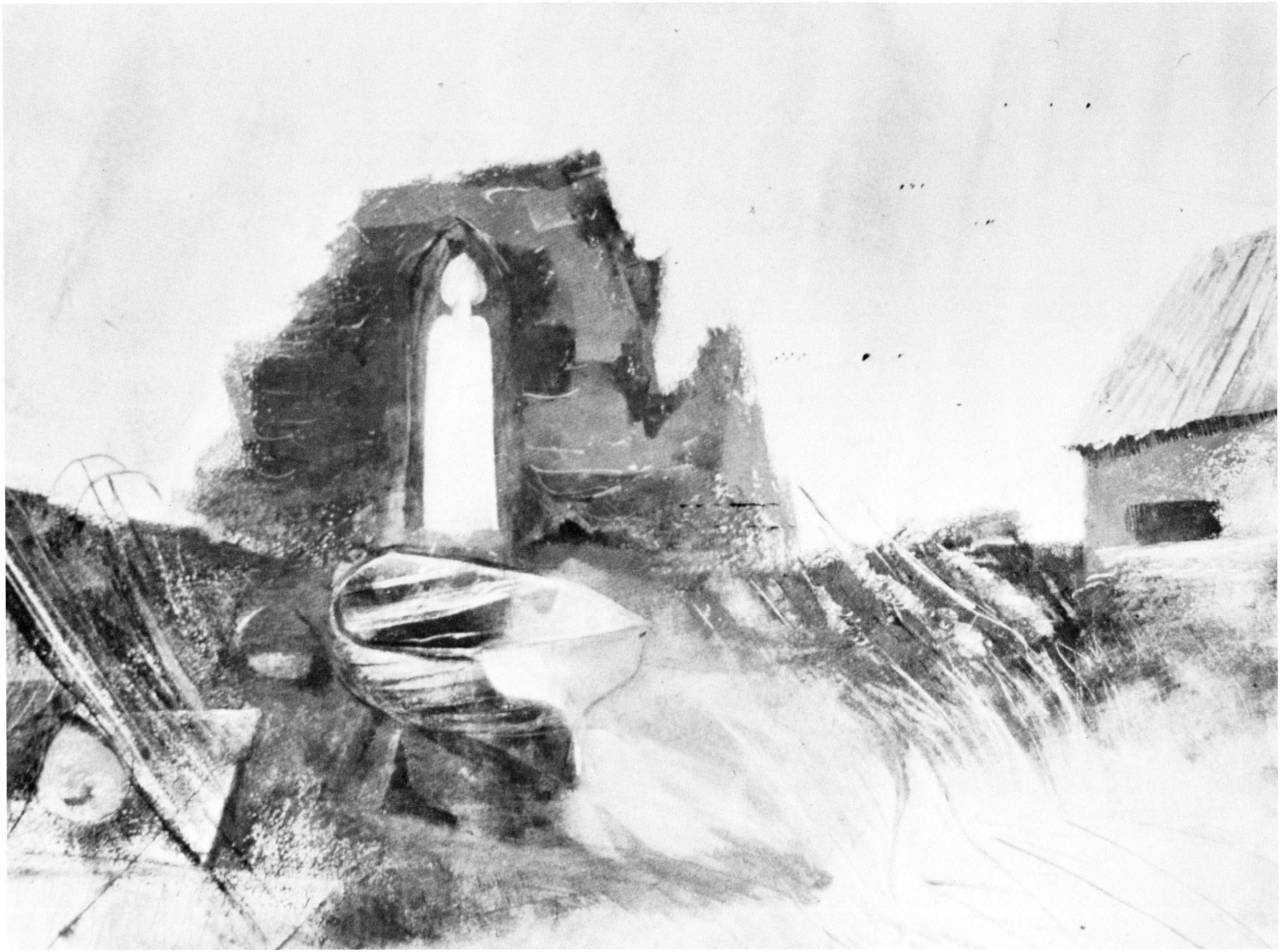

St. John's Point. Size: 19 x 26 inches.

Stage 3
In this painting I've deliberately kept the detail to a minimum, using only the brayer with a sharp penknife for accents. The foreground at the right was kept in a high value to balance the dark stone wall.

Working with two types of oil pigment (crayon and paste) offers a lot of latitude for adjustments late in a painting stage. This helps to keep it from looking overworked.

**picture transformation exercise**

Using the brayer allows you to work in a broad, bold manner both physically and in thought. An excellent way to compare the brayer characteristics with other methods of painting is this:
Select one of your own watercolors or oils that you like or can relate to. Set up the selected painting before you in preparation for painting it again. This time you will use the brayer instead of brushes. Prepare your palette and roll in your background first. Refer to your original painting for mood and inspiration only.

Next, plan your middle value and apply strokes and rolls such as the *up/down and drag,* etc., changing pressure to form the contours and shapes you wish to achieve. Try to create variety by using such procedures as the scraping methods as per page 23 and 24.

With your brayer experiment near completion, compare and see the difference in definition between the two paintings. You'll probably note the brayer handling of your painting is composed of simple forms and tensions. Brayer painting eliminates secondary details not pertinent to the total visual impact.

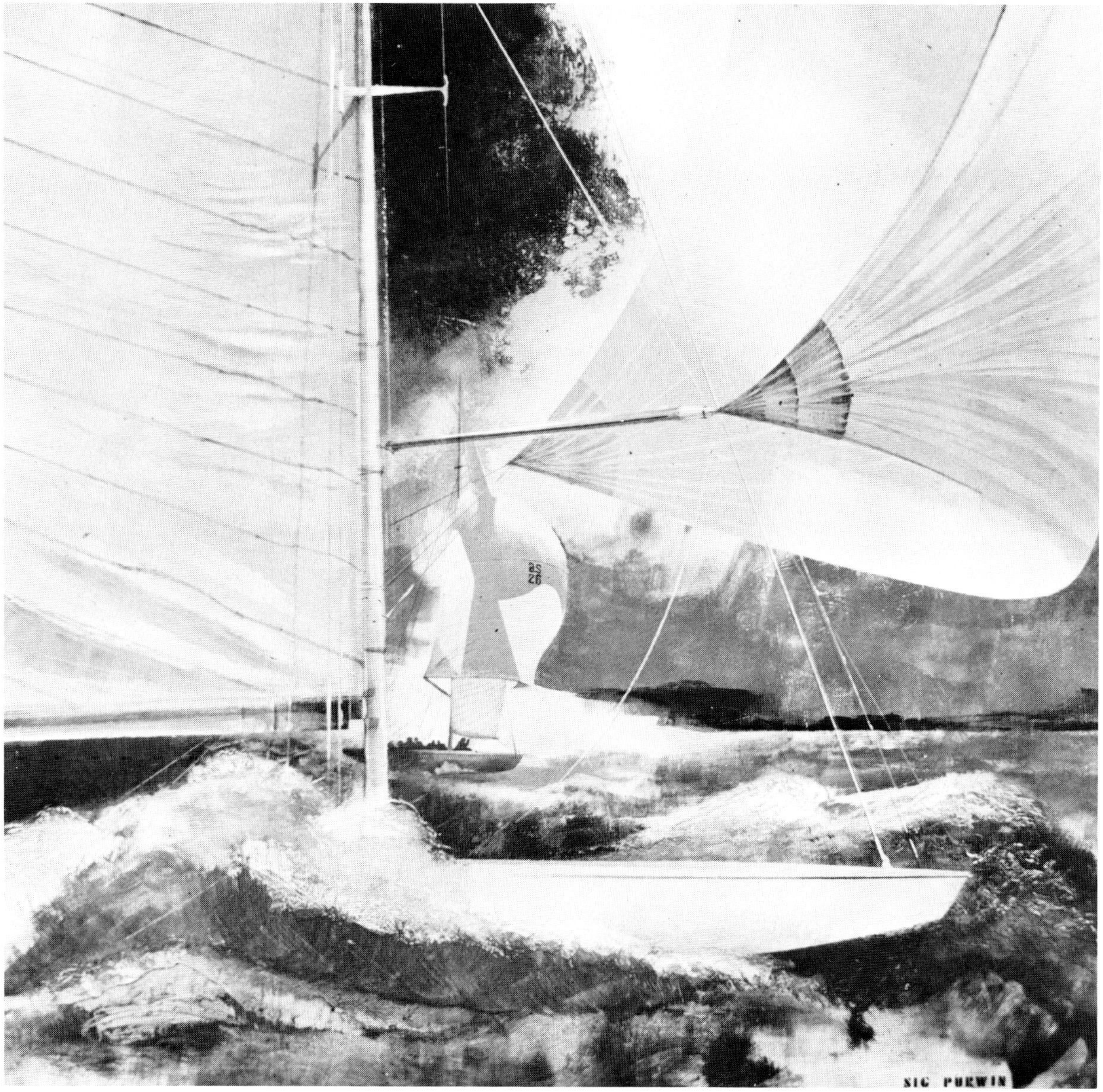


To Catch The Wind

Size: 38 x 38 inches. Brayer, water based paints on gesso-coated plywood.

Nekoosa Paper Corporation calendar art.

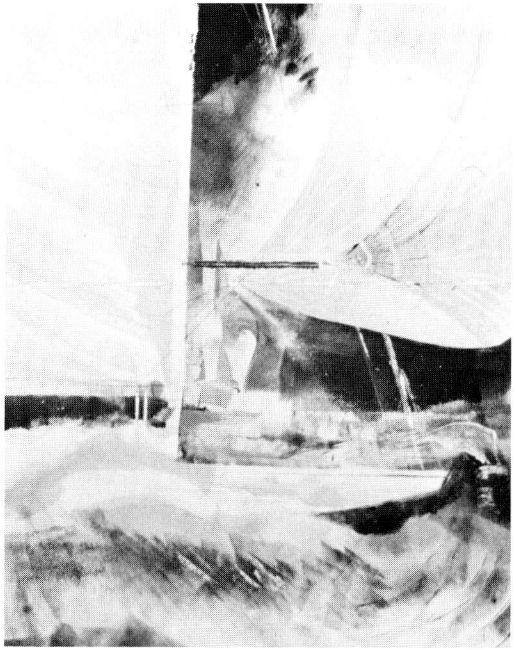

Mini-brayer color sketch.

Size: 9 x 7½ inches.

# outdoor painting

## brayer painting outdoors

Prior to your first outdoor adventure as a brayer painter, I suggest you first experiment with the brayer indoors. Here the convenience of materials and work space is assured. Refresh your memory of the different strokes and rolls. Better still, take the book along with you outdoors. Check your list of materials and equipment for your trip. You should have these items:

Plastic palettes
Two or three brayers
Scrapers (razor blades, knife)
Rags or paper towels
Container & water (turpentine)
Paints or inks (water or oil base)
Paper or other painting surfaces
Portable easel, chair, table

For years, I painted outdoors without even an easel. I just plopped down on the ground with my drawing board wherever it suited me and proceeded. If a tree stump or a rock were near at hand to serve as an easel, all the better. Lately, I've succumbed to the use of those lovely portable easels, stools and even tables that are on the market for outdoor painters. They are nice but you can get along without them.

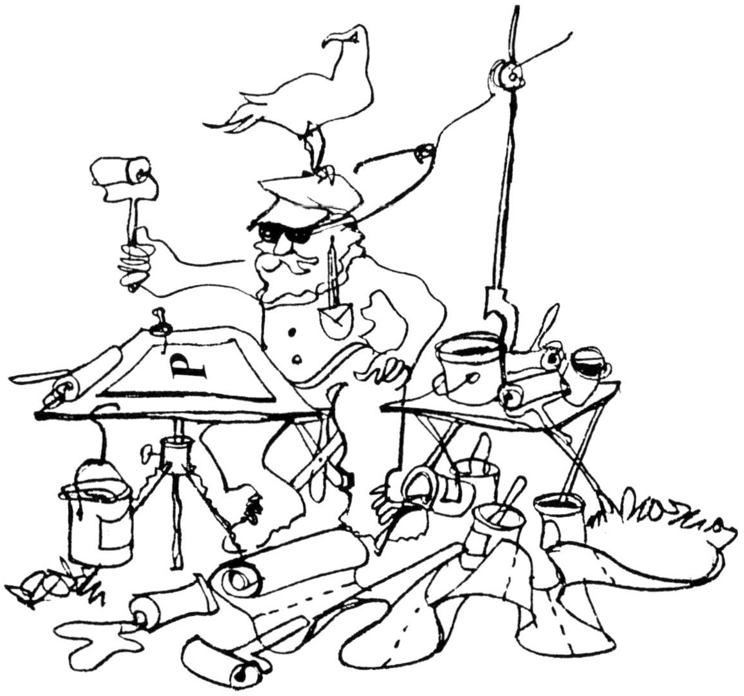

## paints

I prefer to use water soluble inks or paints for outdoor painting or when travelling for demonstration workshops. They're quick-drying and convenient. For starters I suggest these basic colors:

| | |
|---|---|
| Reds | alizarin crimson, vermilion |
| Blues | ultramarine blue, cobalt blue |
| Yellows | yellow ochre, lemon yellow |
| Browns | burnt sienna, raw sienna |
| Black | glazing gel. |

I like to use two rectangular plastic panels for palettes, approximately 6 x 14 inches: one for my warm colors and the other for cool colors. Be sure to allow sufficient space for rolling when you lay out your palette.

I use a minimum number of colors (3), light, dark, medium at the start and add others as needed. Color discipline helps to control values. The intermixing of colors without first removing existing paint on the roller is conceivable, but care must be taken to avoid muddying the paint and palette. You can start painting from light to dark or dark to light. In most cases I prefer light to dark when working with thin or transparent paints.

Density and value variances:

1 By varying pressure on the roller you change the density of the color.
2 The amount of paint on the roller varies the value.
3 By mixing gel (a transparent paste) in your paints, you can glaze over the colors.

## on-the-spot brayer sketching

Squint your eyes while looking at the site you plan to paint. Note how the light patterns vary and the color contrasts have shape in depth.

Make your mini-sketches, set up your equipment and go to it. Don't be too explicit, stay loose. Don't try to solve all your challenges at once. Compromise where and when you feel it necessary as your work develops.

*Look twice, paint once,* and stay with your original motif. Enjoy the ease of applying paint from the palette to paper with your brayer. Concentrate on what you want to happen. Stop repeatedly and check your progress. Let the pleasing accidents be part of your total effort. Again, stay loose; feel good about the effects you create. Try to think positively and you will get positive results.

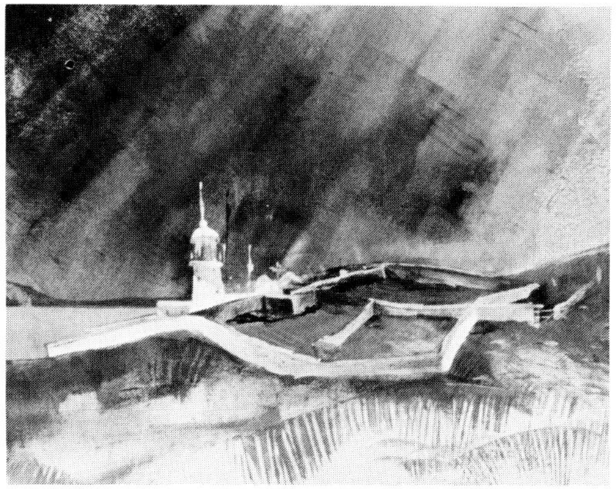

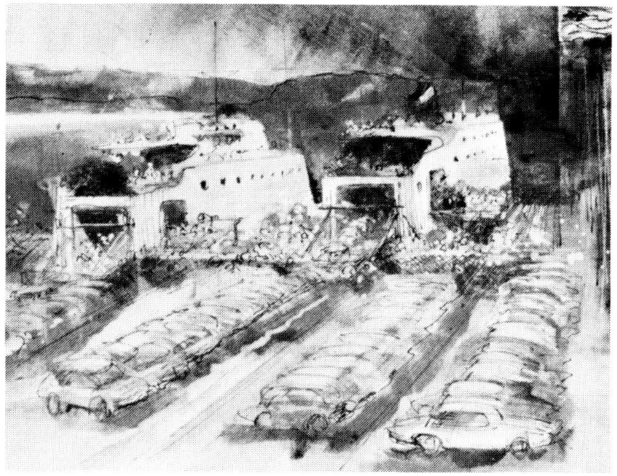

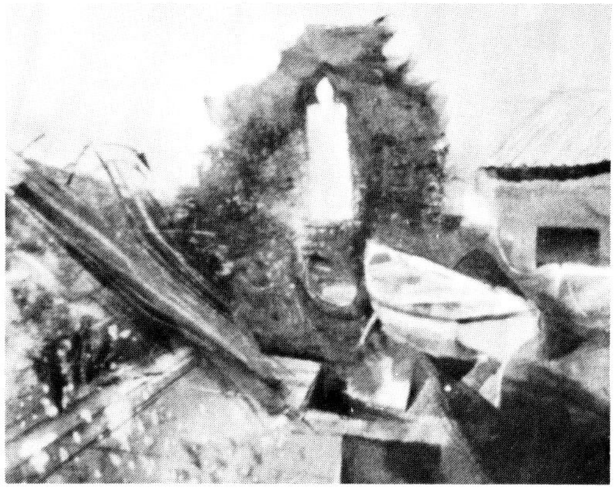

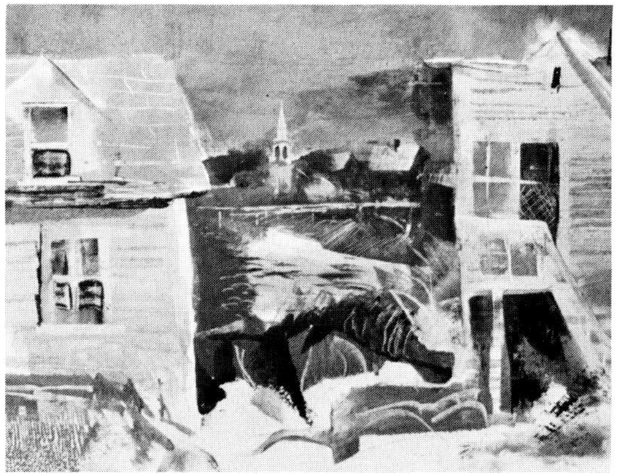

**on-the-spot brayer painting**

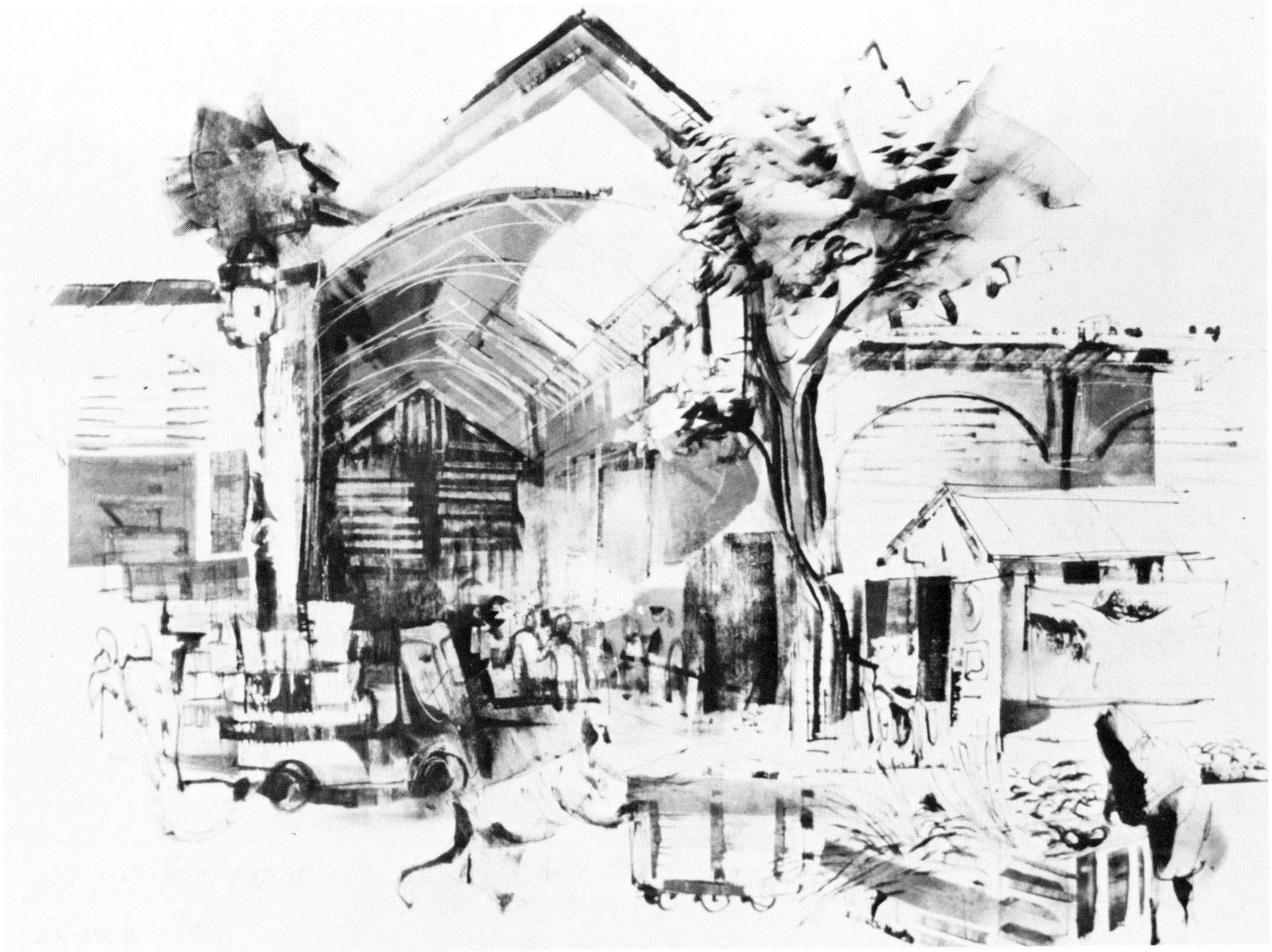

Early morning market in Paris.
Size: 12 x 18 inches, one color, sepia.

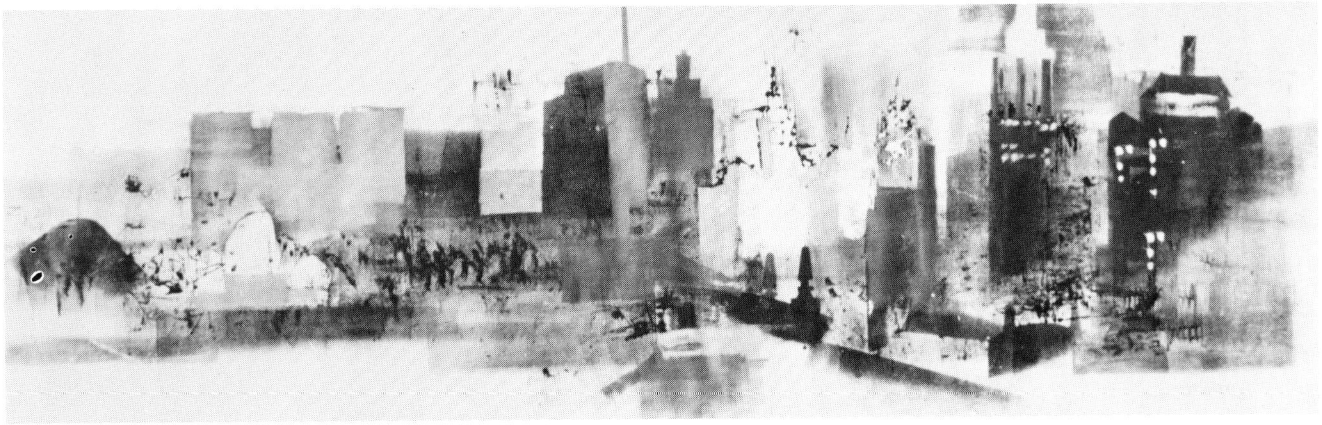

Chicago skyline.
Size: 7 x 18 inches, two colors, black, sepia.

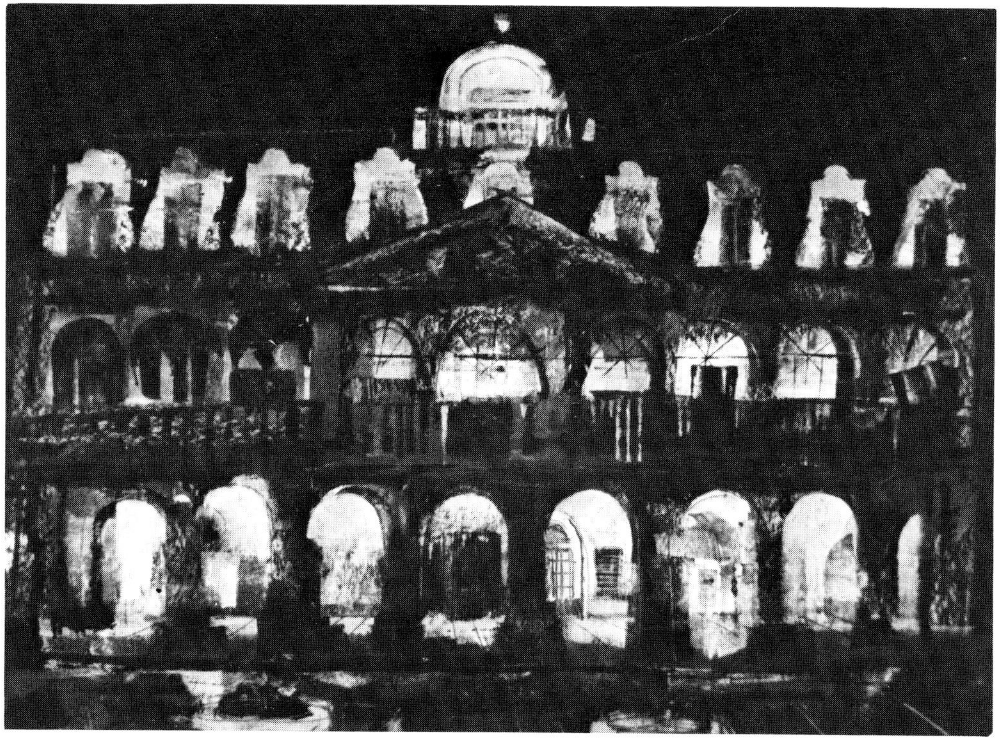

Night Cabildo, New Orleans,
Size: 18 x 24 inches. Opaque white and black on charcoal paper.

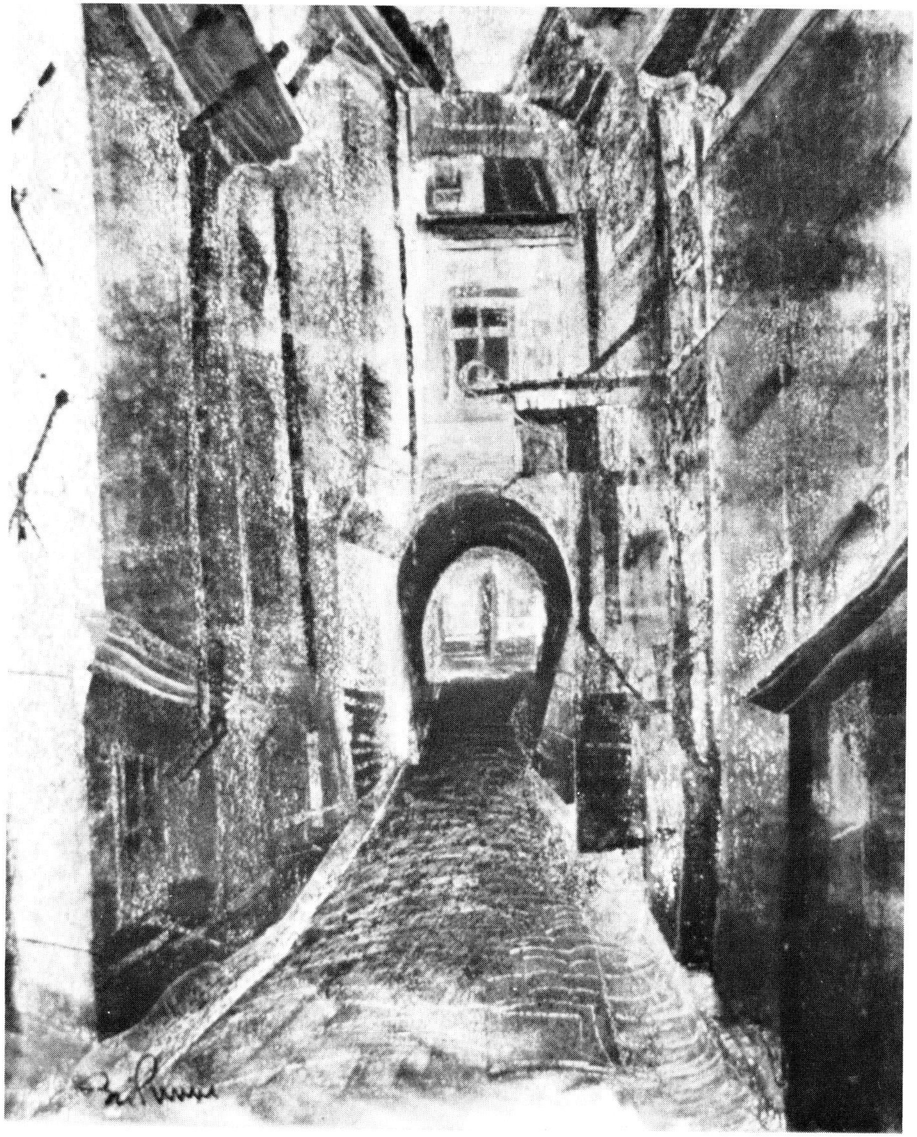

Old Town Alleyway, Stockholm
Size: 24 x 18 inches. Oil crayon base with transparent sepia brayer overtones. Cold press watercolor paper.

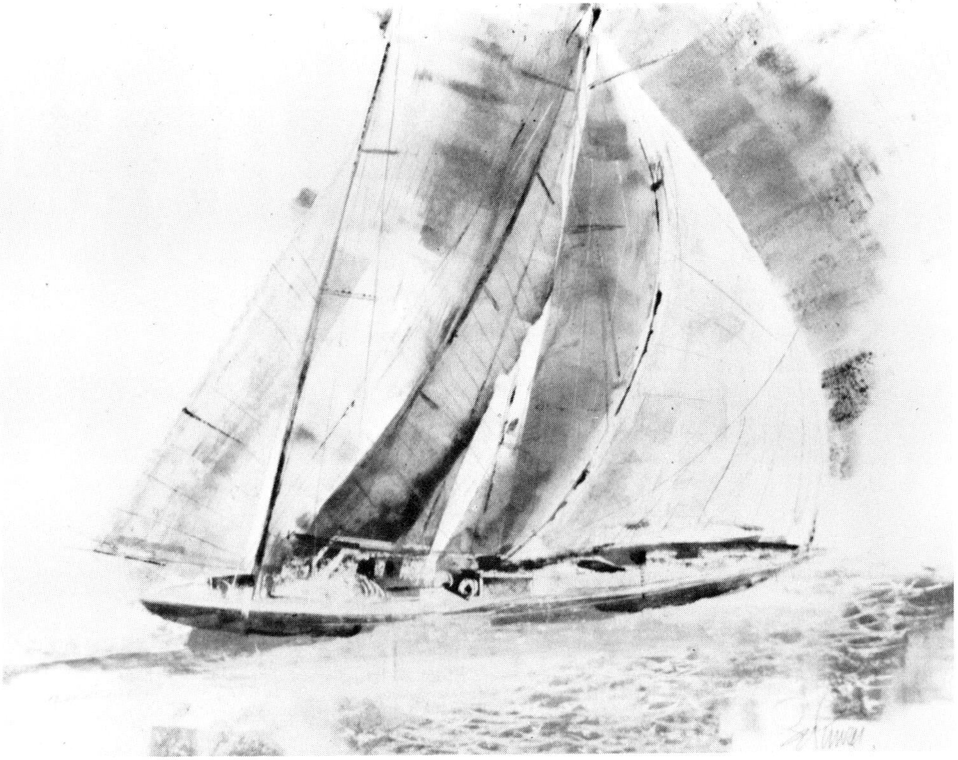

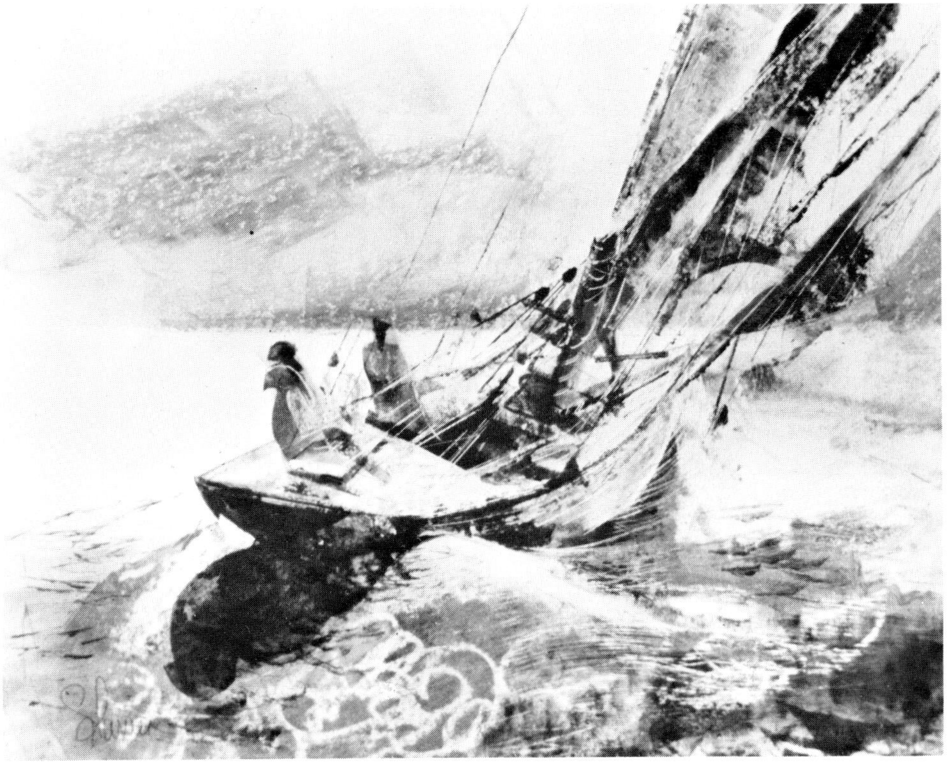

These paintings were done on location at Newport, R.I., famous for its big sailboats and harbors.

The character and mood of sailing is the foremost idea for the paintings. Sailboats in motion require working rapidly, so I had to rely on experience and judgment to keep things under control.

All details were held to mere suggestions in order to keep the composition flowing. The figures at the stern of the boat were handled in the same bold manner as the water and the boat. This helps to make them a definite part of the painting and not a separate afterthought.

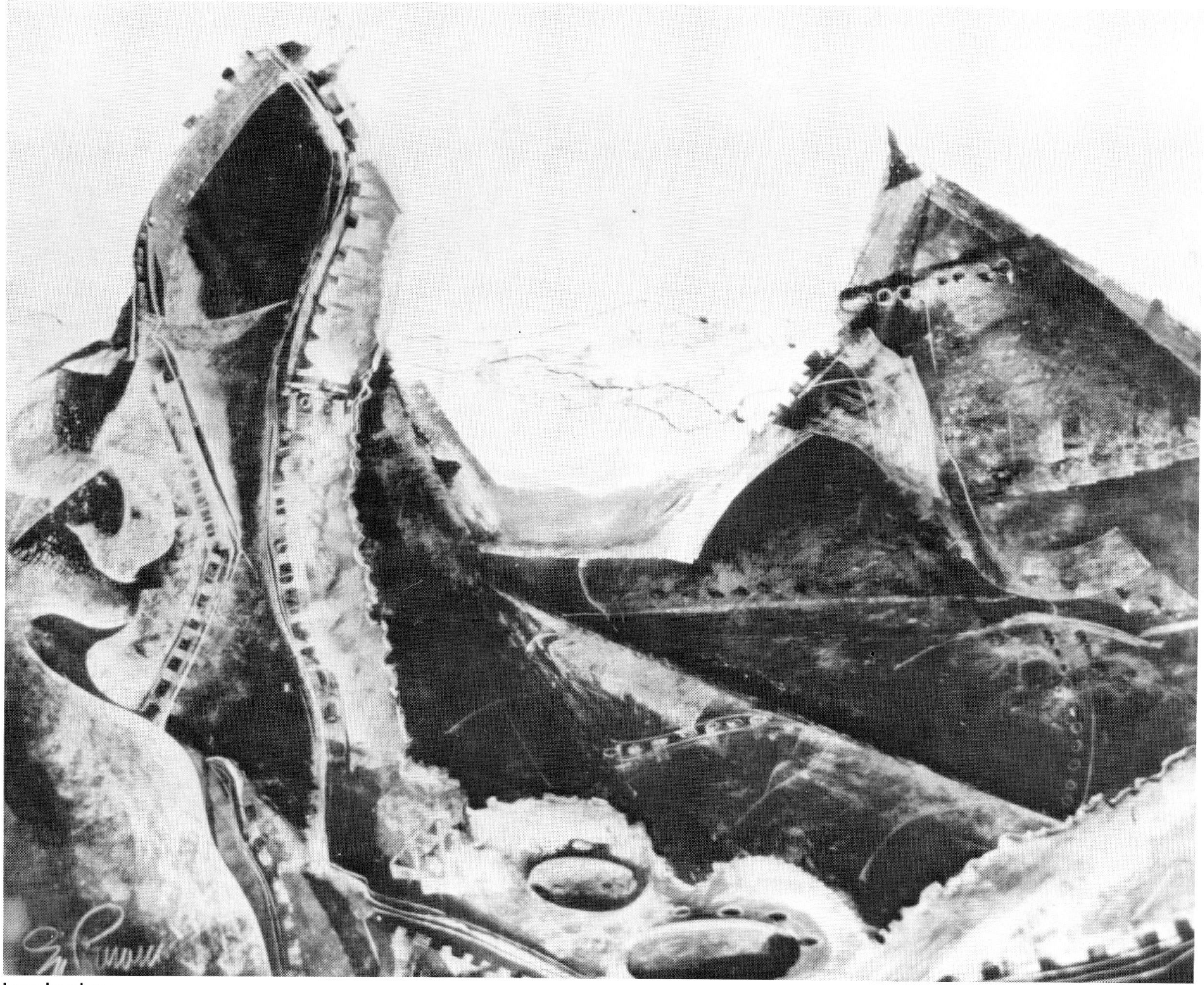

Implosion
Size 26 x 28 inches. Oil crayon base, oil paints on heavy offset paper. Saugus, Calif.

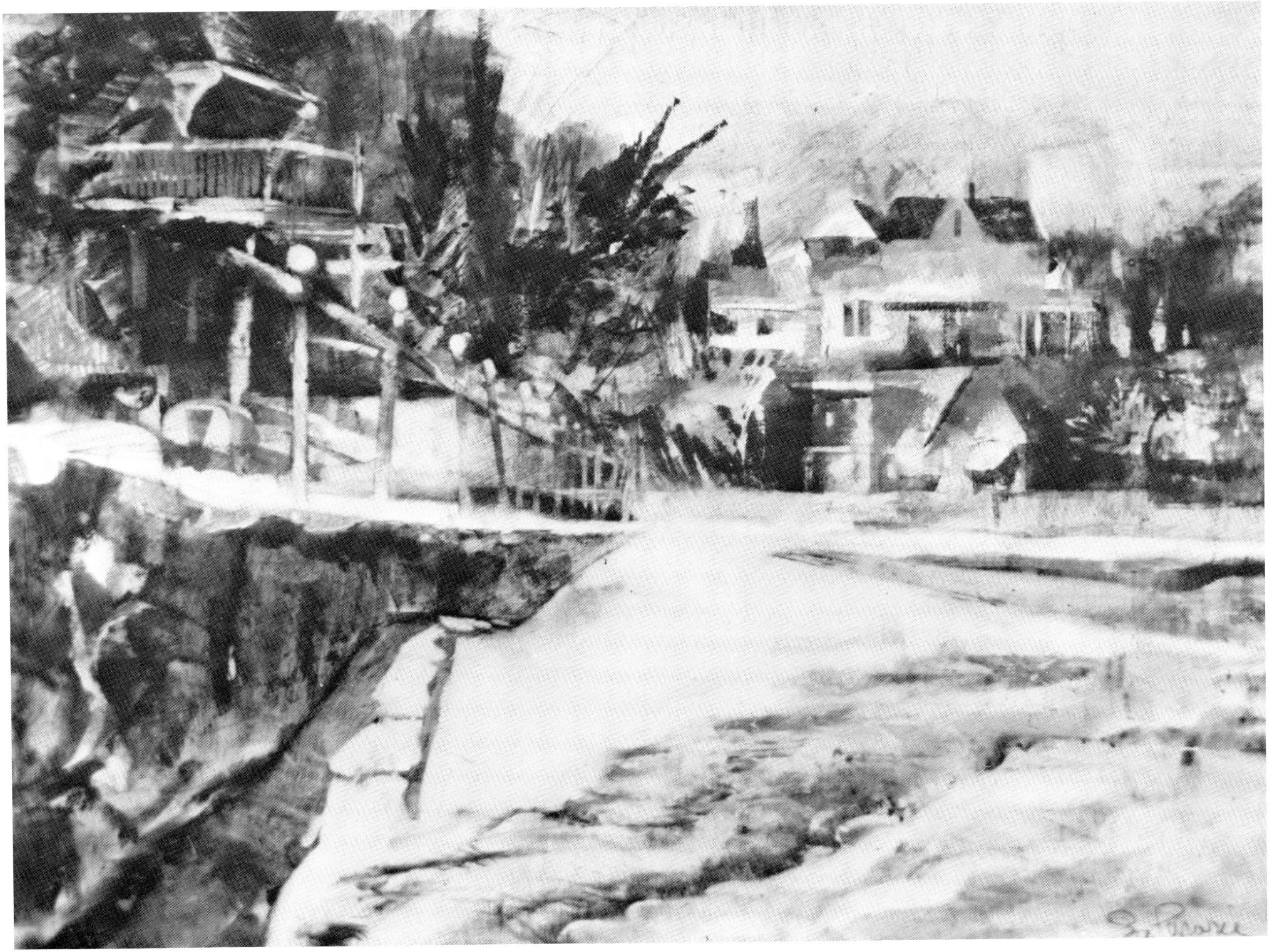

Juniper Point
Size: 18 x 24 inches. Water based paints on three-ply Strathmore paper. Woods Hole, Mass.

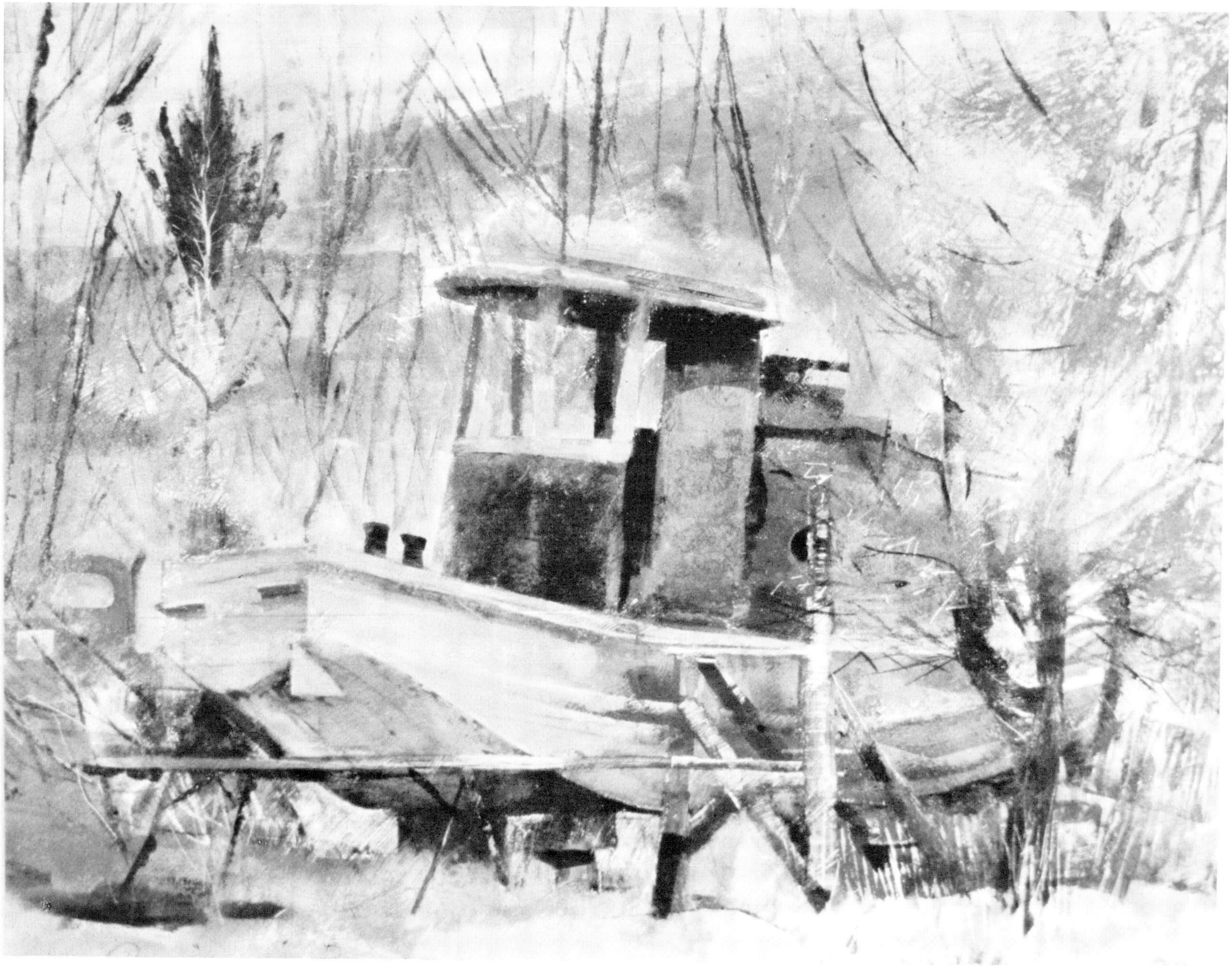

Orange Aid
Size: 18 x 22 inches. Water based paints on a watercolor type paper. Mystic, Conn.

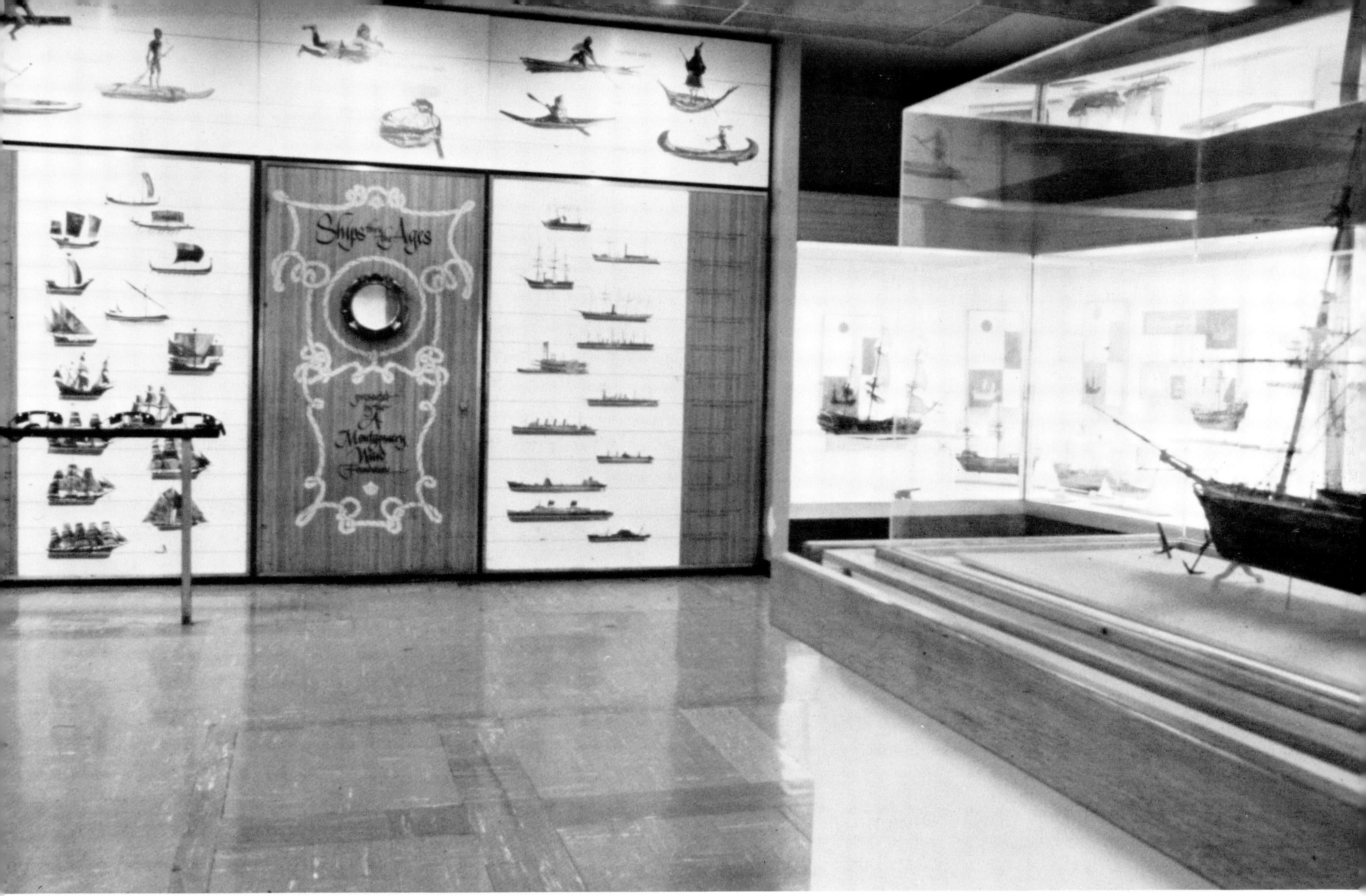


Chicago Museum of Science and Industry

Photography: Stacy Nigrelli

Serigraphs were made from the individual brayer drawings, on 8-foot formica panels. They are hinged to the wall at the museum.

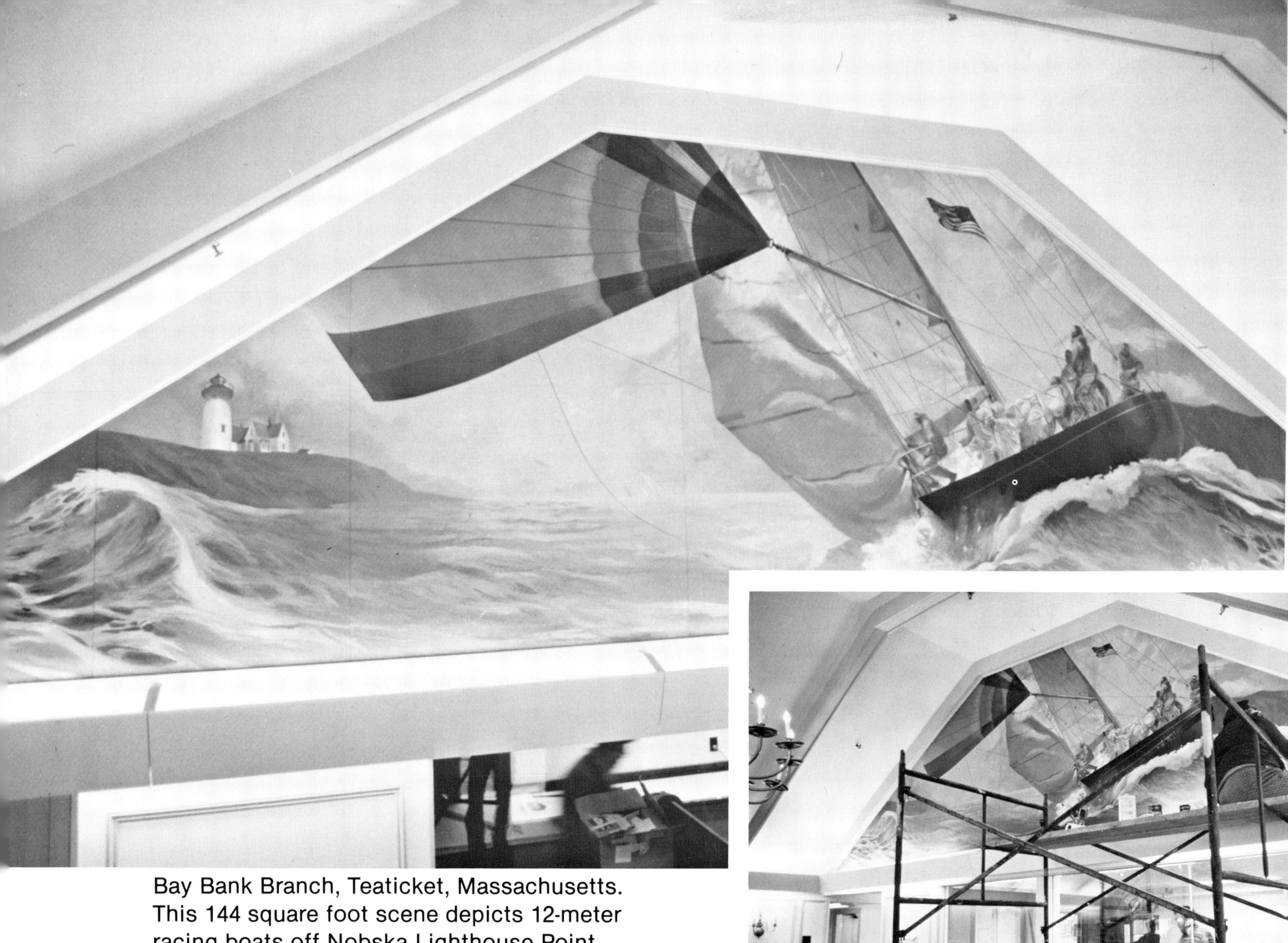

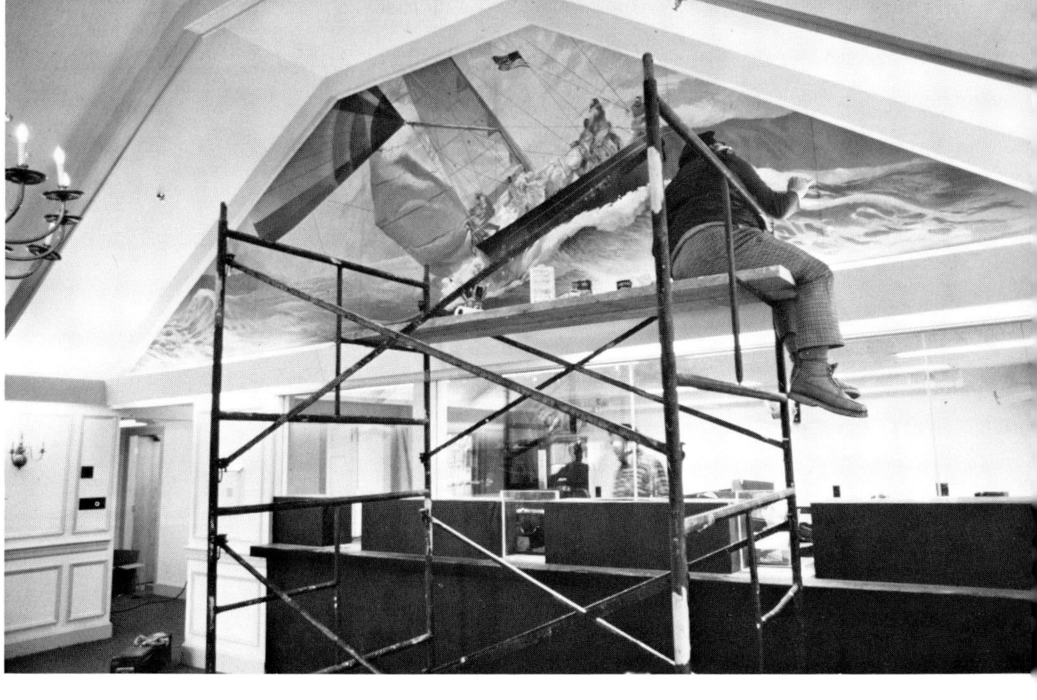

Bay Bank Branch, Teaticket, Massachusetts. This 144 square foot scene depicts 12-meter racing boats off Nobska Lighthouse Point, Woods Hole.



Photography: Michael de Punte

## demonstrations/workshops

# DEMONSTRATE & PARTICIPATE

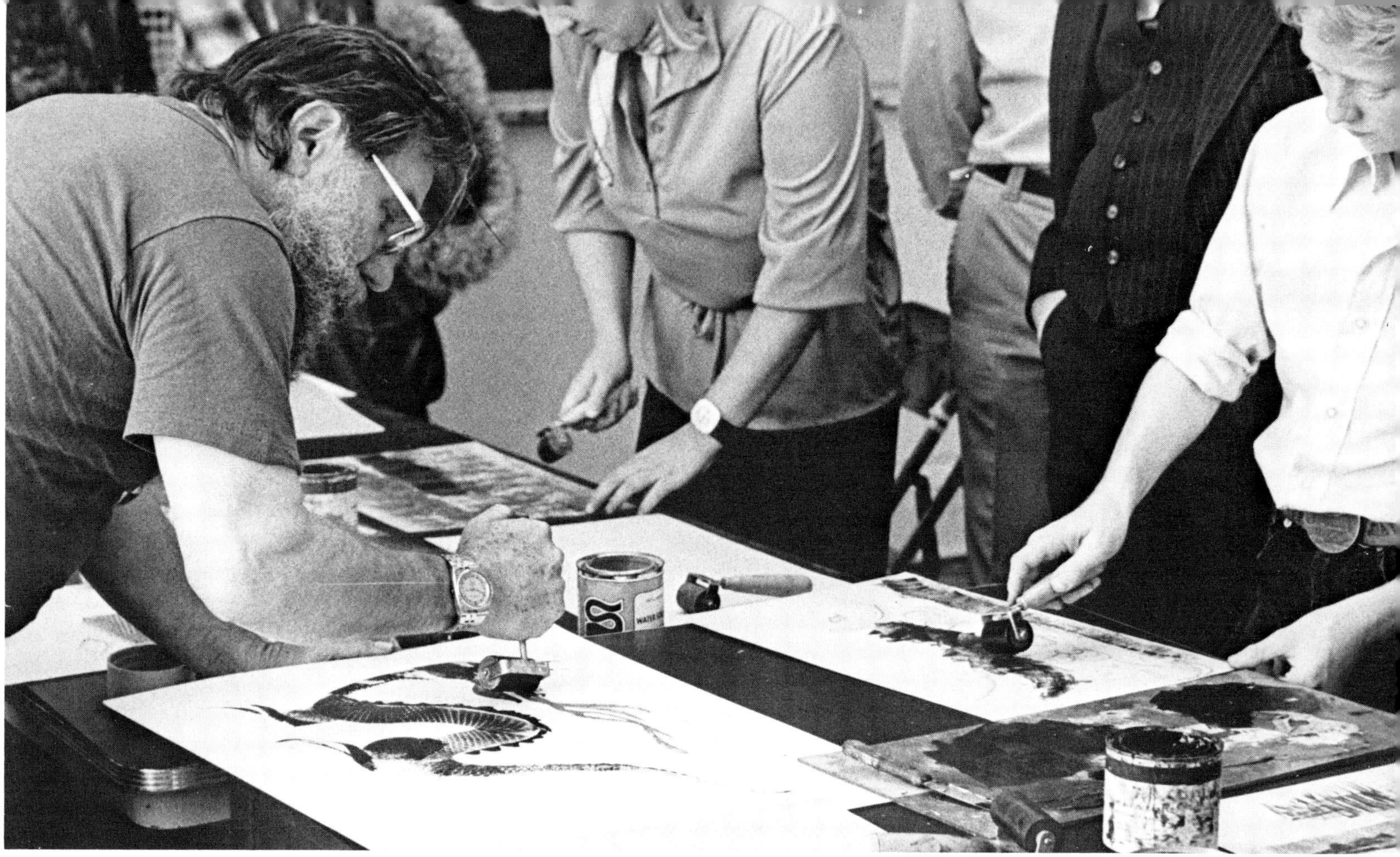

Here I am with students at work.

There's no substitute for *actual participation* in learning your craft, especially *roller art*. Try practicing your rolls and swirls with a dry roller across the paper surface. This is a good way to become familiar with the tool and to gain confidence in selecting various movements. Now repeat the process with a roller full of color. Develop your mental pictures as you work. This is an important step.

**lobster demonstration**

Right at the start, the placement of your first strokes on the paper instantly makes a commitment to your total composition. Therefore, it is important your mental concept be clear at the start. The assistance of a thumbnail sketch gives you some guidelines for looking and planning your arrangements.

In combining two parallel colors on the palette, orange and Van Dyke brown, I pick them up with the brayer and apply my first major stroke on the paper, adding lines to accent the shell segments on the lobster tail. A razor is used for scraping away paint areas. Tilt roller edges for color accents.

Demonstration work must be kept simple, with the subject and the objective as distinct as possible. You must hold the interest of the viewers at all times and sustain their attention throughout the session.

If a workshop is to follow your demonstration, be sure someone is keeping track of the time. Give your audience enough leeway to put into practice their new found directives. Try to keep them at it while they are motivated.

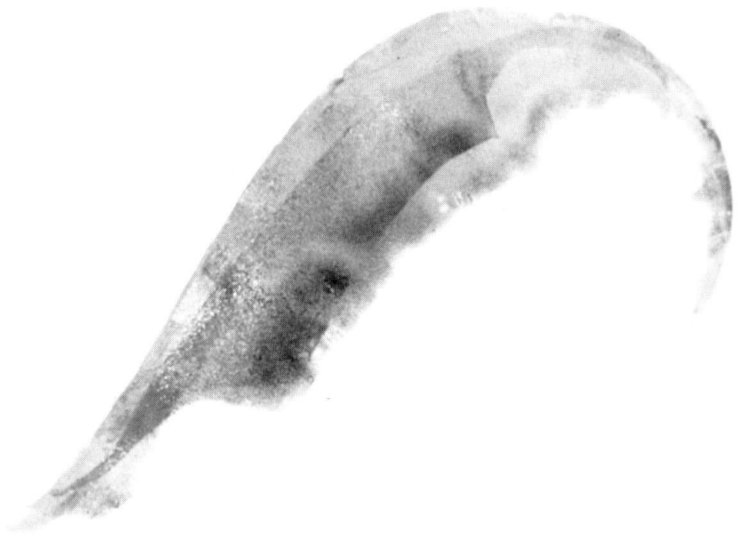

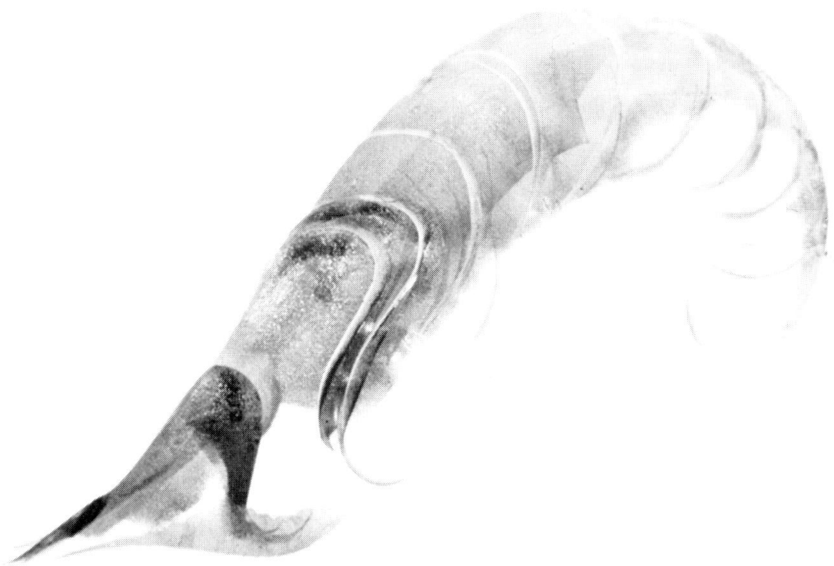

The first stroke placement sets the character and starts the composition. It is important to pre-plan your work carefully.

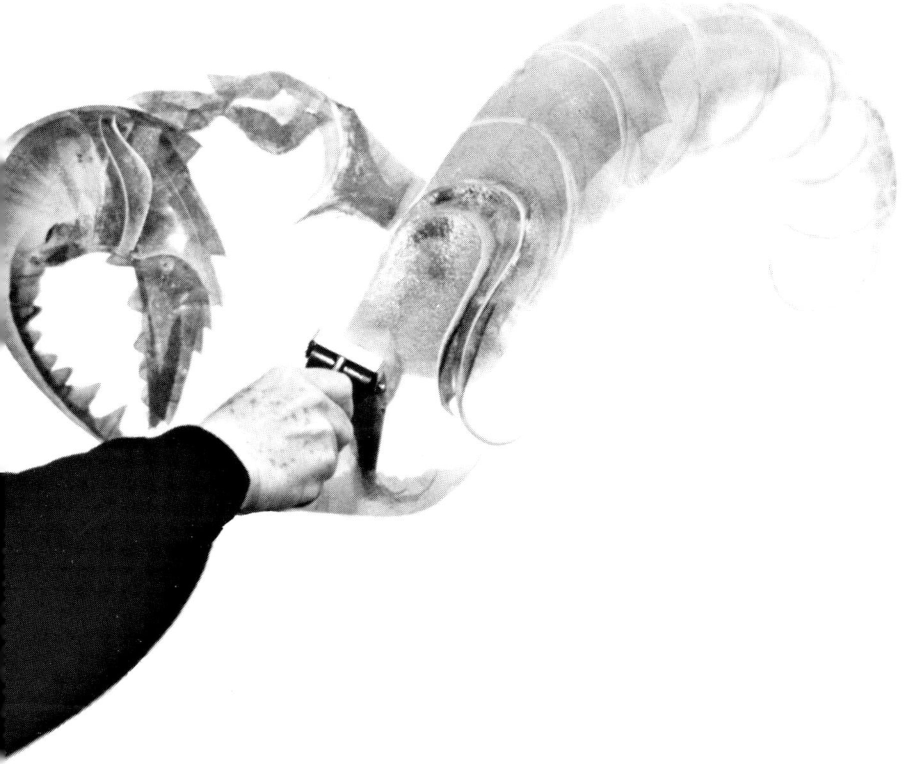

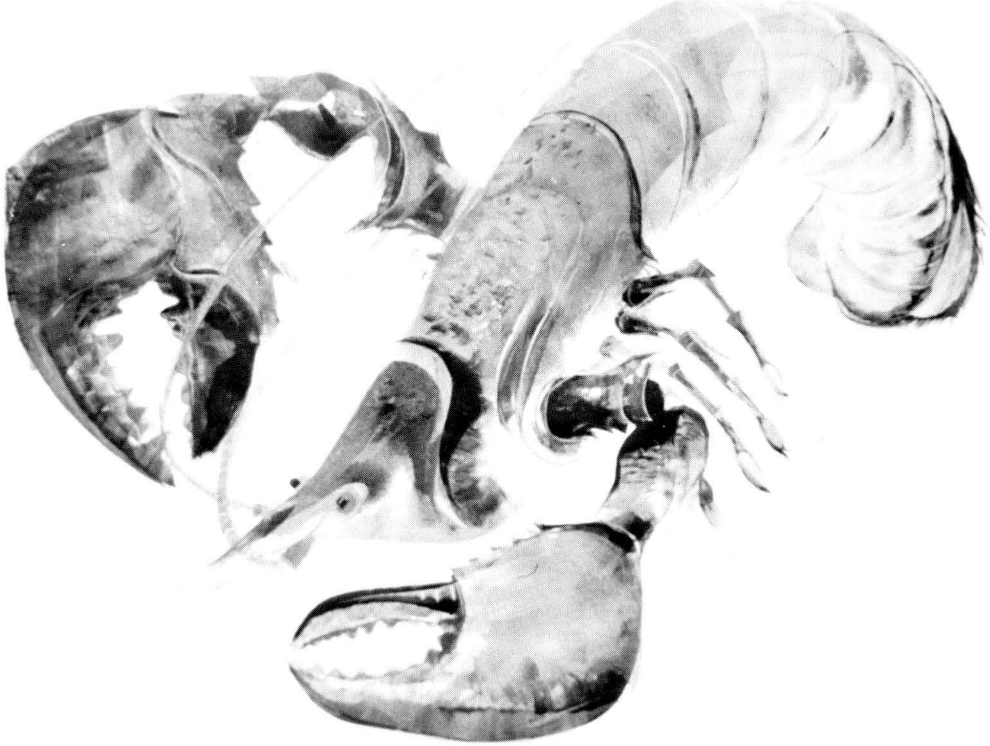

During most of my demonstrations with various groups, the subject is suggested on the spur of the moment from the audience. So quick mental concepts of different subject matter must be as much a part of your equipment as your art materials and tools. A thumbnail sketch of the subject would have been helpful for accuracy in this instance, but time would not allow it. But the stimulation of the challenge and its fulfillment usually makes up for such deficiencies.

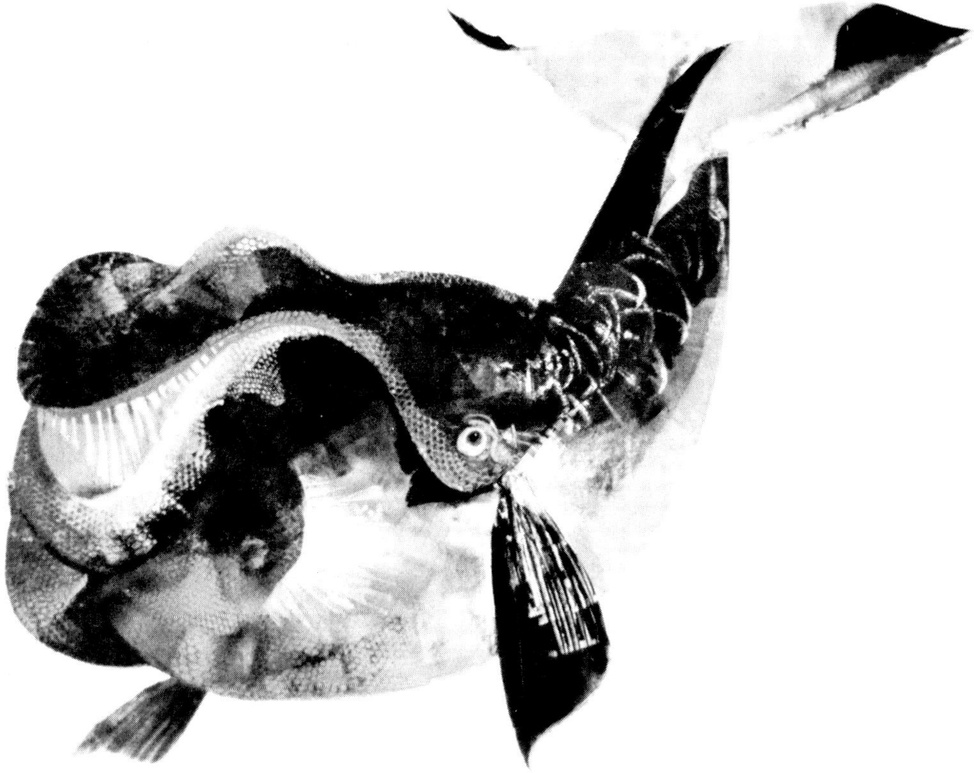

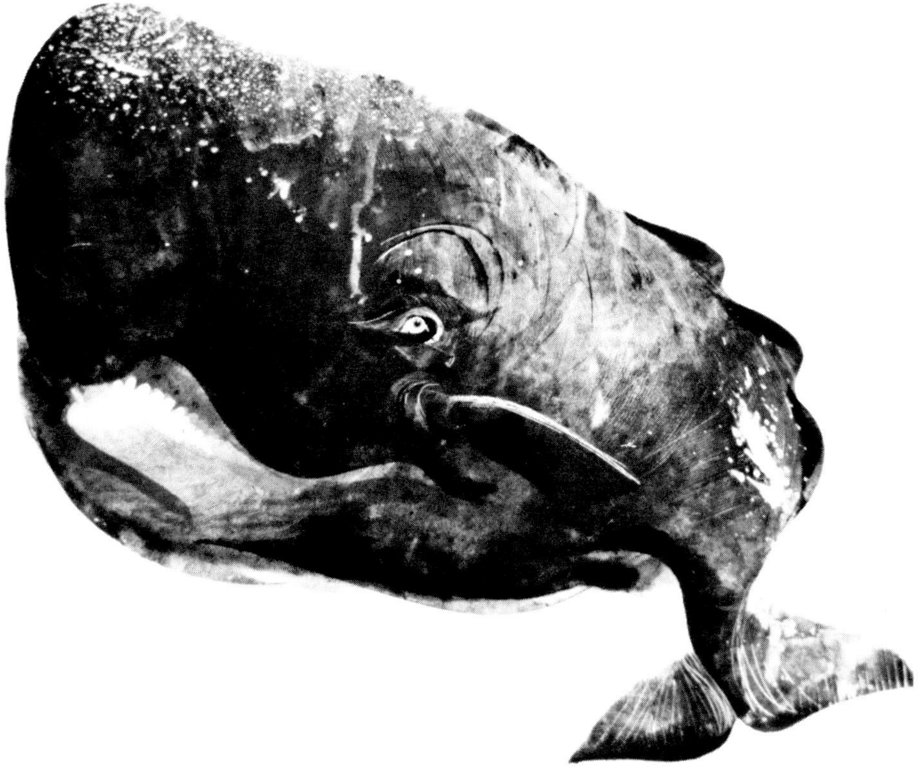

Right Whale Size: 22 x 28 inches.

These demonstration paintings incorporate many of the stroke techniques illustrated in the preceding sections.

Sperm Whale Size: 22 x 28 inches.

Roller scraping: (baleen, flukes, fins) Impressions: metal and chalk, (body and head textures) Spatter and blotting: (heads and bodies).

**sailboat demonstration**

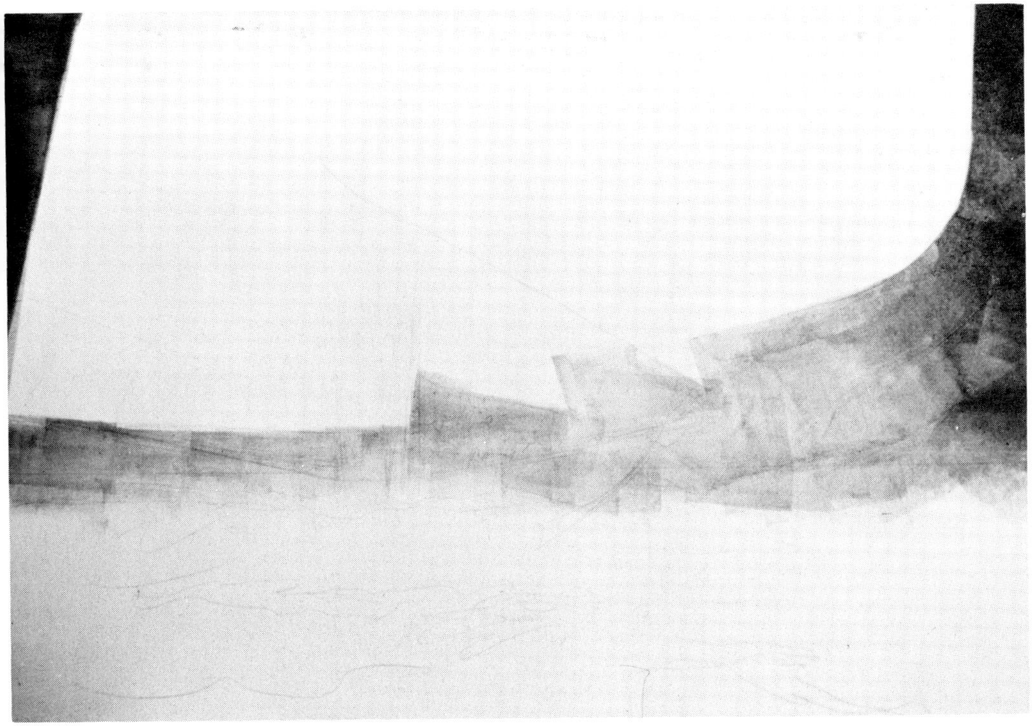

Stage 1
The structural plan for this painting was to silhouette the bulky, billowy sails against the sky and sea.

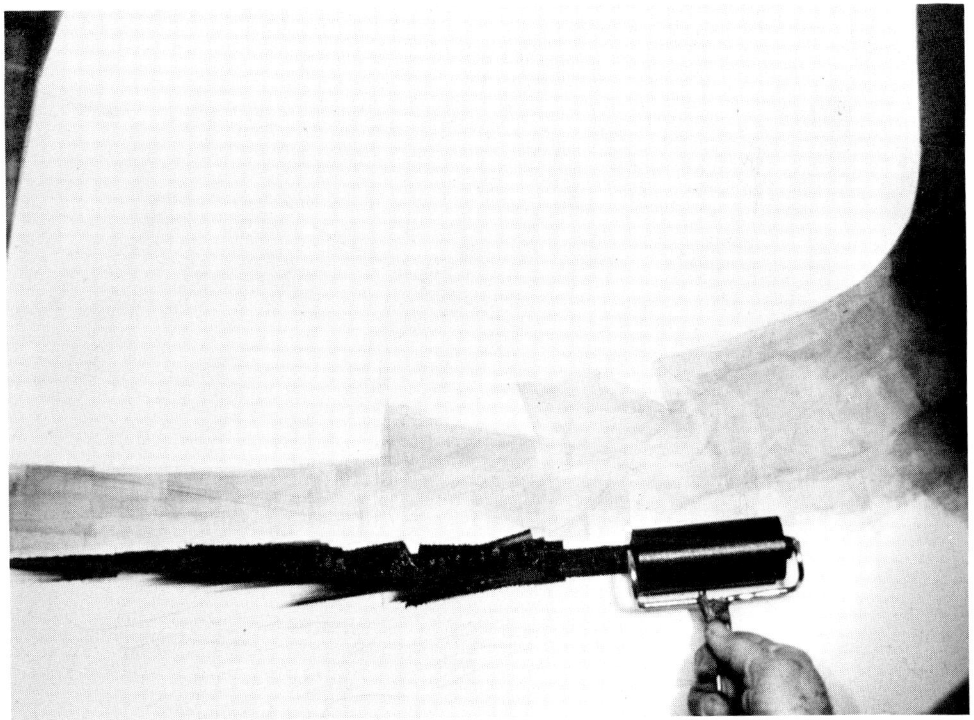

Stage 2
With a strong dark value, I immediately commit the placement for the ship's hull with one stroke. I then begin rendering the sea with the *up/down and drag* strokes.

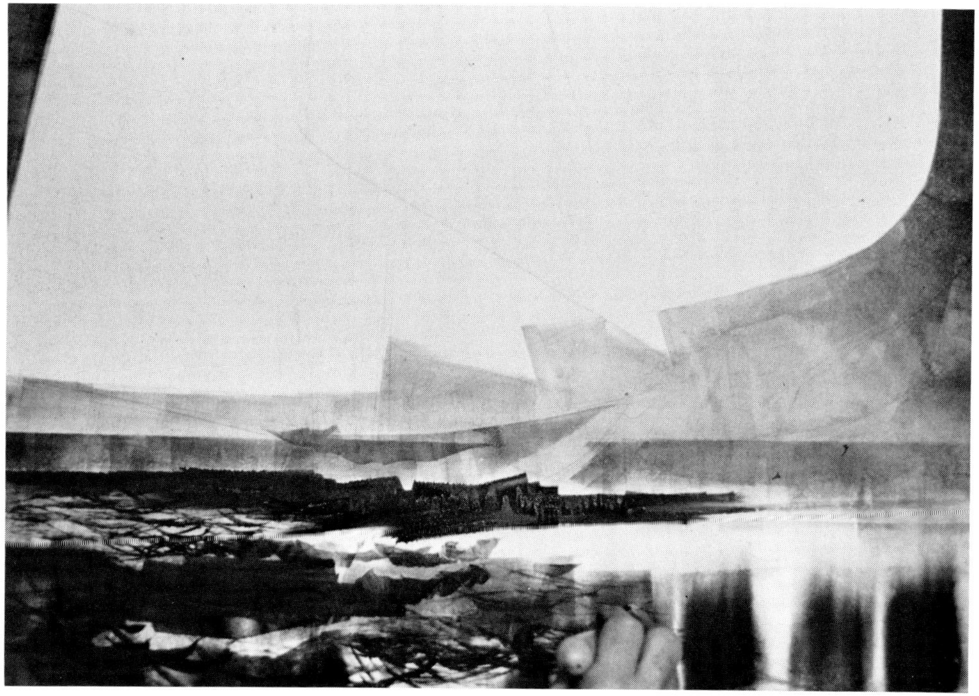

Stage 3
I then establish an undertone for the sea and accent the fore area with vertical as well as the conventional horizontal strokes with the brayer.

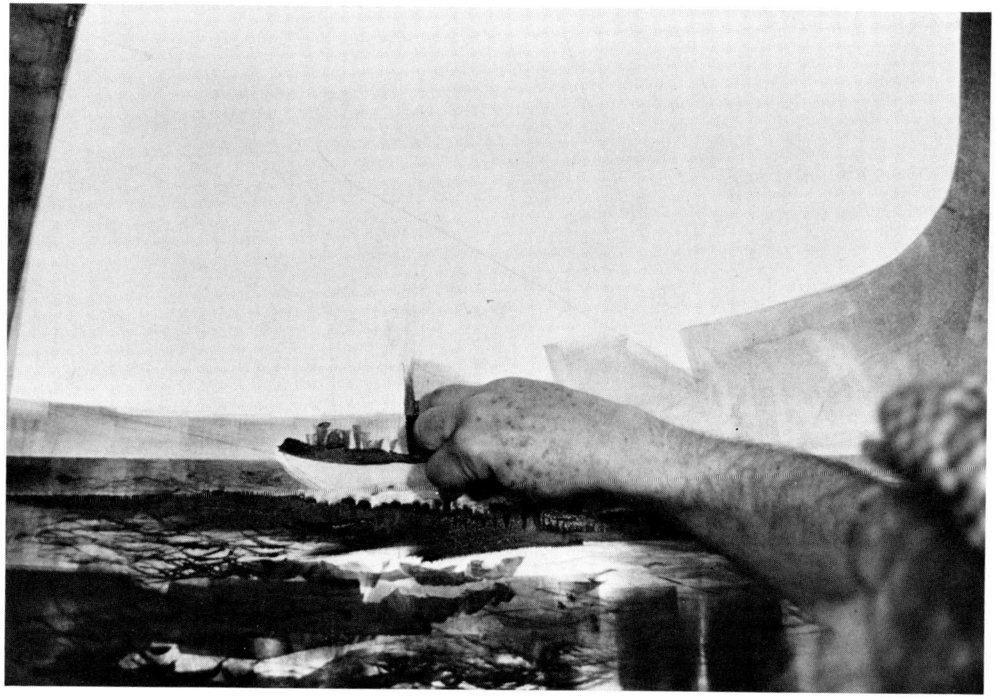

Stage 4
While the area is still wet, I scratch in with a razor blade the wave crests that are immediately below the hull, and the stern of the ship in sunlight.

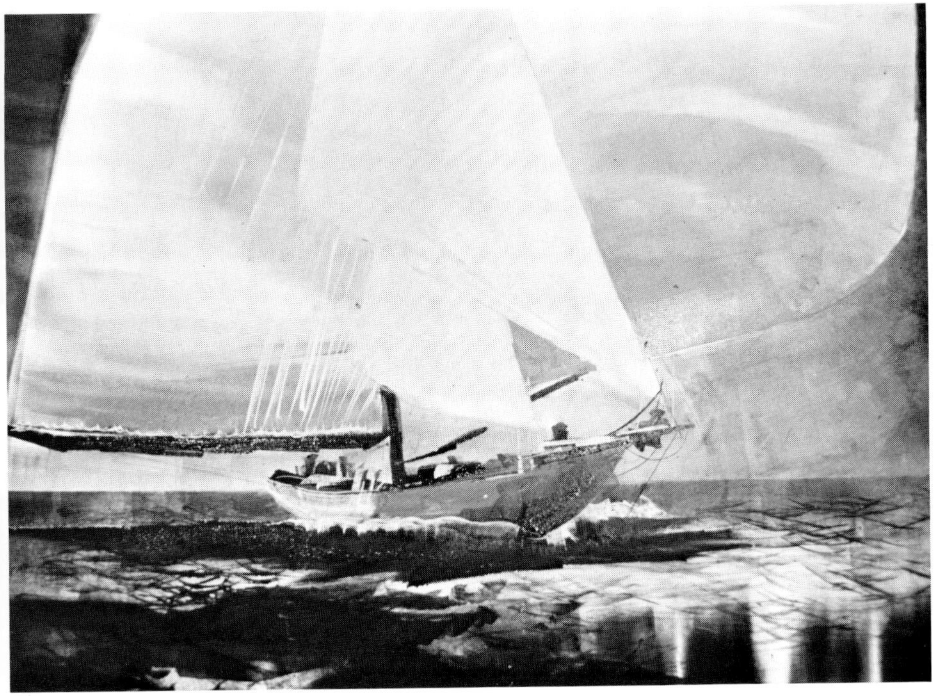

Stage 5
Next, the large mainsail is developed. Stenciling is used on the jib to suggest the light of the sun and the effect of the breeze. The boom, mainmast and the subtle deck details are indicated.

Size: 22 x 28 inches. Water base inks on chrome coat stock.

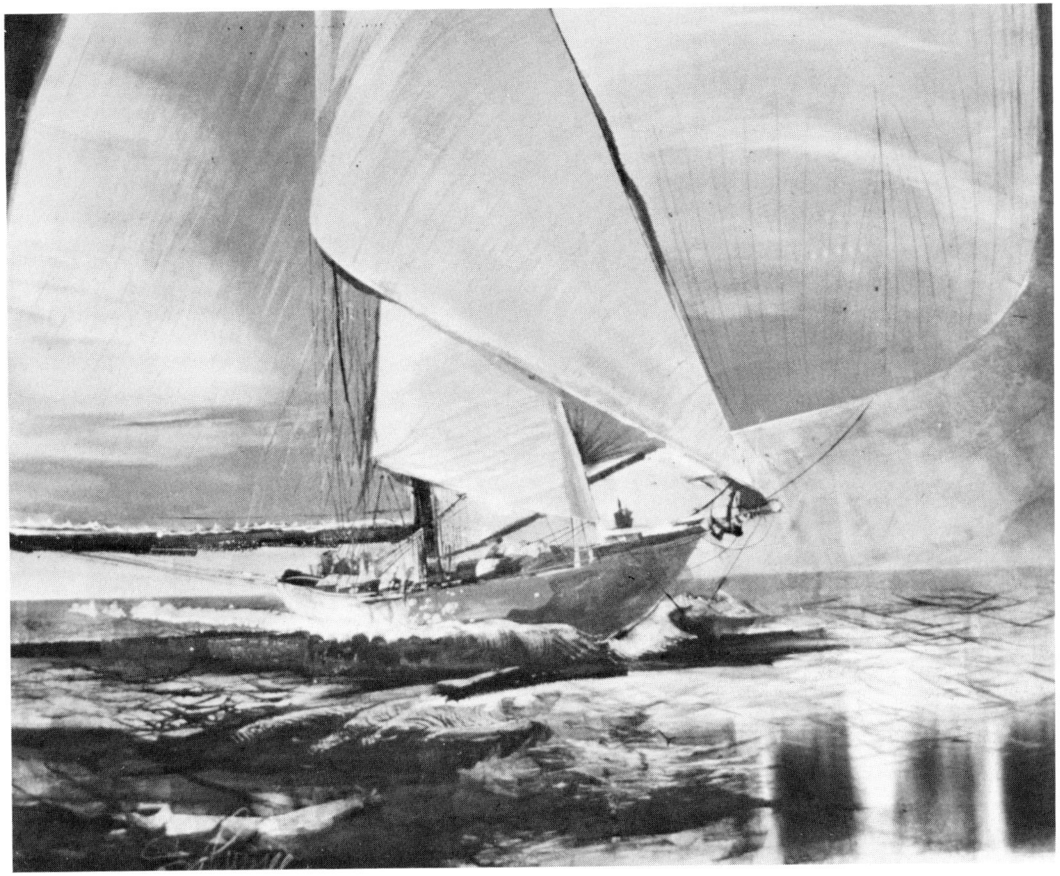

Stage 6
In this final stage of painting I accent the superstructure and rigging with a dark color by picking up the paint off the palette with a razor blade and applying it to the painting. Also, I do some razor scratching and brayer-on-edge accents on the sail seams.

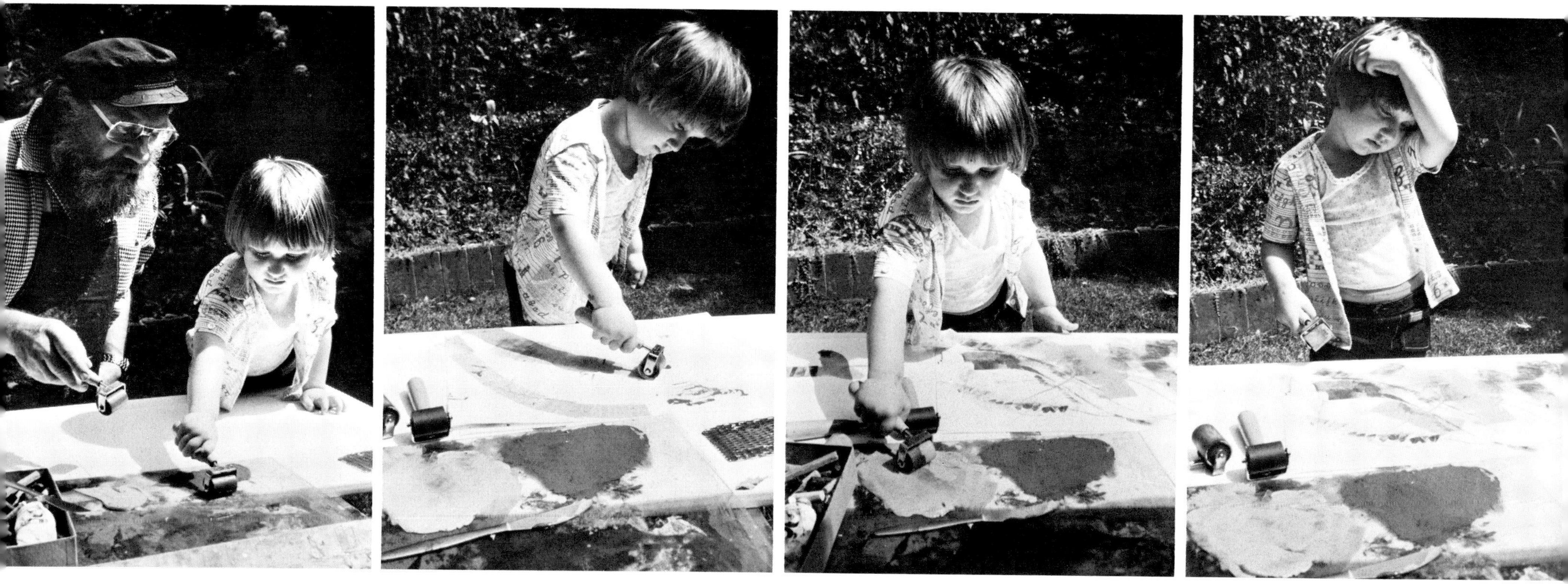

Jack Finley photographer

## Summation

Creative expression is largely spiritual — a language of human spirit. The brayer drawing methods used here can be readily tailored for application to any status of ability. It may, perhaps for the first time, bring out graphic creative intuitions and incentives you never knew you had. Whatever the case, you are sure to surprise yourself with what you are able to create.

# dialogue

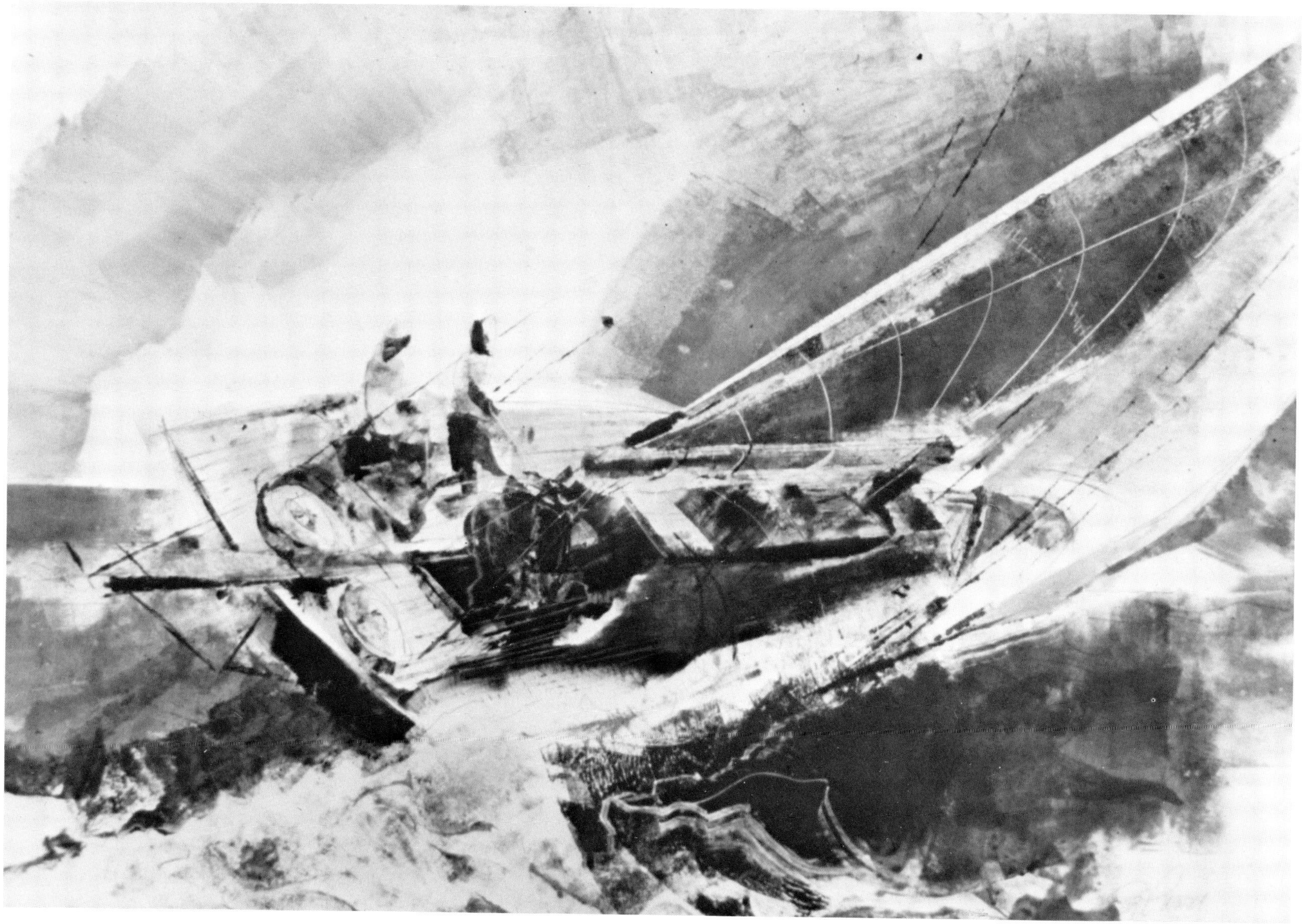

Sailing
20 x 30 inches. Brayer oil painting and scribing
on 80 lb. offset paper.

**excerpts taped during teacher/workshop seminars**

Q *What is a brayer and how did you begin working with the brayer?*

S I discovered the brayer in a class project at the Institute of Design in Chicago many years ago. The brayer is a printer's term for the tool used for braying (spreading) ink on a type plate. As a young designer in the industrial field (before the advent of magic markers), hard pastels were the popular medium for quick sketch concepts. Then came the brayer (roller); it was a natural tool to do the job quicker and better. Plus, I fell in love with its potential, its versatility. This led to much experimenting with various paper surfaces and sizes. In time I began doing workshop demonstrations for audiences of all ages and backgrounds — art groups, industrial management groups and eventually high schools and university art schools, both here and abroad. Today the brayer is still one of my favorite tools.

Lee Side
Size: 28 x 32 inches. Transparent oil on 80 lb. chrome coat stock.

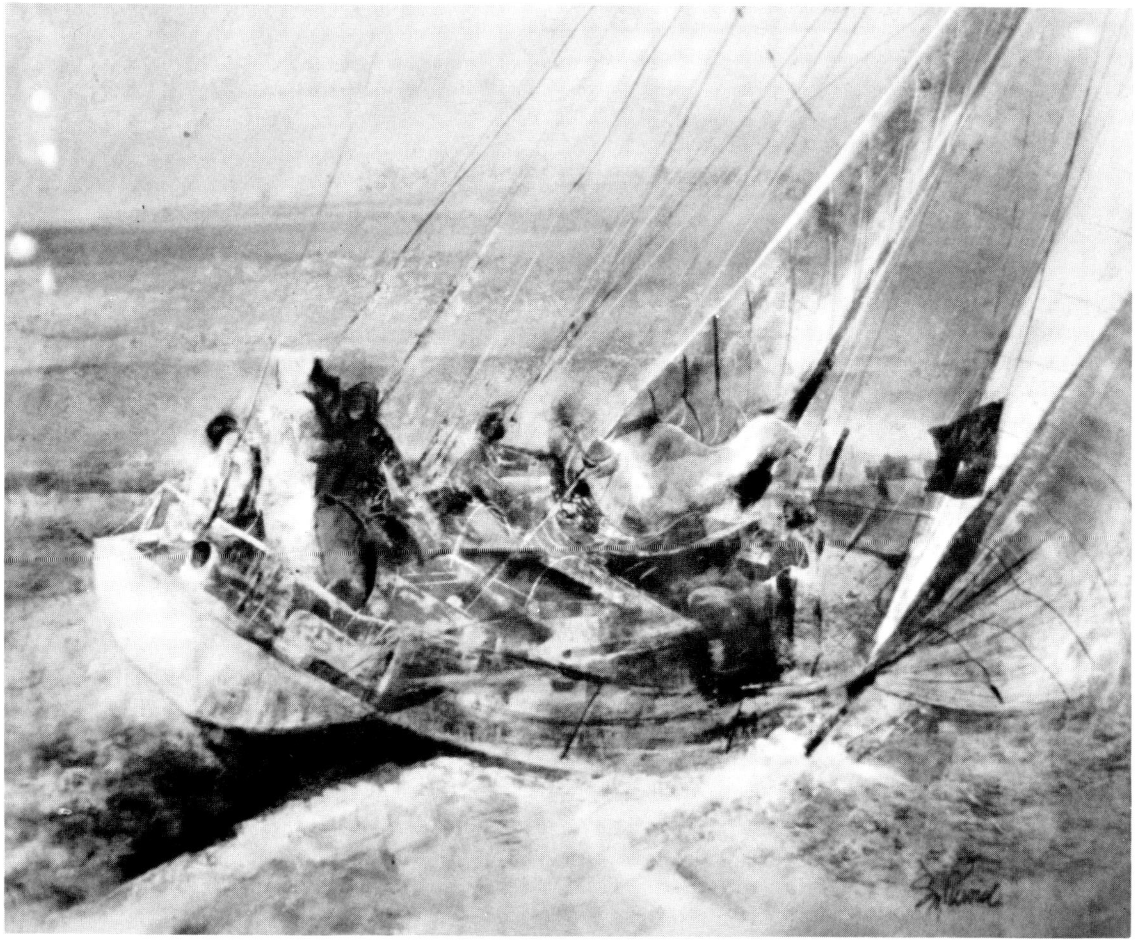

Q *Why use a roller in your graphics?*

S The roller makes a unique, spontaneous image on contact with the paper surface. The composition of the tool provides a flexibility that allows you to experience an immediate visual result.

Q *Does it take a long time to acquire this pictorial ability?*

S Time is a personal measure. Practice on a trial and error basis is a much better barometer for acquiring skills than a clock or a calendar.

Q *What are some of the basic supplies necessary?*

S A roller or brayer (soft rubber, gelatin, or the new plastic type); paints, inks and papers. The foremost tool is the one holding the handle of the brayer.

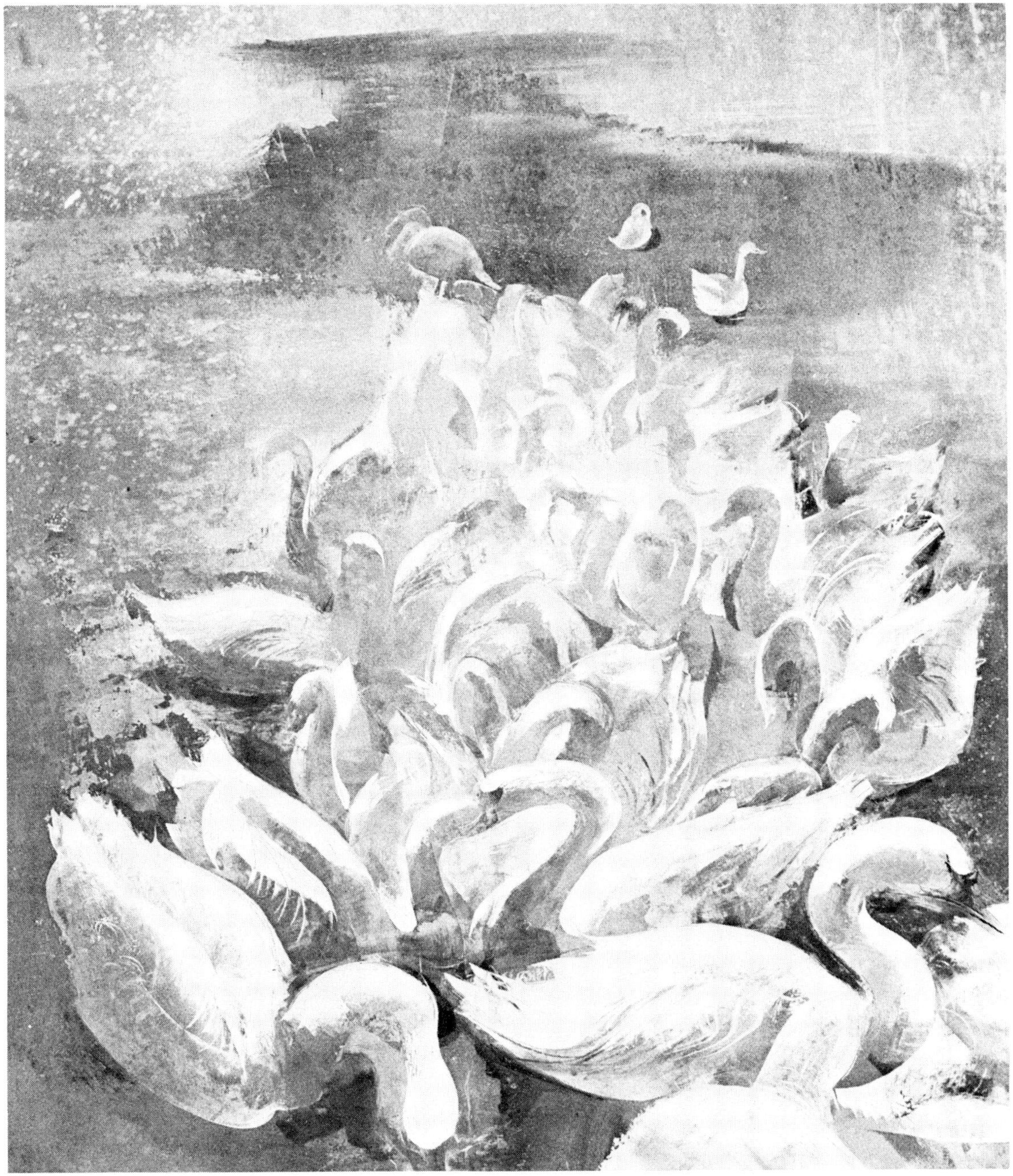

Swans in the Sun
Size: 28 x 24 inches. Brayer with oil on paper and scribing with sharp knife.

Q *Is it really necessary to be able to draw well to enjoy the brayer effectively?*

S No, but the ability to draw certainly helps! To be able to express in a visual manner simple forms and shapes is a utopian reward for the person involved. The novice can experience this — maybe for the first time — the ability to transmit to paper symbols and forms heretofore restricted to the more experienced talent. It's a quick breakthrough for the beginner who has never before tried graphics with a brayer.

Q *What about its usage? Is it restricted in any way?*

S If there are restrictions, I haven't found any. I've painted large wall murals and wall decor by attaching the brayer to a long pole to reach heights without scaffolding. I've used the same tool for illustrative art, covering all types of subjects: sports, animals, architectural renderings on all types of surfaces. The brayer is not a substitute tool or technique but another form in itself. No other tool can simulate the brayer. Why should it?

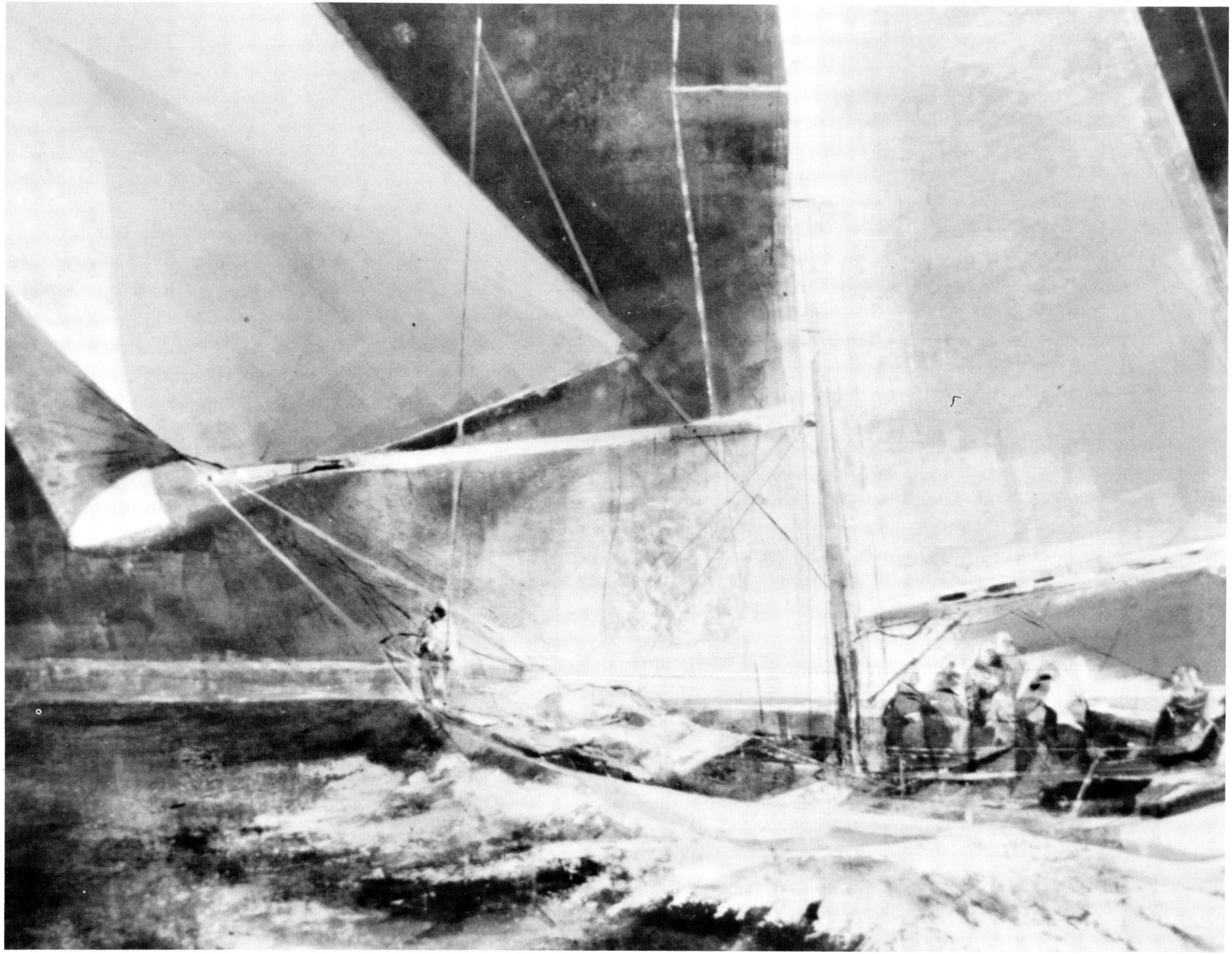

Dusk Before Dark
Size: 28 x 32 inches. Water based inks on heavy offset paper.

Q *Is this roller art medium the only medium you work in?*

S No, but I have found it to be one of the most stimulating techniques I know of. I draw with a pencil, markers and ball-point pens, sketching outdoors wherever I travel. I find sculpture, especially metal wire sculpture, a three-dimensional extension of line drawing. It is an exceptional way to help study and clarify line drawing. It helps you to understand form beyond the two-dimensional surface of the paper. But that's another whole area of exploratory work. Let's stay with our current subject, roller art.

Q *You spoke about painting in various sizes or different paint media. What about your brayer sizes?*

S Various sizes of brayers and roller density are important parts of my equipment. I purchase brayers from all over the world; from soft rubber ones to the more practical 6 x 1½-inch made of gelatin.

Brayers are a very practical tool, easy to clean and transport. I use water soluble inks when I paint on location. They are convenient and easy for clean-up outdoors.

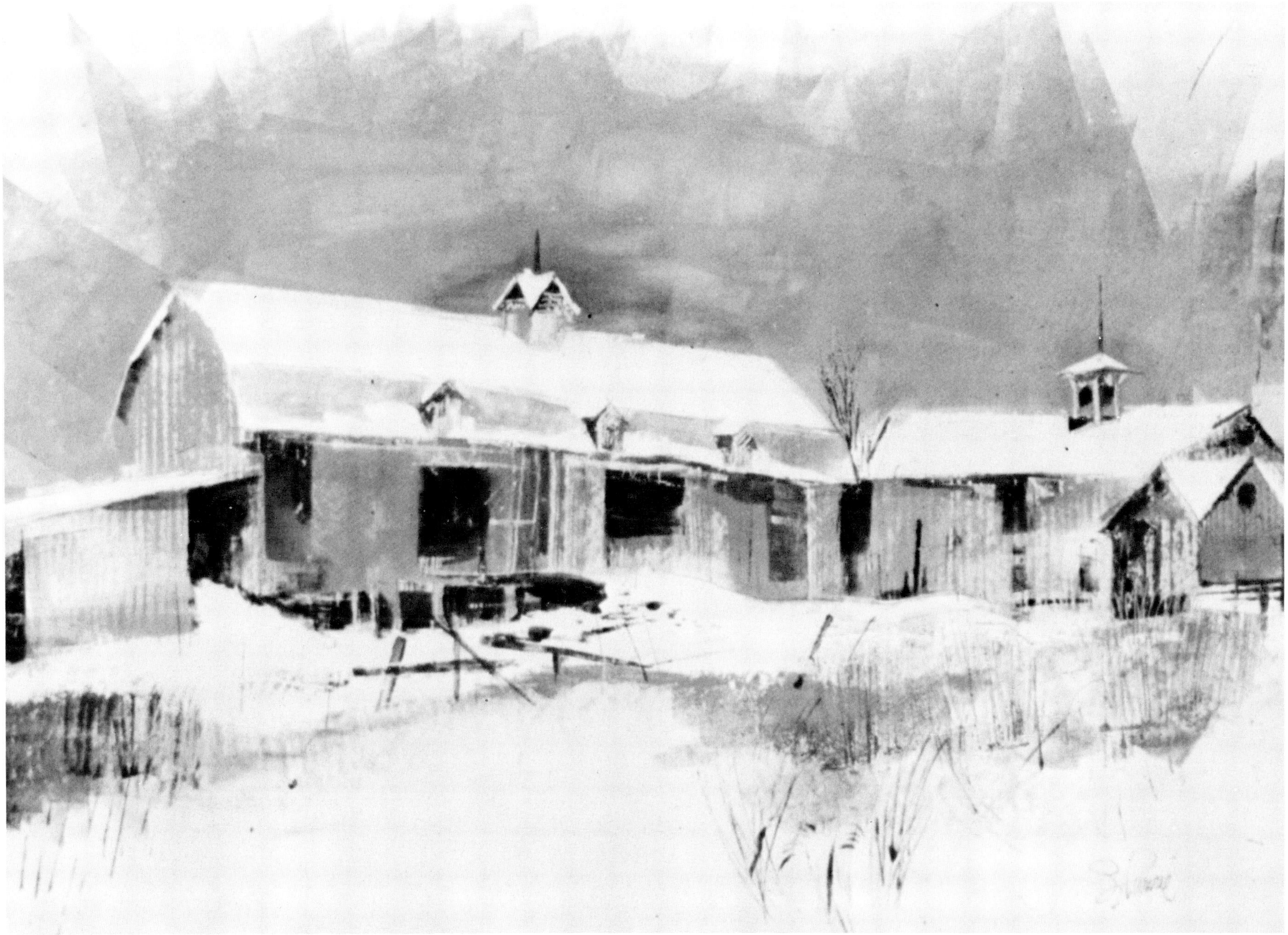

The Mendon Farm
Size 18 x 24 inches. Brayer with water based paints and chalk resist. 80 lb. coated paper.

PAINTINGS FROM THE COLLECTIONS OF:

Mr. and Mrs. John Allen
Mrs. Ann Bengtson
Dr. and Mrs. Thomas Hutchinson
Mr. and Mrs. Ron Hilbrecht
Mr. and Mrs. Wesley Lazott
Mr. and Mrs. Wm. Moore Jr.
Mr. and Mrs. Wm. Moore III
Mr. Richard Sears
Mr. and Mrs. Myron Toomey
Mr. and Mrs. Millard Wells
Bay Bank Merchants, Falmouth, Mass.
Intercraft Industries Corp., Chicago, Ill.
Museum of Science and Industry, Chicago, Ill.
Nekoosa Paper Company, Port Edwards, Wis.